FAVOURITE RECIPES
from
HUDSON AND HALLS

D0609875

CONTENTS

FOREWORD

We have cooked together for nigh on twenty years – some of it good . . . some of it not so good! Compiling this book has taken us back into the past, which has brought us to the present with the realisation of how progress and the advent of so many new cooking aids and ideas have altered eating habits.

A greater variety of vegetables is available than was the case in the not-so-distant past, cuts of meat have become more interesting, and cooking equipment has taken on a new aspect. The only thing that has remained constant is the desire to eat, and to eat well and to entertain friends.

Twenty years of cooking have afforded us a large library of books, magazines and cuttings. Ten years of cooking on television has given us a marvellous opportunity to gain an insight into people's culinary likes and dislikes.

This book is a compilation of recipes prepared and enjoyed by a great many people. We hope you will enjoy them too.

We have talked very little about spirits, other than as additions to various dishes. If you have butlers and cellarmen to cosset your cellar and your palate, there is nothing we can say to enlighten you. For the average person, our rule of thumb is basically, drink a wine that you like and that suits your pocket.

Once there were rather snobbish, strict rules about white wine with white meat and red wine with red meat. It would be a waste of money to drink a delicate white wine with a very highly seasoned duck – you would never taste the wine, even though poultry is considered white meat. We would suggest a white Burgundy, but in preference a good red Burgundy. Likewise, a fine white wine is excellent with poached fish with a delicate sauce – but what is the use of such a wine with a whole mullet, floured and fried in groundnut (peanut) oil and dressed with a sauce of ginger, soy and garlic? Then a red is better.

Simply, if a dish is highly spiced, to our taste a good heavy red is appropriate, and with delicate, light food, a white. How could you drink wine with curry? Try chilled beer instead. A chilled sherry goes well with soup, a sweet Sauterne with fruit and cheese.

When it comes to cooking with wine, the better the wine the better the end result – and the less disastrous the effect on your system.

In the end, to our minds, successful cooking comes down to simplicity, ease of preparation and, of course, the use of prime quality ingredients – cheap stays cheap! Good food need not be complicated. Nothing is more delectable than toast and a perfectly poached egg . . . and a poached egg ain't easy!

SOUPS

Soups can precede a meal, or be a meal in themselves. We sometimes even have them for breakfast, and certainly enjoy them late at night. Cold or hot, soups are far better homemade than out of a can or from a packet. The advent of the food processor, and to some extent of the microwave, has helped to make soup preparation easy.

We are very keen on pure vegetable soups at any time of year, as they provide plenty of vitamins. The basis of these is onions sautéed in oil and butter, a fresh vegetable, such as pumpkin, cauliflower, parsnips, tomato or carrot, good homemade chicken stock, and sometimes cream added to give a little more body.

One thing that we do stress is the use of well flavoured stock wherever possible. It's a good idea to keep chicken stock in the freezer ready for these occasions (p. 183). In some cases you can save vegetable-cooking water to use as a stock base in soups. You can even use leftover cooked vegetables, for instance potato or cauliflower, to thicken a soup rather than using too much high-calorie flour.

Thick soups can be a meal in themselves. Cooked chicken or sausage or frankfurters added to a chunky vegetable soup makes for an easily digested and nutritious meal when served with brown bread, a green salad and fruit and cheese.

Many puréed soups can be served cold, and with the addition of some cream are really superb. Remember that cold soups should be seasoned a little more than hot as chilling tends to diminish the flavour. Also only soups that have little butter or fat in them can be served cold, as chilling causes the fat to congeal and float on the top. (Chicken stock, for example, must be chilled after you have strained it, to enable you to remove all the fat from the top.)

Little additions add nice individual decorative touches to soups. Thin shreds of pancakes or omelettes are good as edible garnishes, as is the traditional chopped parsley. Small croûtons, fried bread cubes, or tiny cooked herb dumplings do wonders for pea and ham soup or a simple cream of vegetable soup. If you are going to make cooked additions such as dumplings, remember to keep them small, as they will have to fit into your mouth in one easy bite.

You can easily ring the changes on a lot of the soups mentioned here. For instance, our Creamy Potato Soup has all kinds of interesting variations.

If you have some good stock to start, a few vegetables and some meat, you can create a soup. Be careful if you are using prepared stock cubes. They can be very salty. When it comes to seasonings, we really prefer to let people add salt and pepper at the table, rather than go in boots and all at the cooking stage.

We didn't mention some of the normal stand-bys like Vichyssoise or Cock-a-Leekie, and, of course, good clear beef consommé, as recipes for these are easy to find. And we are afraid we couldn't do Borstch, as we both hate it . . .

Fish Ball Soup with Spinach

This really is a fantastic soup – every time we have it, we enjoy it that much more! And it's a dish that can be prepared in advance (if you are doing this, add the fish balls just before serving). We often make extra fish balls and freeze them for later quick use. If you do this, freeze them on a tray, then put them in a polythene bag – this way they won't stick together. Thaw them in the fridge overnight, otherwise they will lose their moisture and break up. If spinach isn't available, use lettuce leaves.

500 g/18 oz WHITE SKINLESS FISH, SUCH AS COD

2.5 ml/½ tsp SUGAR

1.25 ml/¼ tsp SALT

1.25 ml/¼ tsp GROUND WHITE PEPPER

PINCH OF CHINESE FIVE SPICES

7.5 ml/1½ tsp CORNFLOUR

1 EGG WHITE, LIGHTLY BEATEN

3 SPRING ONIONS, FINELY CHOPPED

1.2 litres/2 pints (5 cups) CHICKEN STOCK, PREFERABLY HOMEMADE (p. 183)

2 CARROTS, COARSELY CHOPPED

2 STALKS CELERY, COARSELY CHOPPED

4 SPRIGS FRESH PARSLEY

30 ml/2 tbsp GROUNDNUT (PEANUT) OIL

KNOB FRESH ROOT GINGER, PEELED AND VERY FINELY SLICED

LARGE HANDFUL WASHED SPINACH LEAVES

15 ml/1 tbsp DRY SHERRY

15 ml/1 tbsp LIGHT SOY SAUCE

To make the fish balls, cut the fish into fairly small pieces and place in the bowl of a food processor fitted with the steel blade. Add sugar, salt and pepper, five spices, cornflour and lightly beaten egg white. Blend to a paste. Scrape out into a clean bowl and stir in the finely chopped spring onions. (We prefer to chop these by hand as they must be really fine.) Cover a baking tray with greased greaseproof paper, wet your hands and roll teaspoonfuls of the fish paste into balls – not too big. Cover with another sheet of greaseproof paper and chill for an hour or 2.

To make the soup, bring chicken stock to the boil, then add carrots, celery and parsley. Simmer for 5-10 minutes, then strain, discard vegetables and return stock to saucepan to gently reheat.

In a small, heavy-based pan, heat the groundnut oil, drop in the finely sliced ginger and stir fry for about 2 minutes. Don't let it brown! Tip into the heated stock (be careful, as the liquid boils up suddenly when the oil hits the stock). Slice the spinach leaves into strips and drop into the simmering stock. Cook 1 minute, then stir. With a slotted spoon add the fish balls and cook until the soup reaches boiling point again (being cold they will have chilled the soup). At this stage they are done; they mustn't be overcooked. Add the sherry and soy sauce, stir gently and serve at once. This soup has a delightful fresh flavour and looks most attractive *Serves* 6.

Pumpkin Soup

When making vegetable soups it's important to sauté the vegetables before adding the stock, as the soup then has a rounder, nuttier flavour.

50 g/2 oz BUTTER

50 ml/2 fl oz (¼ cup) VEGETABLE OIL

2 or 3 LARGE ONIONS, QUARTERED

1 LARGE CLOVE GARLIC, FINELY CHOPPED

1 MEDIUM PUMPKIN, PEELED, SEEDED AND DICED

2.5 ml/½ tsp CURRY POWDER

1.2 litres/2 pints (5 cups) CHICKEN STOCK, PREFERABLY HOMEMADE (p. 183)

2 BAY LEAVES

SALT AND FRESHLY GROUND BLACK PEPPER

50 ml/2 fl oz (¼ cup) MEDIUM-DRY SHERRY

CREAM (OPTIONAL)

In a large, heavy-based enamel or stainless steel pan, heat the butter and oil over fairly high heat, then sauté the onions and garlic for about 5 minutes – do not let them brown. Add the diced pumpkin and stir fry for a further 5 minutes. Add the curry powder and stir fry for a few minutes, until the flavour has burst. Add the chicken stock and bring to the boil. Add the bay leaves and salt and pepper, lower the heat, cover and simmer about 20 minutes, until the pumpkin is soft. Remove bay leaves and blend until smooth in a food processor with the steel blade (you may have to do this in batches).

Return to the pan and stir well. Add more pepper and salt to suit your palate and stir in the sherry. Add the cream (if used). Reheat (taking care not to let boil if cream is used) and serve. *Serves* 6.

Creamy Potato Soup – Plus

Perhaps a strange name for a recipe, but this soup has so many variations that it should be a stand-by in anyone's repertoire. The recipe was given to us many years ago by a good friend who lives in Miami. It easily feeds 6 to 8 people and makes for a hearty, warming meal when you add French bread (either plain or garlicked), a good mixed salad and a dessert cake to follow. This soup doesn't have a lot of thickening agent in it, as the potato starch gives it body.
You can halve the quantities to make a smaller amount, or change the added extras slightly to suit your own palate.

100 g/4 oz BUTTER

1 LARGE ONION, FINELY CHOPPED

1 TO 2 STALKS CELERY, INCLUDING SOME OF THE TOPS, FINELY CHOPPED

3 TO 4 POTATOES, FINELY CUBED

7.5 g/¼ oz (¼ cup) FINELY CHOPPED FRESH PARSLEY

2.5 ml/½ tsp SALT

1.25 ml/¼ tsp GROUND WHITE PEPPER

1.25 litres/2 pints (5 cups) CHICKEN STOCK, PREFERABLY HOMEMADE (p. 183)

1 litre/1¾ pints (4 cups) MILK

45 ml/3 tbsp CORNFLOUR

50 ml/2 fl oz (¼ cup) WATER

50 ml/2 fl oz (¼ cup) SINGLE (LIGHT) CREAM

1 SLICE BUTTER, TO GARNISH

EXTRA FINELY CHOPPED FRESH PARSLEY, TO GARNISH

In a very large, heavy-based pan, melt the butter and cook the onion and celery over moderate heat, about 10 minutes, stirring often, until the onion is soft. Add the potatoes, parsley, salt, pepper and chicken stock. Cover and simmer gently about 30 minutes, until the potatoes are tender. Stir occasionally and try not to let it come to a full boil. Stir in the milk and wait until it comes back to a gentle simmer. Mix the cornflour and water together, then add to the pan. Bring back to simmering point and cook for 5 minutes. Pour in the cream, stir to mix well and pour into a heated tureen. Drop the slice of butter on the top and sprinkle over some parsley. Ladle out into mugs or soup bowls. Add extra seasoning at the table, if desired. *Serves 6-8.*

Now for the variations that can be made from this basic recipe:

Mushroom and Potato

Stir in 250 g/9 oz thinly sliced small mushrooms when you add the chicken stock. Finish with the butter and the parsley to top the soup once it has cooked, and you can, if you like, sprinkle over a little crumbled crisp bacon as well.

Shrimp and Potato

Add 2 or 3 cans, each about 200 g/7 oz, of shrimps just before adding the cornflour and water, but replace the water to mix with the cornflour with the drained liquid from the cans. Or you can use about 500 g/18 oz frozen prawns, thawed. Both variations seem expensive, but they will serve a fair number of people.

Crab and Potato

Add 2 bay leaves when you add the chicken stock, and 3 cans, each about 200 g/7 oz, of crab meat when adding the cornflour mixture. Remove the cartilage, and use the juice from the cans to mix with the cornflour.

Minced Mussel and Potato

Leave out the butter at the beginning of the recipe and cut 5 rashers of streaky bacon into small dice. Cook for about 5 minutes, then add the onion and celery and continue cooking as instructed. Add 450 g/1 lb (3 cups) of finely chopped cooked mussels just before adding the milk. Heat through thoroughly before thickening and adding the cream.

Fish and Corn Chowder

Proceed as for Minced Mussel, but add only 150 g/4 oz (1 cup) of minced mussels. When you add the mussels, also add about 500 g/1 lb of firm white fish fillets, cut into 2.5-cm/1 inch cubes and a large can of sweetcorn, about 450 g/12oz plus the liquid. Stir in the milk and heat through before thickening and adding the cream.

Beef and Noodle Soup

This is a little bit different, worth a try. By fresh paprika we mean not an old jar you have had hidden at the back of the cupboard! Nothing tastes as awful as stale paprika.

500 g/18 oz LEAN MINCED BEEF

2 ONIONS, SLICED INTO RINGS

1 LARGE CLOVE GARLIC, FINELY CHOPPED

1 GREEN PEPPER, CORED, SEEDED AND CHOPPED

2.5 ml/½ tsp CARAWAY SEEDS

15 ml/1 tbsp FRESH PAPRIKA

50 ml/2 fl oz (¼ cup) MEDIUM-DRY SHERRY

400 g/14 oz CAN WHOLE TOMATOES

1.25 litres/2¼ pints (6 cups) GOOD BEEF STOCK, OR MADE WITH BEEF STOCK CUBE

100 g/4 oz (2 cups) UNCOOKED EGG NOODLES

SALT AND FRESHLY GROUND BLACK PEPPER

SOUR CREAM, TO SERVE

FINELY CHOPPED FRESH PARSLEY, TO GARNISH

In a large, heavy-based pan, using no fat, stir the beef, onions, garlic and pepper over moderate heat until the meat has lost its pink colour. (Takes just a few minutes.) Drain off any excess fat. Stir in the caraway seeds and paprika, then add the sherry. Now add the can of tomatoes with their juice plus the beef stock. Cover and simmer for 20 minutes. Add the noodles and cook, uncovered, for about 10 minutes, until noodles are just tender. Add salt and pepper to taste. When serving add a dollop of sour cream to each bowl and sprinkle with a little finely chopped parsley. *Serves 4.*

Chilled Cream of Parsley Soup

50 g/2 oz BUTTER

1 LARGE ONION

2 STALKS CELERY

2 LARGE POTATOES, PEELED AND CUBED

1 litre/1¾ pints (4 cups) CHICKEN STOCK (p. 183)

SALT AND FRESHLY GROUND BLACK PEPPER

1 BUNCH FRESH PARSLEY, ABOUT 25 g/1 oz (1 cup) LEAVES

100 ml/4 fl oz (½ cup) SINGLE (LIGHT) OR DOUBLE (HEAVY) CREAM

EXTRA FRESH PARSLEY SPRIGS OR LEMON SLICES, TO GARNISH

Melt the butter in a large saucepan. In a food processor with the steel blade, finely chop the onion and celery. (We always string the celery with a vegetable peeler first – a processor never quite gets rid of those strings and you don't get a really smooth soup.) Tip the chopped vegetables into the melted butter, mix well, cover, and sweat over moderate heat for 10 minutes. Stir occasionally, but do not let brown. Add the cubed potatoes, stir and cook, uncovered, for a further 5 minutes. Add the chicken stock and salt and pepper. Simmer gently for 15 minutes or until the potatoes are tender. Place the parsley in the food processor and process until fine. Carefully add the cooled soup and blend until smooth (you may have to do this in 2 stages if the bowl of your processor isn't large enough). Rinse out the saucepan and return the blended soup to it. Add the cream, stir and reheat until it is just coming to the boil. Remove from the heat and cool, then refrigerate, covered, overnight.

Check the consistency the next day and if too thick add a little more cream, or if you consider it to be too rich, thin with milk. Pour into your container and pack with the picnic – don't forget something to drink it out of!

If serving at a dinner, don't thin with the extra cream – pour a little on top of each bowl and garnish with more parsley or a fine slice of lemon. *Serves 6.*

Creamed Mussel Soup

It is considered chic to leave the reserved mussels in their shells and put them in the soup. We think this rather dumb, as you have to plunge your fingers in the hot soup, pick up a scalding-hot mussel, prise it open and eat it! You can use a half mussel shell to drink the soup. We have always wanted to be at a dinner party where they are served this way, and watch a lady in a white satin evening dress coping – however large the table napkin . . .

3 kg/6¼ lb CLEANED MUSSELS

30 ml/2 tbsp FINELY CHOPPED FRESH DILL

30 ml/2 tbsp FINELY CHOPPED FRESH PARSLEY

SALT AND FRESHLY GROUND BLACK PEPPER

4 EGG YOLKS

225 ml/8 fl oz (1 cup) SINGLE (LIGHT) OR WHIPPING CREAM

Steam the mussels as described on page 52, *except* use 200 g/7 oz chopped onions and 350 ml/12 fl oz (1½ cups) dry white wine. Remove from liquid, take from their shells and reserve 24 and the stock. In a processor with the steel blade, purée the mussels with the strained liquid (you may have to do this in batches). Put the purée in a heavy-based saucepan with the dill, parsley and salt and pepper to taste. Mix well and heat, stirring regularly, until nearly boiling.

While the soup is heating, whisk the egg yolks with the cream. When the soup is hot, whisk a little of the soup into the egg yolks. Whisk well. Now add this to the soup, whisking well (this stops the eggs curdling). Heat the soup to boiling point, stirring all the time, but *do not let it boil*. Ladle into heated serving bowls, add the reserved mussels and serve at once. Serves 6.

Minestrone Alla Milanese

There are many varieties of Minestrone (an Italian vegetable soup, basically). This recipe is the one we use most. A bit time-consuming in its preparation, but the end result is very gratifying . . . and very filling. The Pagnotta (p. 158) is an ideal bread to serve with this soup.

100 g/4 oz (⅔ cup) DRIED WHITE HARICOT BEANS, SOAKED OVERNIGHT

75 g/3 oz (½ cup) DRIED PEAS

125 g/4 oz FATTY SALT PORK, FINELY CHOPPED

3 SPRIGS FRESH PARSLEY, FINELY CHOPPED

2 LARGE CLOVES GARLIC, FINELY CHOPPED

1 LARGE ONION, FINELY SLICED

250 g/9 oz MILD BACON, RINDED AND CUT INTO THIN STRIPS

3 LARGE POTATOES, PEELED AND CUBED

3 CARROTS, DICED

3 STALKS CELERY, STRUNG AND SLICED

2 COURGETTES, THINLY SLICED

2 LARGE TOMATOES, SKINNED AND CHOPPED

2.5 ml/½ tsp SALT

2.5 ml/½ tsp FRESHLY GROUND BLACK PEPPER

1 SMALL CABBAGE, FINELY SLICED

200 g/7 oz (1 cup) LONG-GRAIN RICE

20 ml/4 tsp FINELY CHOPPED FRESH BASIL, OR 10 ml/ 2 tsp DRIED

FRESHLY GRATED PARMESAN CHEESE (THE AMOUNT IS UP TO YOU – WE LIKE PLENTY!)

Drain the soaked beans, cover with plenty of fresh water and cook about 20 minutes, until just tender. Drain and keep aside.

Soak the dried peas in hot water about 10 minutes, until they are fat and round. Drain and keep aside.

In a large heavy-based pan, sauté the pork, parsley and garlic over moderate heat until the fat starts to exude from the meat. Add the onion and sauté until soft but not brown. Add the bacon strips and the drained cooked beans. Stir fry for a few minutes, then add all the vegetables, except the cabbage and peas. Raise the heat and stir fry for a further few minutes. Cover with 2.5 litres/4½ pints (12 cups) water, add salt and pepper to taste (don't forget you have used salt pork) and bring to the boil. Lower the heat, cover and simmer for 1½ hours.

Add the cabbage and peas, cook for 15 minutes. Add the washed rice, stir very well and cook for 20 minutes.

Sound the gong – it's ready. Just before serving, stir in the basil, ladle into large soup plates and serve with a bowl of freshly grated Parmesan cheese. *Serves 6 to 8.*

Mulligatawny

There are many versions of this curry soup, which dates from the days of the Raj in India. This one is very easy and quick. The chicken is optional. You can use shredded leftover chicken, or poached chicken breasts, cut into strips. If you are adding chicken and consider the soup may be too thick, omit the rice. Once a can of tomato purée is opened, and only a little used, as in this recipe, the unused portion will spoil quite quickly. It is best removed from the tin as soon as possible. The best idea is to spoon the leftover paste into an ice cube tray and freeze immediately. Pop out when frozen and store in a polythene bag in the freezer, ready to use when required.

30 g/1¼ oz BUTTER

1 ONION, FINELY CHOPPED

1 CARROT, FINELY CHOPPED

10 ml/2 tsp GOOD CURRY POWDER

2.5 ml/½ tsp POWDERED CUMIN

1.25 ml/¼ tsp GRATED NUTMEG

1 COOKING APPLE, PEELED, CORED AND COARSELY CHOPPED

10 ml/2 tsp TOMATO PURÉE (PASTE)

2.5 ml/½ tsp GARAM MASALA

65 ml/2½ fl oz (⅓ cup) MEDIUM-DRY SHERRY

15 ml/1 tbsp CRUMBLED BEEF STOCK CUBES

1 litre/1¾ pints (4 cups) WARM WATER

275 g/10 oz (2 cups) COOKED LONG-GRAIN RICE

COOKED CHICKEN, SHREDDED (OPTIONAL)

225 g/8 oz (1 cup) YOGHURT

In a large, heavy-based saucepan, melt the butter, add onion and carrot and stir fry over moderate heat until just softened. Stir in curry powder and stir fry for 2 to 3 minutes (this lets the flavour buds burst). Add cumin, nutmeg, apple, tomato purée and garam masala. Stir well to mix and cook for 1 to 2 minutes. Add sherry and stir quickly to mix. Add beef stock cubes and warm water, stirring very well to blend. Bring to the boil, cover and simmer for 10 to 15 minutes. Blend the soup in a food processor fitted with the steel blade. Return to saucepan, add cooked rice and chicken and reheat gently. Serve in heated soup bowls. Divide the soup equally between bowls, topping each with yoghurt. *Serves 4.*

Gutsy Onion Soup

This is a natural for cold winter days, but is also ideal when you have been working hard and want
something really nourishing to give you back a bit of vitality. The addition of brandy gives this
version its extra zing.

50 g/2 oz UNSALTED BUTTER

5 LARGE ONIONS, FINELY SLICED

1 CLOVE GARLIC, CRUSHED

15 ml/1 tbsp SOFT BROWN SUGAR

FRESHLY GROUND BLACK PEPPER

15 ml/1 tbsp PLAIN FLOUR

50 ml/2 fl oz (¼ cup) BRANDY

1.2 litres/2 pints (5 cups) BEEF STOCK, PREFERABLY HOMEMADE (p. 182)

6 SLICES FRENCH BREAD, CUT DIAGONALLY

EXTRA BUTTER FOR SPREADING

175 g/6 oz (1 cup) CHEDDAR OR EMMENTHAL (SWISS) CHEESE, GRATED

45 ml/3 tbsp GRATED PARMESAN CHEESE

Melt the butter over moderate heat in a heavy-based saucepan and add the onions and the garlic. Cook them, with the lid on, for a few minutes, until they soften. Add the sugar, raise the heat slightly and continue cooking, stirring from time to time, until they turn a dark brown. Do not let them burn. The addition of the sugar will increase the risk of burning, so be careful. Stir in the pepper and flour and cook for 1 minute. Carefully add the brandy and boil it until it evaporates slightly. Heat stock separately and pour in. Simmer the soup for 10 to 15 minutes.

Meanwhile, spread both sides of the slices of bread with a little butter and place them on a baking sheet in a 180C/350F/Gas 4 oven for about 10 minutes, until they start to turn golden brown. Remove and leave to cool slightly. Mix the grated cheese with the Parmesan and divide equally between the slices of baked bread. Ladle the soup into 6 heatproof bowls and top each with a cheese-laden bread slice. Grill until the cheese melts and bubbles. Serve straight away. (Be careful when you start to eat as it is scaldingly hot.) *Serves 6.*

Crab and Egg Soup

When making our Prawn Curry (p. 47) from fresh peeled prawns, we always boil up the peels with a small sliced onion, a few stalks of parsley and a little chopped carrot and celery, then strain through a very fine sieve to make a stock for later use. If you have this stock on hand it is ideal for this recipe. Use about 225 ml/8 fl oz (1 cup) as a replacement for 225 ml/8 fl oz (1 cup) chicken stock. When we originally tried a soup similar to this in Singapore, a small jug of very dark sharp vinegar was served to counteract the sweetish taste of the soup, using only about 2.5 ml/ ½ tsp per serving. The name of the vinegar is Tientsin, but failing that, a good squeeze of sharp lemon juice can be used. Purely personal taste really, and we don't always use it.

200 g/7 oz CAN CRAB MEAT

1 litre/1¾ pints (4 cups) CHICKEN STOCK, PREFERABLY HOMEMADE (p. 183)

SALT, TO TASTE

2.5 ml/½ tsp GROUND WHITE PEPPER

6 CHINESE MUSHROOMS, SOAKED, DRAINED AND SLICED

10 ml/2 tsp LIGHT SOY SAUCE

10 ml/2 tsp SUGAR

10 ml/2 tsp SESAME OIL

60 ml/4 tbsp CORNFLOUR

100 ml/4 fl oz (½ cup) WATER

2 EGGS, SIZE 1, BEATEN

If you haven't any chicken stock, simmer together a little more than 1 litre/1¾ pints (4 cups) water with a chicken stock cube and a small packet of chicken wings for about 30 minutes, then strain, leave to cool and de-fat before using in this recipe.

Remove the crab from the can, take out any cartilage, and flake lightly. Bring the chicken stock, salt, pepper, mushrooms, soy, sugar and sesame oil to the simmer in a large saucepan and simmer for about 3 minutes. Add the crab meat. Mix the cornflour and water together to make a smooth paste, then add to the soup, stirring. Simmer gently another 2 minutes. Increase the heat slightly and, still stirring in a circular motion, quickly pour in beaten eggs in a stream. They will form threads. Remove from the heat and serve immediately. *Serves 4.*

Carrot and Peanut Butter Soup

It may sound like a peculiar combination, but we can assure you that it is really moreish. The amount of peanut butter you use is virtually up to you, but do use the creamiest peanut butter you can buy, rather than one of the crunchy types. We have found this a good soup to freeze. Cool completely and place in well sealed plastic freezer boxes. Leave to thaw right through before reheating.

50 g/2 oz BUTTER

1 LARGE ONION, COARSELY CHOPPED

5 LARGE CARROTS, DICED

2.5 ml/½ tsp SALT

6 GRINDINGS BLACK PEPPER

20 ml/4 tsp CRUMBLED CHICKEN STOCK CUBES

750 ml/1¼ pints (3 cups) WATER

65 ml/2½ fl oz (⅓ cup) MEDIUM-DRY SHERRY

30 ml/2 tbsp SMOOTH PEANUT BUTTER

JUICE OF ½ LEMON

SOUR CREAM (OPTIONAL)

Melt the butter in a heavy-based casserole or saucepan with lid and sauté the onion and carrots over moderate heat for about 5 minutes, stirring to coat them with the butter. Sprinkle in the salt, pepper and chicken stock cubes. Pour in the water and stir until the liquid comes to the boil. Cover and simmer gently until the carrots and onions are soft.

In a food processor fitted with the steel blade, purée the soup in 2 batches, or use a food mill, blender or sieve. Return the purée to the saucepan, add the sherry and bring back to a gentle simmer. Whisk in the peanut butter and adjust seasoning. At this stage add more peanut butter if you wish and extra water should you wish to thin the soup down a little. Finally, stir in the lemon juice and serve straight away. Do not be tempted to serve large portions at first as it is filling and rich. You can always go back for seconds. You can, if you wish, stir in a little sour cream just before serving. *Serves 6.*

SAVOURIES AND STARTERS

The days of soup, fish, starter, main course, pudding and finally cheese and biscuits have generally gone by the board unless it is a special 'blow-out' occasion. This section isn't just for those who still like to have several courses to make up a complete meal. Many of these dishes can be used as a light main course for lunch, or perhaps 2 or 3 can be served together as a main course for an evening meal.

Certain of the dishes, such as Spinach Gnocchi or Stuffed Mushroom Caps for example, can be used to accompany main course meats or fish.

Simple dishes like Bread and Onion Pudding are the stuff that armies could have marched on, and have the advantage of being made from ingredients that are staples in most kitchens.

An art well worth mastering is the making of good thin pancakes. The recipe in this section has more butter than most call for, but we can assure you that they remain tender, moist and flexible, even after they have been frozen and thawed. They are a definite must to have in the freezer as a stand-by to help you make quick savoury or sweet dishes.

Crustless Quiche

This is a very easy and quick dish to have for lunch or as the first course to a main meal. It can be varied by adding one of the following to the ingredients: chopped ham, chopped cooked bacon, sautéed onion slices, cooked quartered mushrooms or even slivered sliced salami.

90 g/3¾ oz (¾ cup) PLAIN FLOUR, SIFTED

2.5 ml/½ tsp SALT

8 GRINDINGS BLACK PEPPER

40 g/1½ oz BUTTER, SOFTENED

4 EGGS, SIZE 1, LIGHTLY BEATEN

450 ml/ ¾ pint (2 cups) MILK

75 g/3 oz (½ cup) BRAN

200 g/7 oz TASTY CHEDDAR CHEESE, GRATED

Sift the flour, salt and pepper into a large bowl, then rub in the butter as though you were about to make pastry. Add the eggs, milk and bran and mix well with a whisk. Stir in the grated cheese and at this stage add any of the other suggested flavourings, if you want to.

Rub a deep quiche dish inside with a little butter to grease. Set the oven to 160C/315F/ Gas 2½. When the oven has reached its temperature, stir the mixture one more time to distribute the solids and pour into the prepared quiche dish. Bake in the middle of the oven, about 30 minutes, until golden brown and well risen. Leave to cool slightly, in which case the quiche will sink slightly. Cut and serve either hot or cold. Will serve 4 to 6 as part of a meal with some vegetables or salad.

Egg Rolls with Pork Filling

These can be used as part of a full Chinese meal, but we prefer to serve them as a light, tasty first course, especially prior to perhaps a main fish dish. They can be served hot or cold – either way, they really are delicious. Either mince the pork a little at a time in a food processor fitted with a steel blade (it should be partially frozen for this) or grind it through the finest blade of a mincer. The Chinese five spices are an integral part of the flavour of this filling and can be purchased from most delicatessens as well as Chinese supermarkets and Asian shops.

250 g/9 oz PORK, FINELY MINCED

7.5 ml/1½ tsp (LIGHT) SOY SAUCE

5 ml/1 tsp CORNFLOUR

12.5 ml/2½ tsp DRY SHERRY OR GIN

5 ml/1 tsp SALT

1 EGG, LIGHTLY BEATEN

PINCH OF CHINESE FIVE SPICES

4 EGGS, SIZE 1

7.5 ml/1½ tsp GROUNDNUT (PEANUT) OIL

SPRING ONIONS, TO GARNISH

In a bowl combine the minced pork, soy sauce, cornflour, sherry or gin, salt, beaten egg and the five spices. Mix well; set aside. Beat the 4 eggs together until well combined, but not fluffy. Take a fairly large non-stick frying pan and heat 5 ml/1 tsp groundnut oil. When it is hot, after about 30 seconds over a high heat, pour in half the beaten egg and swirl round to coat the base of the pan. Pour off into a small bowl any runny egg mixture that hasn't set. Remove the pan from the heat once the base has been covered to form a thin omelette and leave for about another 30 seconds so that it sets. You don't want to overcook this, just get it to the stage where it has set enough to remove from the pan. A non-stick pan makes it easier to slide out. Don't cook the other side, just slide the omelette onto a plate or board. Return the pan to the heat and add the other 2.5 ml/½ tsp oil. Heat the pan again and pour in the remaining beaten eggs. Again swirl round on the base, tip out any egg that doesn't set and reserve, then slide omelette onto a plate or board.

Let the thin omelettes go cold before attempting to spread the pork mixture over them. This allows them to firm up somewhat and they are less likely to be torn. Spread the pork mixture evenly over the uncooked sides of the 2 omelettes and roll them up fairly tightly like a Swiss roll. Brush the edges of the last part of each roll with the reserved beaten egg and press to seal so that they won't unroll while being cooked.

Place the rolls on a plate and then in a steamer and steam over simmering water for 20 minutes. If you haven't a steamer, place a cake rack or trivet in a large oven dish or casserole, pour in a little water to come just below the rack, cover with a lid or a sheet of foil and simmer gently on the hob. When you place the plate containing the pork rolls on the rack, make sure the water below does not boil over onto the plate or this will ruin the egg rolls. Remove from the steamer and when cooled slightly cut into diagonal slices about 1 cm/½ inch thick. Scatter with sliced spring onions. *Serves 4.*

Salmon Tartlets

These are best made as individual small tartlets rather than a larger one, which would be a quiche. They are fairly rich, and 1 per person, together with a vegetable such as asparagus or broccoli, makes a very good light meal. Use the best quality tinned salmon for more flavour. You may prefer a little more dill than the recipe states, but be careful not to overpower the salmon.

213 g/7½ oz CAN RED SALMON

15 ml/1 tbsp CORNFLOUR

2 EGGS, SIZE 1

100 ml/4 fl oz (½ cup) SINGLE (LIGHT) CREAM

SALT AND FRESHLY GROUND BLACK PEPPER

1.25 ml/¼ tsp DRIED DILL

15 ml/1 tbsp LEMON JUICE

1 SLICE BREAD, TURNED INTO CRUMBS

6 x 10 cm/4 inch PASTRY SHELLS, PARTIALLY BAKED

Mash the salmon and the juices together and place in a bowl. Mix the cornflour, eggs, cream and salt and pepper together in another bowl, then add to the salmon. Add the dill, lemon juice and breadcrumbs and mix in with a spoon. Divide equally between the pastry shells and bake at 180C/350F/Gas 4 for about 15 to 20 minutes until the filling has just set. Serve hot with lemon wedges and a green vegetable or salad. *Serves 6.*

Curried Seafood Filling

This is quite a versatile filling, and we used to ring the changes on how we served it when we ran our own seafood restaurant. The season dictated how it was served, but it could be stuffed into very thin pancakes and then baked, or placed in large buttered mushroom caps and baked. Some people consider it a sin to treat good fresh fish and scallops in this manner by adding curry powder. We don't, and neither will you when you taste the end result and realise that this is a versatile dish indeed.

75 g/3 oz BUTTER

10 ml/2 tsp GOOD CURRY POWDER

250 g/9 oz FIRM WHITE FISH FILLETS, SUCH AS COD, MONKFISH OR HADDOCK, SKINNED AND CUBED BUT NOT TOO SMALL

125 g/4 oz SCALLOPS, CUT INTO 2 OR 3 PIECES DEPENDING ON SIZE

100 g/4 oz CAN SHRIMPS, DRAINED

30 ml/2 tbsp PLAIN FLOUR

100 ml/ 4 fl oz (½ cup) DRY WHITE WINE OR DRY VERMOUTH

100 ml/4 fl oz (1 cup) CHICKEN STOCK, PREFERABLY HOMEMADE (p. 183)

100 ml/4 fl oz (½ cup) SINGLE (LIGHT) CREAM

SALT AND FRESHLY GROUND BLACK PEPPER

2.5 ml/½ tsp GARAM MASALA

Melt the butter in a large, non-stick frying pan and add the curry powder. Stir for 2 minutes over moderate heat to release its aroma. Add the cubed fish and the scallops and cook for 2 minutes, then add the drained shrimps. Sprinkle over the flour and keep stirring for another minute. As the shrimps are canned, they will disintegrate into a mush, but don't worry as the flavour will still be there. Add the wine or vermouth and let it bubble briskly, then add the chicken stock. Add the cream, season with a little salt and pepper and then add the garam masala. Stir until it bubbles, cook for 1 more minute and remove from the heat. Leave to cool.

Stuffed Pancakes

Take 12 cooked pancakes (p. 34). With a slotted spoon, place a good 15 ml/1 tbsp of the mixture on each pancake and roll up into a cylinder. Place side by side on a large buttered ovenproof dish. Over the tops of the pancakes drizzle the sauce left behind when you removed the solids to the filling, and bake at 150C/300F/Gas 2 for about 15 to 20 minutes, until heated through. Serve as a starting course. *Serves 6.*

Stuffed Mushroom Caps

Choose about 12 fairly large mushroom caps, wipe over carefully and remove the stalks. Brush the insides and outsides of the mushrooms with some melted butter and divide the chilled mixture equally between them to fill the cavities, mounding the filling slightly. Place side by side in a shallow ovenproof dish and bake at 180C/350F/Gas 4 for about 15 to 20 minutes until bubbling. Serve as a starter. *Serves 6.*

Baked Smoked Mussels

Smoked mussels can be purchased in cans, like sardines. This starter is very well flavoured and is simple to prepare.

250 g/9 oz CAN SMOKED MUSSELS

2 CLOVES GARLIC, CRUSHED

25 g/1 oz BUTTER

1 STICK CELERY, FINELY CHOPPED

2.5 ml/½ tsp CURRY POWDER

50 ml/2 fl oz (¼ cup) SINGLE (LIGHT) CREAM

A LITTLE SALT AND FRESHLY GROUND BLACK PEPPER

JUICE OF ½ LEMON

2 SLICES WHITE BREAD, CRUSTS REMOVED

50g /2 oz BUTTER, DICED

LEMON WEDGES, TO SERVE

Drain the mussels and cut into small pieces. Put the garlic, 25 g/1 oz butter and chopped celery in a saucepan and cook over low heat for about 5 minutes. Add the curry powder and cook, stirring, for another 2 minutes. Add the cream, salt and pepper and the chopped mussels and bring just to boiling point over moderate heat. Remove from the heat and tip into an ovenproof dish just large enough to hold the mussels in a single layer. Sprinkle with the lemon juice. Turn the slices of bread into crumbs in a food processor and sprinkle over the mussels to cover completely. Dot with the remaining 50 g/2 oz butter, diced, and bake at 200C/400F/Gas 6 about 20 minutes, or until the crumbs are browned. Serve with lemon wedges. *Serves 4.*

Spinach Gnocchi

There are several types of gnocchi made from flour, semolina or potato. This one is made from ricotta cheese. These small dumplings, for that is really what they resemble, are very light and make an ideal first course. We have often read that they can be made well in advance or frozen for use later on, but we disagree as we have found from experience that they tend to lose their light, delicate texture and become rather stodgy. You can make the mixture a day or so in advance and even shape them too, but we still feel that it is best to poach them, drain them, layer them up in a buttered baking dish and cook them straight away. That is particularly true for this recipe, if the dumplings are to retain their fresh flavour.

When buying ricotta cheese make sure that it is moist and creamy and not dry and crumbly. If it is prepacked, look for packages that are hermetically sealed. In really good delicatessens you can buy straight from a bulk supply. We have tried using cottage cheese instead of ricotta for this recipe, but we feel that the texture and flavour are not as good.

1 GOOD-SIZED BUNCH YOUNG SPINACH

500 g/18 oz RICOTTA CHEESE

100 g/4 oz FRESH PARMESAN CHEESE, FINELY GRATED

2 EGGS, SIZE 1

2.5 ml/½ tsp SALT

12 GRINDINGS BLACK PEPPER

SEVERAL GRATINGS NUTMEG

PLAIN FLOUR

60 g/2⅓ oz BUTTER, MELTED

30 ml/2 tbsp FRESHLY GRATED PARMESAN CHEESE

Wash the spinach well in plenty of cold water to remove the dirt and grit. Tear off the stalks and shake the excess water from the leaves. Cook the spinach over moderate heat with only the water that clings to the leaves, or in a microwave oven in a covered casserole or large polythene bag with the end open; microwave on High for 4 minutes, until the leaves are limp. Leave to cool, then squeeze as much water from the leaves as you can and chop very finely. Tip the ricotta into a large bowl and beat with a wooden spoon until smooth. Add the chopped spinach, Parmesan, eggs, salt, pepper and nutmeg and beat all together until well combined. Cover with cling film and chill for about 1 hour.

Bring a large pan of lightly salted water to simmering point. Sprinkle some plain flour on a shallow oven tray, and with a tablespoon take up some of the mixture and dump it into the flour. Sprinkle some flour on your hands and shape the heaped mixture into a cylindrical shape rather than a ball. The mixture is very light and fairly sticky, so coat the dumpling fairly well with flour, not to work into the mixture, just to stop it sticking to your hands.

After shaping about 5 or 6 dumplings, put them in the water and simmer them very gently for about 2 to 3 minutes, until the gnocchi rise to the surface. Transfer carefully (they are delicate) with a slotted spoon to several thicknesses of kitchen paper and drain. While they are cooling, shape another 6 or so and drop them into the simmering water.

Butter a large flameproof dish and place the cooled gnocchi into it, preferably keeping them in a single layer. Continue to shape, cook and drain the remaining mixture until all is used up. The mixture should make about 24 good-sized gnocchi. When all of them have been placed in the buttered dish, drizzle them with the melted butter and sprinkle over the remaining 30 ml/2 tbsp Parmesan. While they are still warm, pop under a grill for 5 to 10 minutes, depending on distance from heat, until the tops start to turn golden brown. Serve on heated plates as a first course or use them to accompany a main dish such as Stuffed Chicken, Italian Style (p. 86) or simple grilled chicken. *Serves 6.*

Walnut and Camembert Pâté

Simplicity itself and easy to prepare. Use as a snack with drinks before dinner, or leave to the end of the meal and serve with some fresh pears and a glass of port.

75 g/3 oz WALNUTS

1 CAMEMBERT CHEESE

125 g/4 oz FULL-FAT SOFT CHEESE, SOFTENED

50 g/2 oz UNSALTED BUTTER

45 ml/3 tbsp KIRSCH

8 GRINDINGS FRESH BLACK PEPPER

The whole procedure is best carried out with a food processor fitted with the steel blade. Chop the walnuts roughly with an on/off action. Do not overchop, as you need a bit of 'crunch' in the end result. Tip out into a bowl.

Cut the camembert, full-fat soft cheese and butter into small pieces and place in the processor bowl. Blend until creamy, stopping from time to time to scrape down the sides of the bowl with a spatula. When thoroughly blended, scrape into the bowl containing the walnuts and mix in the kirsch and the black pepper.

Line a dish large enough to hold the mixture with cling film, leaving some to overhang the edges. Place the mixture into the dish and rap on the top of the work surface to dispel any air. Cover the top with the overhang of cling film and place in the fridge to chill. This is best left overnight to allow the flavours to develop properly.

Turn the pâté out onto a plate, remove the cling film and leave at room temperature for 30 minutes to soften a little. Serve as above or with sticks of crisp celery. If you haven't any kirsch, try calvados or dry vermouth. *Serves 4-6.*

Individual Scallop Pies

This is one of our favourite dinner party starters. It can be prepared the day before and refrigerated. You will need a 225 ml/8 fl oz (1 cup) ramekin per person. If you're a bit short on scallops a few small green seedless grapes mixed with the scallops before the sauce is added make a super addition. Serve this version with a spoon.

APPROXIMATELY 6 SCALLOPS PER SERVING, DEPENDING ON THEIR SIZE (YOU MAY NEED A FEW EXTRA IF THEY ARE SMALL)

10-15 ml/2-3 tsp THICK BÉCHAMEL SAUCE PER SERVING (SEE BELOW)

2 SHEETS FROZEN FLAKY PASTRY, EACH ABOUT 25 cm/10 inches SQUARE (FOR 4 SERVINGS), THAWED

PLAIN FLOUR

1 EGG

Drain the scallops and trim off the sand track (usually black). Divide the scallops between the dishes (don't pack down!). Spoon 10-15 ml/2-3 tsp Béchamel Sauce over each serving.

Lay out the sheets of pastry and let soften. We use a wide champagne glass for cutting the pastry, as the round covers the dish with a little overhang. Dip the glass in flour and gently twist a round from the pastry sheet (you get 2 to the sheet). Wet the rim of the dish, place the pastry round on top and press down. Dip a fork into the flour and score the rim of the pastry to make an attractive edge. (There is enough pastry left over after cutting out the rounds to cut out 1 heart per serving if you want to. Wet one side of the heart and place on top of the pie.) Lightly beat the egg and brush the tops well. Refrigerate for several hours or overnight. Rebrush with egg. Poke a steam hole in the centre of each heart.

Preheat oven to 180C/350F/Gas 4, place oven rack in the upper half of the oven and bake the pies about 20 minutes, until golden brown and puffed. (You may have to give them a half turn to keep the colour even.) Serve at once.

Béchamel Sauce

15 ml/1 tbsp BUTTER

30 ml/2 tbsp PLAIN FLOUR

225 ml/8 fl oz (1 cup) MILK

1 BAY LEAF

PINCH EACH OF GRATED NUTMEG, SALT AND FRESHLY GROUND BLACK PEPPER

15 ml/1 tbsp BRANDY

15 ml/1 tbsp MEDIUM-DRY SHERRY

Melt butter in a heavy-based saucepan, remove from heat and stir in the flour until smooth. Stir in the milk, little by little – the sauce must be smooth. If you prefer, do this with a balloon whisk. Whisk over heat until sauce thickens. Add bay leaf, nutmeg, pepper and salt, stir over gentle heat for 5 minutes. Don't leave it, as it will burn very quickly. Whisk in the brandy and sherry and leave to cool. Gently lay a film of cling film over the top of the sauce to stop a skin forming.

Oyster and Bacon Kebabs

This is a bit fiddly to prepare, but can be done in advance and kept in the refrigerator for the final preparation and cooking. Perfect to have with drinks before a meal.

36 FRESH OYSTERS, BOTTLED OR FRESHLY SHELLED

6 BACON RASHERS, RINDED

SINGLE (LIGHT) CREAM FOR DIPPING

PLAIN FLOUR FOR DUSTING

GROUNDNUT (PEANUT) OIL FOR FRYING

TOUCH OF CAYENNE, PAPRIKA OR CHINESE FIVE SPICES (OPTIONAL)

CHILLI SAUCE, TO SERVE (OPTIONAL)

Drain the oysters if bottled. Soak wooden skewers in hot water, to cleanse as well as to make them swell a little. Lay the bacon rashers on a board and stretch gently with the back of a knife. Lay out on kitchen paper and cover with another piece of paper. Place in the microwave and cook on High for 1 minute, or gently fry until just cooked.

Cut the rashers into small pieces but still big enough to fold in half to put on a skewer. Fold a piece of bacon in half and thread on a skewer – not too far up, as you are going to deep fry them. Now gently thread on an oyster, another piece of bacon, another oyster, more bacon, another oyster and finally another piece of bacon. We usually do 3 oysters to the skewer, which is just comfortable to eat and easy to cook. Prepare all the skewers, place on a plate, cover with greaseproof paper, and keep in the fridge until ready to cook.

Pour some cream onto a dinner plate and put some flour on another dinner plate. Dip each kebab in the cream and roll round to coat well, then roll in the flour. Dust very, very lightly in one of the condiments, if you are using one. In a deep-fat fryer or a heavy based saucepan with about 225 ml/8 fl oz (1 cup) oil, fry the kebabs, a few at a time, just a few minutes, until golden brown.

Hand to guests with a sheet of kitchen paper . . . delicious. A little bowl of chilli sauce on the side makes an unusual addition – just drizzle a little along the kebab. *Makes 12.*

Smoked Eel and Shrimp Pâté

200 g/7 oz SMOKED EEL

200 g/7 oz FULL-FAT SOFT CHEESE

30 ml/2 tbsp WORCESTERSHIRE SAUCE

DASH OF TABASCO SAUCE

2.5 ml/½ tsp SALT

2.5 ml/½ tsp GROUND WHITE PEPPER

JUICE OF ½ LEMON

2 EGG WHITES

200g/7 oz CAN SHRIMPS, WELL DRAINED

LEMON SLICES, TO GARNISH

FRESH PARSLEY SPRIGS, TO GARNISH

COOL TOAST TRIANGLES AND LEMON WEDGES, TO SERVE

In a food processor with the steel blade, process the eel, cheese, Worcestershire sauce, Tabasco sauce and salt and pepper to a smooth paste. Add lemon juice and quickly blend again. Scrape out into a clean bowl. Whisk the egg whites until stiff and fold in with the drained shrimp. (Reserve a few shrimp for garnishing.)

Divide the mixture into individual 100 ml/4 fl oz ramekins or elegant glasses and tap gently on a towel on the kitchen surface to settle them. Cover with cling film and refrigerate for several hours until well chilled.

When ready to serve, uncover and decorate each serving with ¼ of a fine lemon slice, a tiny sprig of parsley and a reserved shrimp. Serve with cold toast triangles, lemon wedges and a knife. A little bowl of unsweetened whipped cream, with a little fresh-grated horseradish folded in, is a nice accompaniment. *Should make about 6 small pâtés.*

Note: should you wish to soften the full-fat soft cheese slightly, unwrap it, roughly cube it, place it in a glass bowl and microwave on Medium for 45 to 60 seconds.

Bread and Onion Pudding

When the weather is bleak and dreary and there is nothing in the house to eat, you can usually find a few onions, some bread, milk and eggs. If you haven't any of these, you will have to slip into something warm and go down to the local store . . . the effort will be worth it.

9 SLICES THICK BREAD

350 g/12 oz (2½ cups) ONIONS, DICED

45 ml/3 tbsp BACON FAT

2.5 ml/½ tsp CARAWAY SEEDS

FRESHLY GROUND BLACK PEPPER

450 ml/¾ pint (2 cups) MILK

100 ml/4 fl oz (½ cup) SINGLE (LIGHT) CREAM

3 EGGS, SIZE 1

7.5 ml/1½ tsp SALT

DASH OF TABASCO SAUCE

3 RASHERS BACON, RINDED AND FINELY CHOPPED

GRATED CHEESE (OPTIONAL)

Trim the crusts from the bread and cut each slice in half. In a square ovenproof dish, spread 6 half slices of bread in 2 rows so that there is space between the edge of the slices. (You should choose a dish the right size for this. If it is just too small, trim the slices of bread slightly to fit.)

Sauté the diced onions in the bacon fat in a large frying pan over moderate heat for about 6 minutes or until golden. Spread half the onions over the slices of bread in the dish and sprinkle over 1.25 ml/¼ tsp caraway seeds. Add a few grindings of black pepper, then repeat the bread layer and the rest of the onions, together with the remainder of the caraway seeds and a little more of the pepper. Finally the last slices of bread are placed on top. You now have 6 individual stacked onion sandwiches. Combine in a jug the milk, cream, eggs, salt and Tabasco sauce. Whisk to combine, carefully pour over the bread and sprinkle the chopped bacon over the top.

Place this dish in a larger one and pour in enough hot water to come half way up the sides of the dish containing the bread and onion mixture. Bake at 180C/350F/Gas 4 in the upper third of a preheated oven for 1 hour, or until the custard is set and the top is golden brown. If you wish, you can sprinkle a little grated cheese over the top in the last 15 minutes of cooking time. Remove and leave to cool slightly before serving. This is excellent to serve with a grilled chop, or on its own as a snack. *Serves 6.*

Fried Stuffed Pancakes with Tongue and Mushrooms

Most recipes for pancakes are very ungenerous with the butter. Our recipe has plenty, which makes for a moist pancake that not only is tender and good tasting, but freezes well for those times you have unexpected guests. We have been using this recipe for almost 20 years and it has never failed us yet, nor will it fail you.

One essential is a crêpe pan that is kept strictly for that purpose, one that never sees water. It is said that when you make your first pancake it never turns out well. This is true in most cases, as the first one is really testing the heat of the pan. You will find by experience the right heat to use – write it beside this recipe when you are confident that you have got it right.

Have a large plate ready to place the cooked pancakes on, or greaseproof paper to go between them for freezing, and a ladle or small measuring jug to give you just enough batter to make 1 pancake at a time. Our ladle is just the right size and is about equivalent to about 40 ml/1 ½ fl oz. This recipe will make about 30 pancakes. Stack them with paper in between to freeze in packets of 8, or whatever you find most suitable. To freeze, leave them to cool and put them in plastic bags, remove as much air as you can with a vacuum pump and seal well. To thaw, either leave them at room temperature or remove the tie from the plastic bag and pop them in the microwave on High for about 2 minutes. If they are warmed through slightly the butter content in the pancakes helps you to separate them easily.

Basic Pancake Recipe

275 g/10 oz (2 cups) PLAIN FLOUR

PINCH OF SALT

4 EGGS, SIZE 1

450 ml/¾ pint (2 cups) MILK

150 g/5 oz BUTTER, MELTED AND COOLED

Sift the flour and salt into a large mixing bowl. Break in the eggs, mix together, then add the milk. With an electric hand mixer, a rotary whisk, or even a balloon whisk, whisk the mixture together until it is well combined and totally free of lumps. Watch that you scrape the edge of the bowl and the base so that no flour remains unincorporated. Beat in the cooled melted butter and leave the mixture to stand, covered with a clean tea-towel, for 1 hour. Just before making the pancakes, check the mixture. It should have the consistency of single cream – if it seems too thick, stir in a little water.

Heat the pan with a little non-flavoured oil in it, tip out the oil when the pan is hot and add sufficient batter to just cover the base of the pan when you swirl it round – you want to keep them as thin as possible. Cook for about 40 seconds, or until the top surface loses its wet appearance. With a palette knife, carefully turn the pancake over and cook the other side for about 30 seconds. Try tossing them if you wish – it is good fun, and even if the first few drop on the floor you will get enough practice to do it right in the future. Cook them just until they have dark beige spots on them, not burnt black ones. Slip the cooked pancake onto the plate and put the pan back on the heat source while you measure the next ladle of batter, so that the pan doesn't cool off too much between pancakes. If the first pancake is too dark, lower the heat slightly, or if it takes longer than about 40 seconds to cook, raise the heat slightly. You really will soon get the hang of it and be the world's best pancakemaker.

Filling for 8 Pancakes

8 THIN SLICES COOKED TONGUE

8 THIN SLICES EMMENTHAL (SWISS) CHEESE, CUT INTO STRIPS

4 LARGE MUSHROOMS, THINLY SLICED

30 g/1 1/4 oz BUTTER

PLAIN FLOUR

50 g/2 oz BUTTER

30 ml/2 tbsp GROUNDNUT (PEANUT) OIL

Lay the pancakes on a clean surface, and put a slice of tongue on each. Lay the strips of cheese horizontally across the tongue slices. Fry the mushroom slices in the 30 g/1 1/4 oz butter over high heat for just a few moments and cool a little before dividing equally over the cheese strips. Starting from the side closest to you, roll up each pancake to enclose the filling, tucking in the ends before the final roll so as to make an enclosed package. Dust carefully with flour. Heat the remaining 50 g/2 oz butter with the oil in a large frying pan (preferably non-stick) until bubbling, and fry the pancakes over fairly high heat until golden and crisp on both sides. Serve at once as a starter. *Serves 4.*

Barbecued Marinated Fillet

If you like barely cooked beef, this recipe is the one for you. It's superb made into sandwiches for a picnic, or served elegantly as a starter for a dinner party.

4 SPRING ONIONS, COARSELY CHOPPED

65 ml/2½ fl oz (⅓ cup) SOYBEAN SAUCE

45 ml/3 tbsp DARK SOY SAUCE

30 ml/2 tbsp DARK BROWN SUGAR

15 ml/1 tbsp PEELED AND FINELY CHOPPED FRESH ROOT GINGER

2 CLOVES GARLIC, FINELY CHOPPED

5 ml/1 tsp SALT

5 ml/1 tsp RED PEPPER FLAKES

350 ml/12 fl oz (1½ cups) DARK ALE

1 kg/2¼ lb FILLET OF BEEF, IN ONE PIECE

In a very large glass or ceramic bowl, mix together all the ingredients, except the ale and the fillet. Stir thoroughly until the sugar has dissolved. Add the ale and stir well. Remove all traces of sinew from the fillet (very important), shape it into a neat long roll, and tie it with string in several places. Put the fillet in the marinade and slosh around to coat. Cover and refrigerate for no less than 1 or 2 days. Don't forget to turn the beef regularly – this ensures the meat is well impregnated with the flavours.

Preheat your barbecue (don't have the rack too close to the coals, as you don't want to cause any flare-up). Remove the fillet from the marinade and pat dry with kitchen paper, place on the barbecue and grill for 15 minutes on either side, turning only once. We actually only cook it for 10 minutes either side, but we like it very rare. Really all we are doing is crusting the outside of the fillet. Remove to a plate and let cool, cover well, and refrigerate overnight. It will only keep 1 day with safety.

With an extremely sharp knife, thinly slice the meat across the grain. As this is rather hard to do, pop the covered meat into the freezer for about an hour – this firms it and you can cut it more finely. Serve with fresh French bread and Shallot Butter (p. 38). Or, overlap slices on serving plates and drizzle Mayonnaise Sauce (p. 38) along it.

Throw the marinade away or do another piece of beef, cook, wrap and freeze for later use. Thaw in the refrigerator. *Serves 6 to 12.*

Hot Courgette and Carrot Salad with Gorgonzola and Cashews

The first time we tried this scrumptious dish, walnuts were used. We have found sometimes that if walnuts are not fresh, they can have a rather bitter taste. We suggest cashews or even pine nuts, but if you know that your walnuts are fresh and sweet, use them. Sometimes we have bought some packaged walnuts and unintentionally had them too long, so long, in fact, that they have attracted some nasty little wiggly things. These should not be used under any circumstances. You may use any blue cheese in place of the gorgonzola – Stilton, Danish blue or Roquefort.

8 SMALL YOUNG CARROTS

4 COURGETTES

100 g/4 oz UNSALTED BUTTER

225 ml/8 fl oz (1 cup) SINGLE (LIGHT) CREAM

200 g/7 oz GORGONZOLA

FRESHLY GRATED NUTMEG

SALT AND FRESHLY GROUND BLACK PEPPER

50 g/2 oz (½ cup) CASHEW, PINE NUTS OR WALNUTS, FINELY CHOPPED AND LIGHTLY TOASTED

Trim and peel the carrots and drop into sufficient salted boiling water to cover. Boil until just tender; test after 5 minutes if they are really young carrots – do not let them get too soft. Drain, refresh under running cold water and set aside. Top and tail and wipe the courgettes and boil and refresh as for the carrots. When they are cool enough to handle, cut into fairly fine julienne strips and leave on kitchen paper to drain.

In a heavy-based saucepan, melt the butter and add the cream, bring to the boil and reduce over fairly high heat to half, stirring to prevent it catching. Break the gorgonzola into small pieces and add to the reduced cream and stir until the cheese has melted and the sauce has thickened. Add some grated nutmeg, salt and freshly ground black pepper to taste. Gently stir in the carrots until heated through, then the courgettes (this is why they should not be overcooked when first blanched). Turn carefully to coat with the sauce and serve sprinkled with the toasted chopped nuts.

This will serve 4 easily, but as it is rather rich cut down the portions when serving with a full course meal.

Note: to toast the nuts, just place in a heavy-based frying pan over moderate heat with 5 ml/1 tsp groundnut oil. Stir around until they turn golden, then chop either in a food processor fitted with the steel blade or by hand.

Shallot Butter

45 ml/3 tbsp FINELY CHOPPED SHALLOTS (THESE ARE NOT SPRING ONIONS)

100 ml/4 fl oz (½ cup) DRY RED WINE

100 g/4 oz (½ cup) UNSALTED BUTTER, SOFTENED

30 ml/2 tbsp FINELY CHOPPED FRESH PARSLEY

SALT AND PEPPER

In a small, stainless steel saucepan, simmer the shallots in the red wine for 20 to 25 minutes, or until the wine has evaporated. Transfer to a small bowl and let cool. Combine with the butter, parsley and salt and pepper to taste, cover and chill. You can make this several days in advance, so as to improve the flavour. Cut French bread into diagonal slices, spread with the butter, place a piece of beef on top ... the rest is up to you!

Mayonnaise Sauce

225 g/8 oz (1 cup) MAYONNAISE

15 ml/1 tbsp WORCESTERSHIRE SAUCE

2.5 ml/½ tsp TABASCO SAUCE

2.5 ml/½ tsp DRY MUSTARD

Mix all the ingredients together. If too thick, thin with a little beef stock (65 ml/2½ fl oz (⅓ cup) at most). The consistency should be that of whipping cream.

FISH AND SEAFOOD

———— ⟿ ————

More and more people are turning to fish as a high-protein, low-cholesterol alternative to meat. This is not a definitive section covering all kinds of creatures from the oceans, but rather several suggestions for ringing the changes on familiar species.

Fresh fish and fresh seafoods – and we mean fresh – need very little done to them in the way of cooking to get the maximum enjoyment. A really fresh Dover sole, just briefly sautéed in a little butter and then sprinkled with a few drops of lemon juice is very hard to beat.

The Barbecued Fish in Foil relies very much on the freshness of the fish. The stuffing is just there to give it a hint of flavour. It's the sort of thing that can be cooked on the beach, providing you have the stuffing, skewers and foil to hand. All you need is a fire to place the well wrapped fish on when it has cooled down slightly but still has sufficient heat to cook the fish.

The Spicy Wrapped Fish Cakes are not packaged frozen ones wrapped in banana leaves, but a very savoury paste made from fish, a dish that we had in Singapore. And when we say Rich Oyster Pie, we mean rich!

It sounds silly, but when you buy fish, sniff it. To the passerby, it may appear that you have a peculiar fetish, but fresh fish should really only have the smallest whiff of the sea. If there is even a slight ammonia smell wafting up your nostrils then go to another supplier. When you have found a good supplier, stick to him or her like glue, the same as you would with a very good butcher. Having had our own fish restaurant for several years, we know what fresh is all about. We had an excellent supplier of fish and an excellent one for crayfish – let's hope you strike it lucky also.

It was, and still is surprising to us, that so much frozen fish is offered for sale in the guise of being fresh. If you are going to pound it, poach it, or put it into something which will disguise it in some way, then it's not too bad to buy fish frozen. Mousses made with the addition of eggs or cream are one example. Poaching frozen fish in a flavoured liquid and then making a sauce to coat the cooked fish is another. Frozen scallops can be used successfully. Because of locality we sometimes have to resort to the frozen product, but we do urge you to use fresh fish whenever possible – it's the only way to go for best results.

Barbecued Fish in Foil

Don't overlook the possibility of buying whole fresh fish rather than paying extra for fillets. The whole fish generally work out cheaper than the fillets. If the fish has not been cleaned and gutted, slit along the belly and remove the internal organs. You don't have to cut off the head for this recipe. Rinse well in cold running water and then scrape off the scales. (It's best to do this outside and then wash the area down.) Cut off all the fins as well, being careful not to prick yourself.
This filling will be enough to delicately flavour a fish of about 1 ½-2 kg/3 ¼-4 ½ lb. Please don't be tempted to overcook the fish, and don't place it over extreme heat either. In New Zealand, we barbecue red snapper. It is available in Britain from larger fishmongers, or often frozen in Chinese supermarkets, but sea bream is a delicious, readily available alternative.

SMALL SPRIG FRESH THYME

SMALL SPRIG FRESH SAGE

SEVERAL STALKS FRESH PARSLEY

2 SLICES BREAD, CRUSTS REMOVED

SALT AND FRESHLY GROUND BLACK PEPPER

JUICE OF ½ LEMON

2 TO 3 TOMATOES, PEELED, SEEDED AND CHOPPED

15 ml/1 tbsp GROUNDNUT (PEANUT) OIL

1 FRESH WHOLE FISH, SUCH AS SEA BREAM OR RED SNAPPER, CLEANED, TRIMMED AND SCALED

EXTRA GROUNDNUT OIL FOR BRUSHING

Break off the tender parts of the fresh thyme, sage and parsley and chop in a food processor fitted with the steel blade. Break up the bread and, with the motor running, drop pieces through the feed tube and process until you have fairly coarse crumbs. Add a little salt and pepper, the lemon juice and the prepared tomatoes, plus the 15 ml/1 tbsp oil. Continue to process until the mixture is well combined, but try not to turn it into a mush. Place this stuffing in the cavity of the fish and then either sew or pin the cavity opening to hold it in. Brush both sides of the fish generously with the extra oil and wrap up well in the double thickness of foil, folding the edges on the top so that none of the juices will seep out during cooking. Heat your barbecue to moderate. (We admit now that after years of blowing embers to get the jolly thing hot we converted several years ago and invested in a gas barbecue. We have never regretted it, and it's safer too, with no sparks to start fires.)

After about 20 minutes, open the package carefully and check whether it is cooked by inserting the tip of a knife. If the flesh has turned white and flakes easily it is done. Take off the skin and remove the top flesh from the bone, then remove the bone and take off the lower flesh. Spoon the accumulated juices over the flesh to moisten and add flavour. Serve straight away. *Serves 4 to 6.*

Fillets of Sole in Wine Sauce

There has been a trend for some time now to use fruits with meats or fish. Sometimes this is taken to the extreme where you imagine the dish should have been called 'Hot Fruit Salad with a Touch of Pork', rather than the other way round. We believe the fruit should enhance the flavour of the beast, fowl or fish it is served with, not be the star attraction.
This dish is the dried fruit version, you could say, of sole Véronique.

45 ml/3 tbsp SEEDLESS SULTANAS

8 SMALL DOVER OR LEMON SOLE FILLETS

PLAIN FLOUR FOR DUSTING

30 g/1 1/4 oz BUTTER

A LITTLE SALT AND FRESHLY GROUND BLACK PEPPER

15 ml/1 tbsp LEMON JUICE

50 ml/2 fl oz (1/4 cup) DRY WHITE WINE

50 ml/2 fl oz (1/4 cup) DRY MADEIRA OR SHERRY

Soak the sultanas in hot water to plump and soften them. Dust the sole fillets in the flour and shake off the excess. Heat the butter in a large pan, preferably non-stick, and add the fillets, together with a little salt and pepper, plus the lemon juice and soaked and drained raisins. Cover the pan and cook the fish over gentle heat for about 10 to 15 minutes, depending on the thickness of the fillets. Try not to overcook them. If they are fresh, and they should be, it is better to undercook rather than overcook. Half way through the cooking time, carefully turn the fillets over with the aid of a fish slice. When nearly done, add the wine and Madeira and quickly bring the mixture to the boil and simmer for 2 minutes, then serve straight away with the sauce from the pan spooned over the fillets. *Serves 4.*

Baked Fish with a Sour Cream Sauce

This dish takes quite a time to prepare, but can be made well in advance, then baked just before serving. It is extremely rich and filling and the taste is superb.

60 ml/4 tbsp BUTTER (YOU MAY NEED MORE)

4 BONELESS FRESH FILLETS, SUCH AS COD

PLAIN FLOUR FOR DUSTING

2 HARD-BOILED EGGS, SLICED

12 MUSHROOMS

4 LARGE POTATOES, PEELED AND THINLY SLICED

SOUR CREAM SAUCE (OPPOSITE)

SALT AND FRESHLY GROUND BLACK PEPPER

60 ml/4 tbsp FRESHLY GRATED PARMESAN CHEESE

Heat a large, heavy-based frying pan and melt 15 ml/1 tbsp butter over moderate heat. Dust the fillets with flour and shake off the excess. Gently fry the fillets on both sides for a few minutes, until lightly golden. Do not overcook, as you are going to bake this at the end – the same applies to the rest of the ingredients.

Lightly butter an ovenproof serving platter and lay the fillets out, slightly apart. Lay the hard-boiled eggs over the fillets in overlapping slices. In the same frying pan melt 15 ml/ 1 tbsp butter and over gentle heat sauté the mushroom caps for a few minutes. Lay 3 of these on top of the egg on each fillet.

Add the rest of the butter to the frying pan (this is where you may need a little extra butter or a touch of groundnut oil), heat the pan to fairly hot, sauté the finely sliced potatoes until golden brown, and drain on kitchen paper. Place the potatoes round the edge of the serving platter (not on the fish).

Now make the sauce.

Sour Cream Sauce

30 ml/2 tbsp BUTTER

15 ml/1 tbsp PLAIN FLOUR

175 ml/6 fl oz (¾ cup) FISH OR CHICKEN STOCK, PREFERABLY HOMEMADE (pp. 182, 183)

250 ml/9 fl oz (generous 1 cup) SOUR CREAM

SALT

In a small, heavy-based saucepan, melt the butter over moderate heat, stir in the flour and mix well. Remove from the heat, whisk in the stock, return to the heat and cook for 5 minutes, whisking all the time. Stir in the sour cream and, again stirring all the time, cook a further 5 minutes. Do not let it boil as it can curdle. Taste it for salt and add some if required, but no pepper. (This is also a very nice sauce to use over freshly cooked vegetables, sprinkled with cheese, then grilled until the cheese is golden brown.)

Finishing the dish. Let the sauce cool a little, then carefully spoon over the fillets, making sure you mask them completely (this stops them drying out in the final cooking). Season to taste. Sprinkle a tablespoon of cheese over each individual fillet. When ready to cook, preheat oven to 150C/300F/Gas 2, place dish in the centre of the oven and bake for about 20 minutes. Serve some of the potatoes with each portion of fish. We prefer this served not too hot, as we think heat tends to minimise the combined flavours. *Serves 4.*

Parmesan Fish Fillets

For this you need firm white fresh fish. The Parmesan does not overpower the fish, but it does give you a crusty brown coating that protects the fillets when you cook them. In fact it's much nicer than just plain crumbed fried fish. It's best to cut a piece of Parmesan from a block, then grind it in the food processor, rather than grate it. You may wish to alter the amount of Parmesan to suit your own taste when you cook this a second time, but the flavour of the cheese must come through in the finished result.
We are not always of one mind over whether or not to fry the bananas. To have them unfried cuts down the richness of the dish.

4 FISH FILLETS, SUCH AS COD OR SEA BREAM

100 g/4 oz (2 cups) FRESH BREADCRUMBS

90 ml/6 tbsp 'GRATED' PARMESAN CHEESE

ABOUT 50 g/2 oz (scant ½ cup) PLAIN FLOUR

SALT AND FRESHLY GROUND BLACK PEPPER

1 EGG, BEATEN WITH 5 ml/1 tsp OIL AND 15 ml/1 tbsp WATER

4 FIRM BANANAS

JUICE OF ½ LEMON

50 g/2 oz BUTTER

30 ml/2 tbsp GROUNDNUT (PEANUT) OIL

30 g/1¼ oz BUTTER

50 g/2 oz (½ cup) FLAKED ALMONDS, TOASTED

LEMON WEDGES, TO SERVE

Rinse the fish under cold water. Pat dry with kitchen paper. Mix together the breadcrumbs and prepared Parmesan and place on a double thickness of kitchen paper.

Season the flour with some salt and freshly ground black pepper and also place on a double thickness of kitchen paper. Place the egg, oil and water in a shallow bowl or lipped plate. Peel and slice the bananas diagonally and sprinkle with the lemon juice to prevent discoloration.

Coat the fish with the seasoned flour, shake off the excess and dip in the beaten egg. Drain the excess egg and place a fillet in the crumbs. Press the crumbs on both sides firmly and again shake away any excess. Place on a large plate until ready to cook. Repeat with the other fillets. If you wish, you may now cover the prepared fillets with cling film and store in the fridge for up to 4 hours, until ready to cook.

To cook, melt the 50 g/2 oz butter and 30 ml/2 tbsp oil in a large frying pan, preferably non-stick. Cook over moderate heat for about 3 minutes on each side. Transfer to a heated plate and keep warm. If the frying pan is too small to do these all together, the coating of crumbs stops the first batch overcooking while being kept warm, but don't keep too long.

Wipe out the pan with some kitchen paper and melt in it the remaining 30 g/1¼ oz butter. Fry the sliced bananas very quickly on both sides until they are heated through and take on a golden colour.

Put the cooked fish fillets on heated serving plates, place the cooked sliced bananas over them decoratively, and sprinkle with the toasted slivered almonds. Serve straight away together with extra lemon wedges and a crisp mixed green salad. *Serves 4.*

Fish Fillets Steamed with Sesame Oil

Flavourful and simple, that's how we would describe this Chinese-style steamed fish. There is a problem if you want to cook this for a lot of people and don't have a multistoreyed steamer. Therefore we are giving the quantities for 2 people, and you can multiply the amounts, depending on how large a steamer you have. If you haven't a steamer you can improvise by using an ovenproof dish and rack. Put in enough water to almost touch the rack, put the plate and fillets on the rack and cover with foil. The two oils that we mention, groundnut and sesame, are essential to the success of this recipe. They give it its special flavour, so don't be tempted to use other oils.

5 ml/1 tsp SESAME OIL

2 FRESH FILLETS, SUCH AS SEA BASS

SALT AND FRESHLY GROUND BLACK PEPPER

10 ml/2 tsp CORNFLOUR

EXTRA GROUNDNUT (PEANUT) OIL

30 ml/2 tbsp FRESHLY GRATED FRESH ROOT GINGER

30 ml/2 tbsp SHREDDED SPRING ONION

30 ml/2 tbsp GROUNDNUT (PEANUT) OIL

45 ml/ 3 tbsp LIGHT SOY SAUCE

Brush the sesame oil over both fillets on each side, sprinkle with very little salt and pepper and dust with the cornflour, also on both sides. Leave to stand for 30 minutes.

With the extra groundnut oil lightly oil a plate that will hold both the fillets and will fit into your steamer. Put the fillets on the plate and sprinkle over them all the grated ginger and half the shredded spring onions. Place in the steamer, cover and gently steam for 10 minutes, or until just cooked. The cooking time varies slightly, depending on the thickness of the fillets. Near the end of the steaming time, heat 30 ml/2 tbsp groundnut oil until it starts to smoke.

Put the cooked fillets on 2 heated plates, sprinkle with the rest of the spring onions and the soy sauce. Finally, pour the smoking oil over the fillets. Serve immediately. *Serves 2.* *Note:* do be careful with the hot oil. We use the smallest frying pan we have to heat it in, with a lip for easy pouring.

Sole Fillets, Italian Style

This is Italian style because of the anchovy fillets that make up part of the sauce. The anchovy imparts its own special salty flavour to many dishes from Italy. In particular we are referring to tinned anchovy fillets, rather than fresh anchovies, which are quite a different matter altogether. Just a word on tinned anchovies. After you have opened a tin and used only 1 or 2, take the lid off completely, carefully wrap the whole tin in plenty of cling film (making sure you keep the oil from spilling out) and freeze for later use. A convenient alternative is anchovy sauce – it isn't quite as pungent as pounded tinned anchovies, but keeps for a long time, and is handier to use. A mixed salad is best with this dish, and perhaps some very good egg noodles tossed in a little butter and cream, with just a hint of Parmesan sprinkled over them to finish.

12 SMALL SOLE FILLETS

SOFTENED BUTTER

1 SMALL ONION, FINELY CHOPPED

30 ml/2 tbsp FINELY CHOPPED FRESH PARSLEY

A LITTLE SALT AND FRESHLY GROUND BLACK PEPPER

50 ml/2 fl oz (¼ cup) DRY WHITE WINE OR DRY VERMOUTH

1 LARGE EGG, BEATEN WITH 30 ml/2 tbsp WATER AND 15 ml/1 tbsp OLIVE OIL

2 THICK SLICES BREAD, TURNED INTO FINE CRUMBS

45 ml/3 tbsp FINELY CHOPPED COOKED HAM

75 g/3 oz BUTTER, MELTED

4 CANNED ANCHOVIES, DRAINED AND MASHED

ABOUT 25 g/1 oz EXTRA BUTTER

Place the fish fillets evenly over the base of a shallow, greased ovenproof dish, making sure that they do not overlap too much. Sprinkle over them the finely chopped onion and parsley, plus a little salt and pepper.

Carefully pour round the wine or vermouth, cover, and bake in a preheated oven at 200C/400F/Gas 6 for 4 minutes (you are only wanting to partially cook the fish to firm it up a fraction for later). Remove from oven, take out the fish with a fish slice, and set aside to cool completely. Drain the juices into a small saucepan and set aside also.

When the fish has cooled, dip each fillet into the beaten egg mixture, drain off the excess egg and dip into the fresh breadcrumbs, which have been mixed with the finely chopped ham. Lightly brush the same ovenproof dish with a little melted butter and lay each crumbed fillet, slightly overlapping, in it. Pour the melted butter carefully over the fillets and bake, uncovered, at 200C/400F/Gas 6 for about 20 to 30 minutes until lightly golden.

While they are cooking, mash the anchovies in a small saucepan, and heat them together with the extra butter over a low heat. When they are liquid, add the reserved fish cooking juices, mix together and serve a little over each pair of fillets. *Serves 6.*

Prawn Curry

This is a somewhat selfish recipe as it serves only 2 people – us. After we have peeled the prawns we usually make a simple stock from the peels by simmering them in water with a little onion, carrot and celery, plus a few sprigs of parsley. Strain, cool and freeze to use in another dish, such as Crab and Egg Soup (p. 20).

The recipe calls for what seems quite a lot of garam masala, but on several occasions we have actually added slightly more. It depends on whether you are using your own mixture, or a commercial one, and on the age and strength of the mixture. Try the 22.5 ml/1 ½ tbsp as we suggest, and add more next time if it suits your taste. Don't, however, decrease the amount.

Served over plain boiled rice, together with some sliced banana, quartered tomatoes, sliced cucumber in yoghurt and various relishes, this makes a stunning, simple dish. It goes well with Indian-style Cabbage (p. 125).

24 LARGE, RAW PRAWNS, ABOUT 450-600 g/1-1¼ lb

15 ml/1 tbsp BUTTER

1 LARGE ONION, FINELY SLICED

5 ml/1 tsp TURMERIC

22.5 ml/1½ tbsp GARAM MASALA

5 ml/1 tsp CHILLI POWDER

4 LARGE TOMATOES, PEELED, SEEDED AND CHOPPED

175 ml/6 fl oz (¾ cup) WATER

15 ml/1 tbsp LEMON JUICE

2.5 ml/½ tsp SALT

HOT BOILED RICE, TO SERVE

Clean the prawns, peel and devein, then keep to one side. Heat the butter in a heavy-based pan and fry the sliced onion until it starts to turn brown over a fairly high heat, stirring from time to time to prevent it burning. Mix the turmeric, garam masala and chilli powder together with some water to form a paste, then add to the onions. Continue cooking over a lower heat for about 4 minutes to release the flavours. Add the prepared tomatoes and simmer gently until they are soft and pulpy. Add the water and continue simmering for about 8 to 10 minutes. Add the prawns and simmer for a further 8 minutes, until they are just cooked, stirring them round so as to coat them with the curry sauce. Don't cook the mixture over too high a heat as this can toughen the prawns. Add the lemon juice and salt and cook for another 2 minutes. When cooked the prawns will curl up and be pink in colour, though this is a bit difficult to see when they are covered in this magnificent sauce. Spoon over hot rice.

Spicy Wrapped Fish Cakes

The Nonya cooking in Singapore provided us with this recipe while we were there filming a series on the various groups of foods prepared in that country. The original is all prepared and pounded in a pestle and mortar, but we have adapted it to the modern kitchen by using a food processor, which takes out a lot of the hard grind (pardon the pun!). Should you have access to banana leaves use them to wrap the mixture, as the result looks very oriental. Failing that, squares of foil are perfectly adequate.

This makes plenty to serve for a party, so consider halving the recipe for your own family's consumption – although we will warn you now, they are extremely moreish and seem to disappear very quickly once cooked and served.

1 kg/2¼ lb FINE-TEXTURED FISH FILLETS, SUCH AS SOLE

15 ml/1 tbsp CORIANDER SEEDS

3 ONIONS

12 SMALL DRIED RED CHILLIES, SOAKED ABOUT 30 MINUTES IN WARM WATER

4 CLOVES GARLIC

2.5 ml/½ tsp TURMERIC

12 MACADAMIA NUTS, OR ALMONDS

2 STRIPS LEMON RIND, CHOPPED

225 ml/8 fl oz (1 cup) PREPARED COCONUT CREAM

5 ml/1 tsp CHOPPED DRIED MINT

15 ml/1 tbsp SALT

15 ml/1 tbsp DARK BROWN SUGAR

PIECES OF BANANA LEAF OR FOIL, ABOUT 15 cm/6 inches SQUARE, GREASED

Cut the cleaned fish into small pieces and blend to a paste in either a blender or a food processor fitted with the steel blade. Do this a little at a time and make sure you occasionally scrape down the sides of the bowl or container with a spatula. As you process the fish, transfer to a large bowl.

Roast the coriander seeds in a small pan over moderate heat until they start to emit their flavour – do not let them burn or scorch. Grind them finely in a spice mill or pestle and mortar and add to the fish.

Peel and quarter the onions and place in the rinsed processor bowl, again fitted with the steel blade, together with the drained chillies, peeled garlic cloves, turmeric, nuts and chopped lemon peel. Process until the onion is finely chopped and beat this into the fish mixture. Now gradually beat in the coconut cream with a wooden spoon until you have a thick paste. Add the mint, salt and sugar, mix well, cover with cling film and place in the fridge for up to 3 to 6 hours.

Blanch the cut squares of banana leaf in boiling water until they are soft and flexible. This will sometimes take up to 5 minutes, depending on the age of the leaf. Try to use young leaves, which you need blanch only for a short time to sterilise.

Place about 30 ml/2 tbsp of the chilled fish mixture on the centre of each blanched banana leaf or square of foil and fold up, envelope-style, into a package. Secure the banana leaves with thin bamboo skewers which have been soaked for 30 minutes in water. Cook over moderate heat on a barbecue for about 5 minutes either side, or grill for about the same time, being careful not to burn the leaf too much by putting it too close to the heat source. Open the leaf and remove the fish.

These can be served with rice, spread on biscuits, eaten as they are (out of their wrappers), or they can be left to go cold and taken on a picnic. Be warned, they are very hot and spicy.

Oriental Mussel Fritters

1.5 kg/3 lb 5 oz MUSSELS, CLEANED (p. 52)

225 ml/8 fl oz (1 cup) DRY WHITE WINE

2 SPRING ONIONS, FINELY CHOPPED

100 g/4 oz (½ cup) WATER CHESTNUTS, DRAINED AND FINELY CHOPPED

30 ml/2 tbsp CORED, SEEDED AND FINELY CHOPPED RED OR GREEN PEPPER

1.25 ml/¼ tsp FINELY CHOPPED FRESH ROOT GINGER

1 EGG, SIZE 1, BEATEN

50 g/2 oz FRESH, FINE BREADCRUMBS (ABOUT 2 SLICES BREAD)

VEGETABLE OIL FOR DEEP FRYING

LEMON JUICE, TO TASTE

Steam the mussels in a large pot with 225 ml/8 fl oz (1 cup) water and the white wine for 8 minutes, shaking often. Drain them, remove from their shells and coarsely chop.

In a bowl, mix well together the mussels and all the ingredients, but only 15 ml/1 tbsp of the breadcrumbs and not the lemon juice or oil. Roll the mixture into small balls about the size of a walnut and roll in the remaining breadcrumbs. Place on a baking sheet in a single layer, cover and chill at least 1 hour.

In a deep pan heat enough vegetable oil, about 5 cm/2 inches to cook the fritters. Flick a drop of water into the oil; if it foams the oil is ready. Fry about 4 balls at a time, turning regularly, for about 2 minutes, or until golden brown. Remove to a hot plate covered with kitchen paper and drain. Sprinkle with lemon juice and serve at once. *Makes about 28.*

Trout Mousse with Prawn Sauce

We prefer this mousse, or any mousse for that matter, warm, rather than hot, as we think the flavour comes out more – but the sauce must be hot.
If you can't get trout, any good, firm-fleshed fish is fine, but of course you won't get that distinctive flavour.

4 SHALLOTS, FINELY CHOPPED (NOT SPRING ONIONS)

30 ml/2 tbsp UNSALTED BUTTER

500 g/18 oz TROUT FILLETS, SKINNED

4 EGG YOLKS, SIZE 1

225 ml/8 fl oz (1 cup) VERY COLD WHIPPING CREAM

SALT AND GROUND WHITE PEPPER

Sauce

75 ml/5 tbsp UNSALTED BUTTER

1 CARROT, VERY FINELY CHOPPED

1 ONION, FINELY CHOPPED

1 STALK CELERY, FINELY CHOPPED (DON'T FORGET TO STRING IT)

1 SPRIG FRESH THYME

1 SPRIG FRESH FENNEL

4 RAW, UNPEELED PRAWNS (CHOP OFF THE HEADS AND KEEP FOR DECORATION)

25 g/1 oz (¼ cup) FRESH PAPRIKA

50 ml/2 fl oz (¼ cup) COGNAC

15 ml/ 1 tbsp TOMATO PURÉE (PASTE)

450 ml/¾ pint (2 cups) WHIPPING CREAM

SALT AND GROUND WHITE PEPPER, TO TASTE

In a heavy-based pan, sauté the shallots in the butter over moderately high heat, until softened but not browned. Chop the trout fillets into pieces and purée them in a food processor with the steel blade. Add the egg yolks, one at a time, blending each one. Add the sautéed shallots and blend until well mixed – it should be like a paste. To make this mixture even finer, put through a mouli into a large clean bowl.

In another bowl, whip the cream until holding soft peaks (not stiff). *Stir* a third of the cream into the trout purée, then fold in the remainder, with salt and white pepper to taste. Cover the mousse, and chill for 30 minutes.

Butter well four 100 ml/4 fl oz (½ cup) ramekins and divide the chilled mousse between them. Place in a baking pan and fill with hot water half way up the ramekins. Bake in the centre of a preheated oven at 170C/325F/Gas 3 for 25-30 minutes, or until a skewer comes out clean.

While these are cooking, make the sauce. In a heavy-based saucepan, melt the butter over moderate heat and cook the carrot, onion, celery, thyme and fennel for 5 minutes, stirring all the time. Lightly bash the unpeeled prawns with the back of a cleaver or a heavy knife. Add to the vegetables along with the paprika and cook for 10 minutes, stirring occasionally. Add the Cognac and the tomato purée and stir fry for 2-3 minutes. Now stir in the cream, salt and white pepper and simmer for 10 minutes, stirring occasionally.

Remove prawns from the sauce and take off the peels. Discard the peels. Place prawns in a food processor with the steel blade, pour on the sauce and mix until finely blended. Pour back into the saucepan and reheat but do not boil. Bring a small pan of water to the boil, throw in the prawn heads and boil for a few minutes, drain and rinse under cold water.

Unmould the cooked mousses onto individual serving plates, pour a little sauce round (not over) the mousses, and decorate each with a prawn head. *Serves 4.*

Red Snapper Cooked in Coconut Milk

This dish goes well with plain rice, or good old potatoes. Red snapper is abundant in the Pacific waters surrounding New Zealand, so we cook with it often.

350 ml/12 fl oz (1½ cups) PREPARED COCONUT CREAM

2 LARGE TOMATOES, PEELED, SEEDED AND QUARTERED

1 SMALL GREEN PEPPER, CORED, SEEDED AND THINLY SLICED

7.5 ml/1½ tsp TOMATO PURÉE (PASTE)

7.5 ml/1½ tsp FINELY CHOPPED FRESH OREGANO, OR 2.5 ml/½ tsp DRIED

SALT AND FRESHLY GROUND BLACK PEPPER

1.5 kg/3¼ lb RED SNAPPER, OR SEA BREAM, SKINNED AND FILLETED, THEN FILLETS CUT IN HALF CROSSWAYS

25 g/1 oz FINELY CHOPPED FRESH PARSLEY

Place the coconut cream in a stainless steel or enamel saucepan and warm gently. Add tomatoes, green pepper, tomato purée, oregano and salt and pepper to taste. Stir well, bring to the boil and simmer gently for 15 minutes. Add fish fillets, mix in gently to coat with liquid. Cook over moderate heat for 7 to 10 minutes (do not overcook). Season again with more salt and pepper, sprinkle over the parsley, gently stir and serve at once. *Serves 6.*

Steamed Mussels in Egg and Cream Sauce

Such a lot of people don't eat mussels, and they are so delicious. Perhaps it is because a lot of places serve the overly large ones that can be tough; also we think they should be trimmed of their black rims as well – just a fad, but in the larger ones this always seems to be tough and looks ugly.

There are usually plenty of places along the seashore where you can buy freshly picked and bagged mussels in New Zealand, much preferred to bottled shelled ones (though these latter are ideal for a mussel soup).

Cleaning mussels really isn't that bothersome – scrub them well with a stiff brush, remove any beards that are hanging on the outside, place them in a bucket and just cover with fresh water for several hours or overnight. This makes the mussels disgorge any sand that is inside the shell. It is then purely a case of steaming them open in well-flavoured stock. When the mussels have been steamed and have opened (only takes about 8 to 10 minutes), any that have not opened naturally must be thrown away – they are not fresh or good, so do not under any circumstances prise them open and use.

For Steaming the Mussels

65 g/2½ oz (½ cup) FINELY CHOPPED ONION

50 g/2 oz (½ cup) FINELY CHOPPED CELERY

1 CLOVE GARLIC, FINELY CHOPPED

1 BAY LEAF

PINCH OF DRIED THYME

15 ml/1 tbsp FINELY CHOPPED FRESH PARSLEY

100 g/4 oz UNSALTED BUTTER

2.5 kg/5½ lb CLEANED MUSSELS

225 ml/8 fl oz (1 cup) DRY WHITE WINE

FRESHLY GROUND BLACK PEPPER

Egg and Cream Sauce

3 EGG YOLKS, SIZE 1

100 ml/4 fl oz (½ cup) WHIPPING CREAM

10 ml/2 tsp LEMON JUICE

7.5 g/¼ oz (¼ cup) FINELY CHOPPED FRESH PARSLEY

SALT AND FRESHLY GROUND BLACK PEPPER, TO TASTE

In a large enamel or stainless steel pan, cook the onion, celery, garlic, bay leaf, thyme and parsley in the butter, covered, over moderate heat, for about 5 minutes, or until vegetables are just soft. Add mussels, 225 ml/8 fl oz (1 cup) water, wine and several grinds of fresh black pepper. Cover and steam the mussels over moderate-high heat for about 8 minutes,

[52]

shaking the pan vigorously every now and again. Cook no longer than 10 minutes. Remove the mussels and keep warm. Strain the liquid through a cloth-lined sieve into a bowl. Set aside 450 ml/¾ pint (2 cups) of strained liquid.

To make the sauce, put the reserved liquid in a stainless steel or enamel saucepan. Reduce by half over moderately high heat.

Meanwhile, in a bowl whisk together the egg yolks and cream. Whisking all the time pour in, in a stream, 100 ml/4 fl oz (½ cup) of the reduced stock. Now whisk this into the remainder of the reduced stock. Reduce heat to moderate, whisk the sauce constantly until it thickens slightly. Add the lemon juice, parsley, salt and pepper to taste. Whisk to amalgamate.

Put the mussels on heated serving plates and pour sauce over. Serve at once. *Serves 4.*

Mussels with Toasted Almonds

24 MUSSELS, STEAMED AS IN PREVIOUS RECIPE

1 SLICE WHITE BREAD

24 BLANCHED ALMONDS, TOASTED

15 ml/1 tbsp RED WINE VINEGAR OR BRANDY

100 ml/4 fl oz (½ cup) OLIVE OIL

DASH OF TABASCO SAUCE

SALT AND FRESHLY GROUND BLACK PEPPER, TO TASTE

With a slotted spoon remove open steamed mussels to a large dish or board. Remove tops, loosen mussel from base shell and trim off the black rim, if you wish. Cover the mussels with cling film and chill thoroughly. Break the bread in pieces and put in a food processor with the steel blade, add the toasted almonds and chop until fine, add vinegar or brandy, olive oil, Tabasco and salt and pepper to taste. Whizz until well blended to a granulated paste. Spoon this mixture over the mussels, cover and re-chill.

Serve as a cold starter, or, if you want to heat them for a change, preheat the grill and grill just under the heat until the mussels are golden brown. Watch carefully, as this won't take long. *Serves 4.*

Vermouth-flavoured Scallops

This is a good way of using frozen scallops, though fresh are still first choice in our book. If they are frozen, take them out of the freezer and thaw slowly overnight in the fridge.
This is an excellent first-course dish. Because of the lemon juice in the marinade, which becomes the sauce later, they are not quite as rich as one would imagine. They are therefore ideal to serve in double quantities as a main course, with perhaps a fresh green salad to accompany them.

16 TO 20 SCALLOPS, DEPENDING ON SIZE

100 ml/4 fl oz (½ cup) DRY VERMOUTH

30 ml/2 tbsp FINELY CHOPPED FRESH PARSLEY OR CORIANDER

15 ml/1 tbsp LEMON JUICE

5 ml/1 tsp SUGAR

SALT AND FRESHLY GROUND BLACK PEPPER

4 SLICES OF BREAD, CRUST REMOVED

PLAIN FLOUR

2 EGGS, BEATEN WITH 30 ml/2 tbsp WATER

80 g/3¼ oz BUTTER

30 ml/2 tbsp GROUNDNUT (PEANUT) OIL

5 ml/1 tsp CORNFLOUR

50 ml/2 fl oz (¼ cup) WHIPPING CREAM

Remove any sand tracks from the scallops, rinse briefly under cold running water, drain and place to one side.

In a medium-sized glass bowl, combine the vermouth, parsley, lemon juice, sugar and a little salt and pepper. Mix together well and add the drained scallops. Cover with cling film and place in the fridge to marinate for at least 3 hours or up to 12, stirring from time to time to make sure they are well mixed.

Make the fresh breadcrumbs in a food processor fitted with a steel blade, dropping small broken pieces in through the feed tube while the motor is running.

Drain the scallops, reserving the marinade. Dip the scallops individually in plain flour, shake off the excess, then dip into the beaten egg and finally into the fresh breadcrumbs to coat thickly. (Despite all the years we have been trying to breadcrumb things this way, we still get our fingers coated in goo. Many people use 2 forks to work the scallops through each stage of crumbing, but we find we don't save much time or mess by doing it that way. Do it next to the sink and you won't have any real difficulty.)

Thread scallops onto thin bamboo skewers, 4 or 5 to a skewer, and set aside on a plate until ready to cook. If you do this several hours in advance, cover with cling film and keep in the fridge. Remember to bring them out to come back to room temperature before cooking.

Melt the butter and oil over moderate heat in a non-stick frying pan. Carefully place the skewered scallops in the pan and cook until golden, turning half way through. This should take no longer than 4 minutes total. Remove to a serving plate and keep warm while you make the sauce.

Pour into the pan the reserved marinade and bring to the boil, leave to boil and reduce for 2 minutes. Meanwhile, mix the cornflour with 30 ml/2 tbsp water to a paste and add the cream. Pour this into the boiling marinade and whisk or stir until it comes back to the boil and thickens.

To serve, remove the skewers carefully and pour the sauce over the scallops. Let the guests season them at the table. Cooked rice, flavoured with finely chopped spring onion, goes well with this dish. *Serves 4.*

Mussels Steamed in Beer

2.5 kg/5½ lb MUSSELS, CLEANED (p. 52)

350 ml/12 fl oz (1½ cups) BEER

1 CLOVE GARLIC, BRUISED BUT NOT PEELED

PINCH OF GROUND ALLSPICE

2.5 ml/½ tsp CAYENNE PEPPER OR GROUND CHILLI

1 BAY LEAF

3 SPRIGS FRESH PARSLEY

Sauce

150 g/5 oz UNSALTED BUTTER

1 CLOVE GARLIC, CRUSHED

30 ml/2 tbsp LEMON JUICE

2.5 ml/½ tsp DARK SOY SAUCE

5 ml/1 tsp DIJON MUSTARD

15 ml/1 tbsp FINELY CHOPPED FRESH PARSLEY

SALT AND FRESHLY GROUND BLACK PEPPER

Put the first 7 ingredients in a large pan, cover and steam over moderately high heat for 8 to 10 minutes, shaking often. Remove mussels and keep hot. Discard liquid.

To make sauce, melt butter with the garlic in a small saucepan over moderate heat, then whisk in lemon juice, soy sauce, mustard, parsley and salt and pepper to taste. Heat sauce until hot – do not boil. Remove the garlic clove and pour sauce into hot serving bowl.

Serve mussels on heated plates; serve sauce separately. *Serves 4-6.*

Prawns and Pork, Our Style

Having lashed out and bought some raw prawns, we were at a loss as to how to prepare them. We looked to see what else was on hand to turn them into a dish that would go a little further and so make a very substantial meal for 2. Finding some pork pieces we constructed the following.

225 g/8 oz PORK TENDERLOIN OR LEAN PORK PIECES

4 SLICES FRESH ROOT GINGER, FINELY CHOPPED

15 ml/1 tbsp CORNFLOUR

90 ml/2 tbsp LIGHT SOY SAUCE

SEVERAL GRINDINGS BLACK PEPPER

GROUNDNUT (PEANUT) OIL FOR FRYING

2.5 ml/½ tsp SESAME OIL

250 g/9 oz PRAWNS, UNPEELED

8 BABY EARS OF CORN, CUT INTO THIRDS

1 GREEN OR RED PEPPER, CORED, SEEDED AND DICED

2 STALKS CELERY, THINLY SLICED

1 CLOVE GARLIC, CRUSHED

½ CHINESE CABBAGE, SHREDDED

100 ml/4 fl oz (½ cup) WATER

5 ml/1 tsp CRUMBLED CHICKEN STOCK CUBE

5 ml/1 tsp TOMATO SAUCE

2.5-5 ml/½-1 tsp CHILLI SAUCE

10 ml/2 tsp CORNFLOUR

4 SPRING ONIONS, COARSELY CHOPPED

Finely mince the pork, or process until fine in a food processor fitted with a steel blade. If using a food processor, have the meat partially frozen as it makes it easier to turn into a paste. Add the ginger to the pork together with the cornflour, soy sauce and pepper. Mix together well with a wooden spoon. Shape into small balls, about the size of a walnut.

Place about 15 ml/1 tbsp groundnut oil in a wok together with the sesame oil. Fry pork balls until golden, turning frequently to prevent them sticking, about 7 minutes. Remove with a slotted spoon and place on kitchen paper to drain.

Peel and devein the prawns. (Simmer the shells, heads and tails in some water to cover, to make a stock that can be added to fish soups or help make a sauce for another occasion.)

Have all the vegetables prepared and in bowls ready to add to the wok. Heat the wok until fairly hot and add the corn, pepper, celery, garlic and cabbage. Stir fry over high heat for about 2 to 3 minutes. Add the peeled prawns and continue to stir fry for another minute or 2, until the prawns turn pink. Add the pork balls. Mix together the water, stock cube, tomato sauce and the chilli sauce and pour into the pan. Mix the cornflour with a little water and add this also. Cook for another minute, add the chopped spring onions, cook until all is mixed together and hot and serve straight away on plain rice. Add extra soy sauce to season if required. *Serves 2.*

Scallops Véronique

Firstly, let us emphasise that it is a crime to freeze scallops. But it is really the only way that you can sometimes buy them, if you live a long way from the ocean. Providing they have been frozen correctly in the first place and haven't been kept too long in the freezer, they can be turned into many magnificent dishes. If using frozen scallops, leave to thaw in the fridge overnight. Do not be tempted to throw them into hot water to thaw. Drain them and quickly rinse under cold water. This is one of those dishes that should be started and completed all in one go, so have everything ready by your side once you start. You can show off a little should you have a chafing dish that can be used by the side of the table. Never overcook scallops as they become like bullets.

24 SHELLED SCALLOPS, ABOUT 600 g/1 ¼ lb, PREFERABLY FRESH

30 g/1 ¼ oz UNSALTED BUTTER

225 ml/8 fl oz (1 cup) SINGLE (LIGHT) CREAM

30 ml/2 tbsp BRANDY

30 ml/2 tbsp MEDIUM-DRY SHERRY

1.25 ml/¼ tsp SALT

1.25 ml/¼ tsp GROUND WHITE PEPPER

24 SEEDLESS GREEN GRAPES

LEMON SLICES, TO GARNISH

Clean the scallops of any sandy bits, leaving the coral on. In a heavy-based frying pan, melt the butter over moderate heat and tip in the scallops. Cook for about 3 minutes, until they have started to turn opaque, and remove with a slotted spoon to a plate.

Raise the heat slightly under the frying pan and pour in the cream. When the cream comes to the boil, stir and lower the heat and simmer the cream for about 5 minutes. Add the brandy and the sherry, simmering and stirring until the sauce has reduced and thickened enough to coat the back of a spoon. Season with the salt and white pepper. Tip in the grapes. (If you are unable to buy seedless grapes, buy ones with seeds in, cut them in half and remove the seeds. A bit of bind we know, but as this is a simple elegant dish, the whole effect can be ruined if you and your guests have to keep spitting out seeds.)

After the grapes have heated through, add the scallops and any juices that may have exuded onto the plate. Stir until they are heated through and serve immediately in scallop shells or on warm plates, garnished with lemon slices. Serve as a starter. *Serves 4.*

Rich Oyster Pie

*This is a little like our Country Chicken Pie (p. 84). It has most things in it, enough to make it a
meal in itself. Simply serve with a steamed vegetable, such as extra fresh asparagus, or a lively,
lemon-dressed mixed salad.*
*We still say that fresh, and we mean fresh, oysters are best served on their own with perhaps a
sprinkling of lemon juice and some freshly ground black pepper. This recipe is for those who like the
oyster flavour, but cannot face them in their raw state. However, it will also be enjoyed by raw
oyster afficionados who think we are doing the oyster a grave injustice by marrying it with other
ingredients, and indeed subjecting it to the oven. And be warned – this pie is very rich.*

60 RAW OYSTERS

125 g/4 oz BUTTER

4 SPRING ONIONS, CHOPPED

125 g/4 oz BUTTON MUSHROOMS, SLICED

45 ml/3 tbsp FINELY CHOPPED FRESH PARSLEY

SALT AND FRESHLY GROUND BLACK PEPPER

4 HARD-BOILED EGGS

4 ARTICHOKE HEARTS, FRESHLY COOKED OR CANNED AND WELL DRAINED

125 g/4 oz ASPARAGUS TIPS, PARBOILED OR CANNED AND WELL DRAINED

ENOUGH SHORTCRUST PASTRY TO LINE AND TOP A 1-litre/1¾-pint (4-cup) PIE DISH

SINGLE (LIGHT) CREAM, TO GLAZE

15 ml/1 tbsp PLAIN FLOUR

50 ml/2 fl oz (¼ cup) DRY WHITE WINE

30 ml/2 tbsp LEMON JUICE

FRESHLY GRATED NUTMEG

2 EGG YOLKS, BEATEN WITH 50 ml/2 fl oz (¼ cup) SINGLE (LIGHT) CREAM

Place the oysters in a sieve and dip them in a pan of boiling water for 10 seconds, until they
stiffen. Remove and leave to drain. Melt half the butter in a non-stick pan and sauté the
onions, mushrooms and parsley, about 4 minutes, until the onions are soft. Add the oysters
and a little salt and pepper and set aside in a bowl. Melt the rest of the butter in the same
pan and quickly sauté the hard-boiled eggs (whole), the artichoke hearts and the fresh
asparagus tips. If you are using canned asparagus tips instead of fresh, do not add them at
this stage or they will become too mushy. Transfer to the oysters and roughly break up the
eggs and the artichoke hearts. You can now add the canned asparagus, if using. Leave to
cool.

Roll out two-thirds of the pastry and line a well buttered 1-litre/1¾-pint (4-cup) pie dish with it. Fill with the cooled mixture and cover the top with the remaining rolled-out pastry. Crimp the edges together well to seal and cut a small hole in the top of the pastry in the centre to let some of the steam escape during cooking.

Place a metal oven tray in the centre of the oven and preheat the oven to 180C/350F/Gas 4. Brush the top of the pie with a little extra cream to glaze, and bake on the tray for 30 to 40 minutes, until the pastry is well browned. The heated tray will help cook the base of the pastry.

About 10 minutes before the pie is cooked, stir the flour into the same non-stick pan and cook over moderate heat until pale beige in colour (do not let it burn). While stirring the flour, add the wine, lemon juice and a little grated nutmeg. Stir for a few minutes and remove from the heat. Add the egg yolks and cream to the pan. Remove the almost cooked pie carefully from the oven and, with the aid of a small funnel, carefully pour the cream mixture through the hole in the centre of the pie crust. Gently swirl around the cream and return the pie to the hot oven for another 5 to 7 minutes.

When cooked, leave the pie to settle for 10 minutes before serving. *Serves 6.*

MAIN COURSE MEATS

Don't go searching this section for plain roasts, grilled chops, fried steak or sausages as you won't find any. There are plenty of recipe books to tell you how to do that sort of cooking, so we have left it alone.

Everyone cooks a roast to their own particular taste. Some people like it very rare, in the case of beef, for example, and others like it very well done. Lamb, to our taste, should be cooked till pink and moist, but again some like it cooked till it is grey. A good piece of beef, aged by your butcher, can be absolutely delicious when roasted with nothing more than a little dripping to baste it every now and again. Some people douse the meat with lots of wine, or spread mustard over the top, or add generous amounts of herbs and butter to cook the beef in. All these things alter the plain roast and give it an entirely different character.

There are many different approaches to roasting and there is nothing really wrong with any of them, but it does depend on the cut of meat. If in doubt, ask your butcher – he or she wants you to be happy with whatever you purchased and to keep coming back as a customer. Some butchers can be very erratic, but most are true professionals. When we lived in the city, we used to travel a considerable distance to our butcher because his meat was really the best.

Cheaper cuts of beef usually require slow simmering or braising to bring out their flavour and make them tender. You cannot expect to roast a piece of stewing steak and make it come out like choice fillet.

In the case of frying or barbecuing, the only thing we would stress is, do not overcook chops or steaks. And remember that steaks in particular do not take too kindly to being treated roughly on a barbecue. The best method is to place the steaks on the heated rack, preferably having brushed them with a little oil first, do one side for several minutes and, when they are seared, turn them over. Do not overcook, and do not under any circumstances, keep prodding them with a fork or tongs and turning them over and over. The fork tines penetrate the centre of the meat and release the juices that run out each time you turn the steak – you end up with something that is totally dry and as often as not tough.

Steaks or chops are generally fried over a fairly high heat to seal the outsides and leave the centre slightly rare, but chicken pieces and pork chops do better at a lower heat and with a slightly longer cooking time.

Frozen meat must be thawed completely before it is cooked. The best place to do this is in the fridge and not on a window sill in full sunlight. Slow thawing lets less of the juices flow from the meat. To contradict ourselves completely, we do use our microwave oven to thaw meat – but do this carefully and do not let parts of the meat start to cook. Follow the instructions with your microwave.

There is a misconception that if a piece of beef has not been aged before you freeze it it will age in the freezer. This is simply not true.

Meat left at room temperature or stored badly can go off, so don't have too much raw meat stacked in the fridge at any one time. Buy what you need for your requirements, or alternatively freeze the surplus for later use. Make sure you put the date on the label. Too long in the freezer and the meat can be ruined.

When all is said and done, there is nothing nicer than a good piece of meat cooked simply and to perfection for getting the gastric juices going. Many people have drooled over the smell of the humble sausage being grilled, but they have to be good sausages. The same applies to plain roast lamb, beef, pork or chicken – they must be of the best quality. We have always believed that it is better to have less of something which is really top quality than to have a lot of something inferior. Even when buying minced beef (if you don't make your own), make sure that it is of top quality and not filled with an overabundance of fat.

We think the basic thing to remember is that if you try a piece of meat and it is on the rare side for your taste, you can always cook it a little more, but if you have overcooked it in the first place, you can't turn the stove backwards and cook it a little less!

Stir-fried Beef and Spring Onions

*The best thing about Chinese-style food in most cases is that it is quick to cook, very tasty, and easy
on the waistline. As with all dishes of this nature, have all the ingredients for this one prepared in
advance and in separate small or large bowls. A wok is still the best thing to cook Chinese food in,
although we sometimes use a large, heavy-based pan, and we now have a wok-shaped pan that has
a slightly flattened base so that you can use it on an electric cooker as well as on gas. In some
instances people try to reduce the price of the dish by buying cheaper cuts of meat, but as this cooks
so quickly, it is best to buy the meat recommended, in this case rump.
Should you not have sufficient spring onions, use the white parts of young leeks, well washed and
finely shredded. You will need 2 to 3 leeks to make up the quantity, depending on size.*

500 g/18 oz RUMP STEAK, WEIGHED AFTER THE FAT HAS BEEN REMOVED

30 ml/2 tbsp LIGHT SOY SAUCE

15 ml/1 tbsp DRY SHERRY OR GIN

15 ml/1 tbsp CORNFLOUR

2 CLOVES GARLIC, CRUSHED

10 ml/2 tsp SUGAR

15 ml/1 tbsp GROUNDNUT (PEANUT) OIL

275 g/10 oz SPRING ONIONS, SHREDDED, GREEN PARTS AS WELL, ABOUT TWO
BUNCHES

45 ml/3 tbsp DARK SOY SAUCE

ANOTHER 10 ml/2 tsp SUGAR

450 ml/¾ pint (2 cups) GROUNDNUT (PEANUT) OIL

5 ml/1 tsp SESAME OIL

Cut the beef into thin slices across the grain. The slices should be about 4 cm/1½ inch long
by 0.5 cm/¼ inch wide. In a medium-sized bowl, combine the beef strips, light soy sauce,
sherry or gin, cornflour, garlic and the first 10 ml/2 tsp sugar. Mix all together to coat the
beef and leave to marinade for at least an hour, stirring the beef round occasionally. Drain
off any surplus liquid and mix the beef with the 15 ml/1 tbsp groundnut oil to coat the strips.
Have the spring onions or leeks already prepared. Mix together the dark soy sauce and
remaining 10 ml/2 tsp sugar in a small bowl.
In a wok, heat the 450 ml/¾ pint (2 cups) groundnut oil until fairly hot, but certainly not
to the smoking stage, and add the beef strips. Cook for 1 to 2 minutes, until they separate
and change colour. Do this in 2 batches, and stir the beef round as it cooks with either a
slotted spoon or a Chinese wire skimmer. The oil should be hot enough so that when you
put the beef in it starts to splutter, but not too hot. If you are using a sugar thermometer the
heat should be about 180-190C/350-375F. When the beef has changed colour, remove
with a skimmer to a heated plate.

After you have cooked all the beef, drain the oil from the wok, being very careful not to burn yourself. Turn the heat up under the wok and return about 22.5 ml/1½ tbsp groundnut oil to it. When the wok is hot, add the shredded spring onions or leeks and stir fry for 1 minute, return the beef and the soy and sugar mixture and keep stir frying over high heat until the liquid has reduced to a syrupy glaze. Quickly add the sesame oil, toss all together and then serve straight away on a heated plate. This will serve 4 if you are using other dishes to make up a full Chinese meal.

Fillet of Beef with Madeira Sauce

We have always found fillet of beef suits our needs very well. Because you can use it either as steaks or for a roast it is a very versatile cut of beef. There really is no substitute for Madeira as it imparts its own particular flavour. We are talking about a sweet Madeira, not the dry Sercial Madeira that we use in other recipes. You can use a sweet vermouth at a pinch but the end result is not the same. Do not attempt to use cheap steak in this recipe as it will be too tough.

4 THICK SLICES FILLET OF BEEF, OR SIMILAR STEAKS

FRESHLY GROUND BLACK PEPPER

1 RASHER STREAKY BACON, RINDED AND CUT INTO SMALL PIECES

1 SMALL ONION, FINELY CHOPPED

25 g/1 oz BUTTER

50 ml/2 fl oz (¼ cup) BEEF STOCK, HEATED

50 ml/2 fl oz (¼ cup) MADEIRA

25 g/1 oz CHILLED BUTTER, DICED

Prepare the steaks and flatten them slightly with your hand. Leave at room temperature, covered, for at least 30 minutes before cooking and sprinkle a little freshly ground black pepper over them, if desired. Put the bacon, onion and butter in a moderately heated frying pan, preferably one with a non-stick surface. Cook until the onion and the bacon have turned golden brown. Remove these from the pan with a slotted spoon and discard, leaving the flavoured butter and fats in the pan. Raise the heat, and sear the steaks for 2 minutes on either side, and add the stock and Madeira. Lower the heat and continue to cook for another 2 minutes on each side to imbue the steaks with the flavour of the liquid. Transfer the steaks to heated plates, raise the heat of the pan and swirl in the butter pieces. When all the butter has amalgamated with the juices and thickened them slightly, pour over the steaks. Simple steamed potatoes and a green vegetable such as broccoli are ideal to serve with this rather sweetish, rich-tasting steak. *Serves 4.*

Curried Beef Pie

We did this on the show many years ago. How simple, we thought, no one will be impressed with something so homely. You could have knocked us down with a feather when, after the programme went on air, our office was inundated with requests for the recipe. It's terribly easy, and it's one of the answers to the question one used to hear years ago: 'What can I do with a pound of mince?'

60 g/2⅓ oz BUTTER

2 CLOVES GARLIC, CRUSHED

1 LARGE ONION, FINELY CHOPPED

500 g/18 oz MINCED BEEF

1 CARROT, DICED

2 STALKS CELERY, DICED

ABOUT 300 g/11 oz CANNED SWEETCORN, WELL DRAINED

15 ml/1 tbsp CURRY POWDER

SALT AND FRESHLY GROUND BLACK PEPPER

50 ml/2 fl oz (¼ cup) HOT WATER MIXED WITH 5 ml/1 tsp CRUMBLED BEEF STOCK CUBE

15 ml/1 tbsp CORNFLOUR MIXED WITH A LITTLE WATER

15 ml/1 tbsp TOMATO PURÉE (PASTE)

GOOD PINCH OF GARAM MASALA (OPTIONAL)

FLAKY PASTRY, THAWED IF FROZEN, TO COVER

1 EGG, BEATEN

Melt the butter in a large, heavy-based pan, add the crushed garlic, the chopped onion and the minced beef, and cook over high heat until the meat starts to change colour and browns a little. Stir while doing this, so that it doesn't catch. Carefully drain off excess fat and then add the diced carrot, celery, the drained sweetcorn, curry powder, a little salt and pepper and the water mixed with the beef stock cube. Bring to the boil, lower the heat and simmer the mixture for 10 minutes, stirring once or twice. Stir together the cornflour water and the tomato purée and add to the mince, stirring while the mixture returns to the boil and thickens. Leave to cool completely. Place in a round, deep pie dish and sprinkle with the garam masala, if using.

Cut a strip of pastry as wide as the rim to place on the rim of the baking dish. Dampen the pastry strip with water, then top with the remaining rolled out pastry. Seal the edges well and crimp to make a decorative edge. Brush the pie with the beaten egg mixed with a few drops of water and cut 1 or 2 vents in the pastry to let out the stream. Place the pie in the fridge, while you heat your oven to 220C/425F/Gas 7. Bake for 10 minutes, then reduce the heat to 180C/350F/Gas 4 and cook for a further 20 minutes, or until rich golden brown. *Serves 6.*

Scallopini

Instead of the traditional veal, we tried this one with fillet of beef. If you wish to serve more than 2 people increase the number of scallopini and adjust the sauce accordingly. Try this using thinly sliced pork fillet.

4 SLICES FILLET OF BEEF, ABOUT 2.5 cm/1 inch THICK

PLAIN FLOUR FOR DUSTING

25 g/1 oz BUTTER

15 ml/1 tbsp VEGETABLE OIL

3 SPRING ONIONS, FINELY CHOPPED

8 MUSHROOMS, THINLY SLICED

100 ml/4 fl oz (½ cup) BEEF STOCK

45 ml/3 tbsp BRANDY

1.25 ml/¼ tsp DRY MUSTARD

7.5 ml/1½ tsp DRAINED CAPERS (CHOPPED IF YOU WANT A STRONGER FLAVOUR)

2.5 ml/½ tsp WORCESTERSHIRE SAUCE

2.5 ml/½ tsp LEMON JUICE

SALT AND FRESHLY GROUND BLACK PEPPER

FINELY CHOPPED FRESH PARSLEY, TO GARNISH

Trim the fillet of any gristle and surplus fat. Place each steak between pieces of greaseproof paper and gently pound with a heavy meat mallet until about 0.5 cm/¼ inch thick. Place between layers of fresh greaseproof paper and chill for several hours (ideal to prepare in the morning).

When ready to cook, dust the steaks lightly with flour. Heat a heavy-based frying pan over fairly high heat, add the butter and oil. When bubbling nicely cook the floured meat for 1 minute on each side. It should be nice and brown, but pink inside. Place on a heated platter and keep hot in the oven.

In the same pan, make the sauce. Scrape the pan to loosen any bits stuck to the bottom. You may have to add a little more butter if the pan is too dry. Add the onions and mushrooms and stir fry until wilted, only a few minutes. Add beef stock and stir well. Add brandy, mustard, capers, Worcestershire sauce and lemon juice, bring to the boil and simmer, uncovered, until reduced to about half. Pour in any juices that may have accumulated on the plate from the steaks. Taste for pepper and salt. Serve the meat on heated dinner plates, pour over the sauce, sprinkle with parsley, and serve at once. *Serves 2.*

Oxtails with Orange and Walnuts

There is constant argument when we talk about oxtail stews – one of us wants to leave the fat in, the other wants to remove it when it has cooled down. The choice is yours, but about one thing we are both adamant. To get the best flavour, you must cook the oxtail the previous day and leave to cool, then chill overnight before finishing off the dish. This makes removing the fat from the surface of the chilled dish easier.

We omit salt from the list of ingredients so that if you use commercial beef stock cubes, which are usually salty, you shouldn't end up with something too oversalted.

Day 1

2 OXTAILS

PLAIN FLOUR FOR DUSTING

50 ml/2 fl oz (¼ cup) VEGETABLE OIL

2 LARGE ONIONS, SLICED

2 STALKS CELERY, SLICED

4 CLOVES GARLIC, CRUSHED

FRESHLY GROUND BLACK PEPPER

225 ml/8 fl oz (1 cup) DRY WHITE WINE

2 x 230 g CANS TOMATOES IN JUICE

750 ml/1¼ pints (3 cups) BEEF STOCK

PARED RIND OF 1 ORANGE

6 STALKS FRESH PARSLEY

5 ml/1 tsp EACH DRIED BASIL AND DRIED THYME

2 BAY LEAVES

Use a large, covered casserole that can be placed in the oven or on top of the oven. Cut the oxtail into joints and dust with the flour. Heat the oil in the pan, shake the excess flour from the oxtails and brown them in the oil. Do this several pieces at a time so as not to overcrowd the casserole. Remove the pieces with a slotted spoon and set aside.

Place the sliced onions, celery and crushed garlic in the heated casserole. Cook the vegetables over moderate heat until they are softened, and sprinkle with a little freshly ground black pepper. Add the white wine, increase the heat a little and boil the wine for 2 minutes, stirring everything round as you do so. Put the browned oxtail pieces back in the pot, together with the tinned tomatoes and juice, plus the beef stock. While this is coming to the boil, tie the orange rind, parsley, herbs and bay leaves in a clean piece of muslin and add to the pan. When the liquids boil, cover, reduce the heat and simmer for 3 hours, or until just tender. (If there is too much evaporation, top up with a little hot water.) When the oxtail is just tender, remove from heat, leave to cool and place in the fridge overnight.

Day 2

65 ml/2½ fl oz (⅓ cup) RED WINE OR RED WINE VINEGAR

45 ml/3 tbsp DARK BROWN SUGAR

THINLY PARED RIND OF 1 ORANGE

450 ml/¾ pint (2 cups) WATER

50 g/2 oz (½ cup) WALNUT HALVES

10 ml/2 tsp UNSALTED BUTTER

PINCH OF SALT

30 ml/2 tbsp UNSALTED BUTTER

Next day, an hour before serving, remove the fat from the casserole with a spoon (your decision entirely) and place the covered casserole in the oven at 150C/300F/Gas 2.

Boil the red wine or red wine vinegar together with the sugar for 5 minutes. Set aside. Shred the orange rind into fine julienne and boil in the water for 5 minutes; drain and place on a sheet of kitchen paper to drain completely.

Put the walnut halves in a separate pan with the 10 ml/2 tsp butter and stir fry over moderate heat for 3 minutes, then set aside. (We regret all the pans, but these three things can be done in advance, and the end results will make up for the extra bits of washing up.)

When the casserole has heated through, remove the muslin bag and discard. Using a slotted spoon, transfer the oxtail pieces to a large serving casserole. Keep warm.

Mouli or process the cooking liquids, being careful not to burn yourself. Rinse out the casserole and transfer the resulting purée back into it. Add the shredded orange rind and the wine syrup, simmer until the sauce reduces and thickens slightly, then swirl in the 30 ml/2 tbsp butter. Sprinkle the walnuts over the oxtail pieces and pour over the sauce.

Serve with either mashed or plain boiled potatoes to mop up the sauce. (We find we always have a lot of sauce to start with, but after the meal, and with the help of lots of sliced bread, there never seems to be any left...) It's wise to have finger bowls, large extra napkins that can be easily washed later, and a bowl in the centre for the bones. *Serves 4 to 6.*

Rich Meat Sauce

A really good meat sauce to serve over spaghetti or pasta is one of our most used standbys, especially when unexpected guests drop in. It is easy to make up a large batch and then divide it into smaller quantities to freeze for later use. This sauce is also suitable to use to construct a lasagne or to fill pancakes. Additional extras such as fried chopped mushrooms can be added to it when thawed, to be used for a particular dish. Some people like to add a few mashed anchovies, others some strips of ham. To make it a little richer, you can add about 50 ml/2 fl oz (¼ cup) single (light) cream. The quantities are up to you, to suit your own taste, but the sauce is a good base to start from. To get a beefier flavour you might like to add 15 ml/1 tbsp of beef extract. Again, you can change the flavour by using red wine, white wine, sherry or Madeira rather than the sweet vermouth that is suggested here.

30 ml/2 tbsp OLIVE OIL

2 LARGE ONIONS, FINELY CHOPPED

2 CLOVES GARLIC, CRUSHED

2 SMALL CARROTS, FINELY DICED

1 STALK CELERY, FINELY DICED

2 RASHERS STREAKY BACON, FINELY DICED

1 kg/2¼ lb LEAN MINCED BEEF

2.5 ml/½ tsp EACH DRIED OREGANO, THYME AND BASIL

15 ml/1 tbsp CRUMBLED BEEF STOCK CUBES

225 ml/8 fl oz (1 cup) HOT WATER

800 g CAN ITALIAN TOMATOES, PREFERABLY PACKED IN TOMATO JUICE

50 ml/2 fl oz (¼ cup) SWEET VERMOUTH

8 GRINDINGS BLACK PEPPER

8 WHOLE CLOVES, OR 2.5 ml/½ tsp GROUND

45 ml/3 tbsp TOMATO PURÉE (PASTE)

Heat the oil in a very large pan and add the onions, garlic, carrots, celery and bacon. Stir over a fairly high heat until the onions start to turn golden brown. Break up the minced beef and add all at once. Still over a fairly high heat, stir and break up the meat and continue to cook until it has all changed colour (it does not have to go brown). Lower the heat and add the rest of the ingredients, breaking up the tomatoes. Simmer very gently for an hour, preferably covered to eliminate the spattering that can occur. Leave to cool, and then reheat gently and simmer for another hour, stirring occasionally. (Again, have the lid partly covering the pot to stop spattering.) Check for seasoning and leave to cool with the lid off completely. Divide the cooled sauce into suitably sized containers to suit your needs, chill, cover and freeze.

Try to use the sauce within a month. To reheat, thaw overnight in the fridge, place in a saucepan and gently heat until boiling. It is now that you add any other flavours you wish.

If this entire quantity were used, layered with sheets of cooked lasagne, Béchamel Sauce (p. 186), and shredded mozzarella cheese into a completed lasagne, it would easily feed 12 people as a main course.

Italian Meatballs

The thing that sets Italian meatballs apart from the ordinary is the use of grated lemon rind. You can use, if you wish, a combination of beef and pork in about 50/50 proportions, but the recipe we give here is for beef only. You will notice that there is no onion in this recipe. Should you wish, add about half an onion, very finely chopped, or alternatively, add some extra crushed garlic. You can also vary the taste by adding about 2.5-5 ml/ ½-1 tsp dried oregano. When cooked, serve the meatballs with buttered pasta, or add them to a fresh tomato sauce and serve over spaghetti, with plenty of grated Parmesan cheese sprinkled over the top.

500 g/18 oz LEAN MINCED BEEF

30 ml/1 tbsp FINELY CHOPPED FRESH PARSLEY

1 CLOVE GARLIC, CRUSHED

FINELY GRATED RIND OF 1 SMALL LEMON

2.5 ml/½ tsp SALT

8 GRINDINGS BLACK PEPPER

PINCH OF GRATED NUTMEG

15 g/½ oz (¼ cup) FINE FRESH BREADCRUMBS

1 EGG, LIGHTLY BEATEN

OLIVE OIL

Mix the meat and dry ingredients together in a large bowl. Add the beaten egg to bind all together. Cover with cling film and chill for at least 1 hour or up to 6 hours. Heat some olive oil in a heavy-based, non-stick pan, dampen hands and roll the mixture into balls about the size of a golf ball. Fry, turning frequently, over moderate heat for about 5 or more minutes until they are browned. *Serves 4.*

Burgundy Beef

There are lots of variations on this dish, the simplest being possibly the best. The one thing that invariably makes the dish a disappointment is cutting the meat too small and ending up with dryish pieces of meat rather than juicy ones. We once made it in our restaurant days with left-over pieces of filet mignon. What a waste, you may say – and you would be right, because the meat virtually disintegrated, and we were left with this rather thick meat soup. The best cut is a piece of topside or rump, cut into 5 cm/2 inch cubes, no smaller. This can be cooked in a flameproof casserole with a well fitting lid, or in a crockpot or slow cooker. We find these methods preferable to cooking on top of the oven.

100 g/4 oz UNSALTED BUTTER

15 ml/1 tbsp OLIVE OIL

1 kg/2¼ lb TOPSIDE OR RUMP, CUT INTO 5 cm/2 inch CUBES

1 LARGE ONION, FINELY SLICED

15 ml/1 tbsp PLAIN FLOUR

50 ml/2 fl oz (¼ cup) BRANDY

3 CLOVES GARLIC, CRUSHED

1.25 ml/¼ tsp DRIED MIXED HERBS OR BOUQUET GARNI (PARSLEY, THYME, MARJORAM, BAY LEAF, PIECE OF CELERY)

2.5 ml/½ tsp SALT

2.5 ml/½ tsp FRESHLY GROUND BLACK PEPPER

1 BOTTLE RED WINE, PREFERABLY BURGUNDY

150 g/5 oz STREAKY BACON, IN ONE PIECE

25 PICKLING ONIONS

150 g/5 oz BUTTON MUSHROOMS

FINELY CHOPPED FRESH PARSLEY

20 GREEN OLIVES (OPTIONAL), STONED

Melt half the butter and the oil in a heavy-based, flameproof casserole and brown the meat over fairly high heat. Now add the sliced onions to the pan, reduce the heat slightly and cook until they are transparent. Add the flour and continue to stir for a few minutes longer, pour in the brandy and when it has warmed for a few seconds, set it alight with a long match. (A word of warning here. Should you have an extractor fan or hood above your oven, make sure that it is switched off during this flaming operation, so as to avoid flames accidentally reaching it and causing a fire.) Now add the crushed garlic, the mixed herbs or bouquet garni wrapped in some clean muslin, and the salt and pepper. Add enough of the wine to cover the meat and bring it to simmering point. Cover the casserole, put it in a preheated oven at 150C/300F/Gas 2 and cook for 2 hours.

Cut the bacon into small cubes and fry in the remaining butter until it starts to turn golden brown, add the peeled onions to the bacon and cook until lightly brown also. Add this to the casserole and cook for a further 30 minutes. Add the mushrooms whole, if they are small, or sliced if using large mushrooms, and cook for a further 15 minutes. If thickening is necessary, place the casserole on top of the oven, drop in bits of beurre manié (below), and cook at moderate heat, stirring, until the desired thickness is obtained. Add olives for last few minutes. Remove the bouquet garni and serve sprinkled with the chopped parsley.

To cook this dish in a crockpot, when you have added the wine and brought it to a simmer, transfer all the ingredients to the crockpot and cook for 6 hours. Add the browned bacon and onions and cook for another 2 hours, all this on the low setting. Add the mushrooms and cook for a further 30 minutes. (These times are approximate, as room temperature can make a difference. If the meat is not cooked through in the initial stage on the low setting after 6 hours, raise to high and continue on high after you have added the onions and bacon.) If you wish to thicken the sauce at all, and you will find you will have more liquid left when cooking in a crockpot, use a beurre manié, which is equal weights of butter and flour mixed together and dropped in little bits into the dish. Switch the controls to high, add the bits of beurre manié and cook, stirring, for about 15 minutes with the lid off. Add olives, if used, just 5 minutes before serving so that they heat through. *Serves 4.*

Pork Medallions with Calvados Cream Sauce

This is delicious served with Ginger Ribboned Carrots and Vegetable Custards (pp. 137 and 144). It is a meal which is relatively simple to prepare; the carrots can be prepared in the morning and held until you require them – likewise the vegetable custards can be cooked ahead and then reheated. The pork has to be cooked just before serving. We have chosen pork tenderloins – make sure that you trim off the sheath and sinew before cutting them into slices.

2 PORK TENDERLOINS, EACH 150-200 g/5-7 oz, TRIMMED

SALT AND FRESHLY GROUND BLACK PEPPER

PLAIN FLOUR FOR DUSTING

30 g/1 ¼ oz BUTTER

15 ml/1 tbsp GROUNDNUT (PEANUT) OIL

225 ml/8 fl oz (1 cup) CHICKEN STOCK

5 ml/1 tsp CORNFLOUR

50 ml/2 fl oz (¼ cup) SINGLE (LIGHT) CREAM

30 ml/2 tbsp CALVADOS OR DRY CIDER

45 ml/3 tbsp SUGAR

30 ml/2 tbsp WATER

2 APPLES, PEELED, CORED AND CUT INTO EIGHTHS

Slice each tenderloin into 8 pieces, starting from the thickest end. Pound these out to thin medallions, using the side of a meat mallet or a rolling pin. Sprinkle both sides of each medallion with salt and pepper and dust both sides with flour, shaking off the excess. In a non-stick pan, melt the butter and the oil over moderate heat and cook the pork for 3 minutes on each side, until lightly golden brown. Transfer to a plate and keep warm in the oven. Mix together the chicken stock and cornflour and pour into the same pan. Increase the heat and stir, scraping any brown bits from the bottom of the pan. Boil and reduce the liquid by half, then add the cream and simmer for a further 2 minutes. Pour in the calvados and transfer the sauce to a heated sauceboat. In another pan, bring the water and sugar to the boil so that the sugar has dissolved and when it starts to turn pale gold, place in the apple slices and turn frequently until they have slightly caramelised.

To serve, place 4 of the pork medallions in a line, slightly overlapping; arrange a piece of apple on each slice and spoon over some of the sauce. *Serves 4.*

Ham and Cheese Filled Meat Loaf

The cheese can be thinly sliced mozzarella or cheddar. If you wish, you can use processed cheese of any flavour you choose.

750 g/1½ lb MINCED BEEF

2 SLICES BREAD, TURNED INTO CRUMBS

1 EGG, SIZE 1

225 ml/8 fl oz (1 cup) MILK

1 ONION, FINELY CHOPPED

15 ml/1 tbsp WORCESTERSHIRE SAUCE

5 ml/1 tsp SALT

2.5 ml/½ tsp DRY MUSTARD

1.25 ml/¼ tsp FRESHLY GROUND BLACK PEPPER

1.25 ml/¼ tsp DRIED SAGE

1.25 ml/¼ tsp GARLIC POWDER

4 SLICES HAM

4 SLICES CHEESE

Preheat the oven to 180C/350F/Gas 6. In a large bowl mix together all the ingredients, except the ham and cheese. Press half the meat mixture into an ungreased 900 g/2 lb loaf tin. Place 2 of the ham slices side by side, slightly overlapping, top with 2 slices of cheese, another 2 ham slices and finally the other 2 cheese slices. Roll these 4 layers up tightly from the longest side to form a roll and place on the meat in the loaf tin. Top with the other half of the meat mixture, press down firmly and bake in a shallow baking dish in the middle of the oven for 1¼ hours. (The dish will catch any drips.) When cooked, drain off any excess fat from the loaf tin and leave to settle for about 5 minutes. Run a knife around the edges to loosen, then turn out onto a warm plate. Cut into thick slices to serve. *Serve 6.*

Country Pork Pâté

Pork pâtés or terrines, whichever you wish to call them, usually consist of pork, both lean and fat, a binding agent, usually eggs, and some form of alcohol. Of course there are generally herbs and spices mixed in as well to give added flavour. They really are excellent for parties, weekend entertaining, or just good eating generally. This one is made of coarsely minced meats and cubes of fat. The meats are better put through a meat mincer or grinder, rather than into the processor, as you can easily end up with mince that is a combination of overprocessed and underprocessed – part paste and part chunks.

We mention Sercial Madeira, which is not always easy to come by, but if you do see it, buy it. It has a dry flavour, but you can substitute a very good dry sherry if you cannot obtain it. Like a lot of other alcoholic beverages that are used for flavouring, kirsch for example, the original outlay seems a lot, but you generally use so little it is a good investment as there is often nothing that really has the same flavour for a particular recipe.

If you are in doubt as to whether you have flavoured the pâté enough, do the following: mix all the ingredients together and leave for at least an hour before you pack them in the container in which you are going to cook them. Take a 15 ml/1 tbsp or so and fry in a little clarified butter or tasteless oil so that you can taste what the herbs and flavourings are like. Don't forget to leave the pâté for several days after it has chilled to allow the flavours to combine. Remember that chilling has a tendency to diminish the flavour, but that extra pepper and salt can be added when the pâté is served.

500 g/18 oz LEAN PORK, COARSELY MINCED

250 g/9 oz CHICKEN OR PORK LIVER, COARSELY MINCED

250 g/9 oz VEAL, COARSELY MINCED

ABOUT 100 g/4 oz (½ cup) HAM OR TONGUE, DICED

ABOUT 100 g/4 oz (½ cup) PORK FAT, DICED

100 ml/4 fl oz (½ cup) SINGLE (LIGHT) CREAM

50 ml/2 fl oz (¼ cup) SERCIAL MADEIRA OR GOOD DRY SHERRY

1 EGG, SIZE 1, LIGHTLY BEATEN

15 ml/1 tbsp PLAIN FLOUR

7.5 ml/1½ tsp SALT

2.5 ml/½ tsp FRESHLY GROUND BLACK PEPPER

2.5 ml/½ tsp DRIED THYME

1.25 ml/¼ tsp GROUND ALLSPICE

3 BAY LEAVES

6 TO 8 RASHERS STREAKY BACON

Put all the ingredients in a bowl, with the exception of the bacon and the bay leaves. Mix thoroughly by hand or with a wooden spoon. Cook a little of the mixture, as suggested above, and test for flavour. Remove the rind from the bacon rashers and stretch them lengthways with the back of a heavy knife. Arrange the bay leaves in the bottom of a 1.5 litre/2½ pint (6¼ cup) terrine or loaf tin. Line the container with bacon, overlapping slightly and allowing the bacon to extend over sides of container. Fill with the meat mixture and bring the overhanging strips of bacon over the top to cover. Cover with a double strip of lightly buttered foil, plus the lid of the container if it has one. Place the terrine in a larger baking pan and fill with hot water to come two-thirds up the sides of the terrine. Bake at 170C/325F/Gas 3 for 2 hours in the middle of the oven, checking occasionally to ensure that the water doesn't evaporate too much. Remove from the oven, tip the water out of the pan, and return the terrine to the pan so that when you weight it, the pan will catch any exuding fats. Leave the terrine to cool for about 20 minutes, remove the lid, leaving the foil on, and weight it with weights, heavy tins, an iron or whatever, until the pâté is cool. When cold, place the weighted pâté in a fridge, in the pan, and leave overnight. Remove the weights and leave to ripen for 2 days at least before you serve. Run a thin knife round the edges and pop the base in very hot water for a few seconds to loosen it, turn out on a board and serve in thickish slices. *Serves 6-8.*

Pork Tenderloin Marsala

This is equally nice done with scallops of veal, chicken breasts or lamb cutlets that you have really bashed flat.

1 OR 2 PORK TENDERLOINS, PREFERABLY THICK ONES, TOTAL WEIGHT ABOUT
500 g/18 oz

PLAIN FLOUR FOR DUSTING

50 g/2 oz BUTTER

125 g/4 oz MOZZARELLA CHEESE

SALT AND FRESHLY GROUND BLACK PEPPER

ANCHOVY FILLETS (OPTIONAL)

CAPERS, WELL DRAINED

60 ml/4 tbsp MARSALA

100 ml/4 fl oz (½ cup) SINGLE (LIGHT) CREAM

The thicker the tenderloin, the larger the flattened rounds will be. Cut the tenderloins into rounds, about 2.5 cm/1 inch thick, place between greaseproof paper and gently pound out until twice the size. The quantity will depend on how many you wish to serve; we work on 4 rounds per person. Lightly dust with flour and shake off the excess, then put aside until ready to cook.

In a heavy-based frying pan, melt the butter over moderate heat and gently fry the pork rounds until lightly golden brown (you are going to cook them again later on). Lay them separately on a flat platter. Slice the mozzarella to fit the pork rounds. (If you want to be extra flash, you could cut these slices with a scone cutter, to make rounds.) Season the pork with salt and pepper and place a piece of cheese on each round. Drain the anchovy fillets, lay 2 anchovy fillets on each pork round. Drain some capers, 4 for each round, and place these on top.

At this stage you can leave them until you are ready to finish them, so they are ideal to prepare in the morning or the night before – but don't wash out the pan, you want the juices. When ready to serve, gently heat the pan and juices, place in the dressed pork rounds, cover and reheat for about 10 minutes, or until the cheese has softened visibly. Remove to a heated serving platter and keep hot in the oven.

Add the Marsala to the pan and stir any stuck bits off the bottom of the pan, bring gently to the boil, then add the cream, stir over moderate heat until sauce has thickened slightly and reduced. Serve the sauce over the platter of pork rounds or serve on individual plates. *Serves 4.*

Lion's Head Stew

This is a very traditional Chinese stew. The pork balls are meant to represent a lion's head and the Chinese cabbage the mane. Call it what you will it is delicious and very easy to prepare and cook. All the ingredients must be very fine so that the balls will stick together, as you are using neither flour nor egg to bind the mixture. We suggest you heat the wok before adding the oil, as the Chinese do.

We like to use gin for a change. Some Chinese prefer it to sherry in place of rice wine, on account of its dryness. Dried shrimps are available from Chinese supermarkets.

500 g/18 oz MINCED PORK, NOT TOO LEAN

100 g/4 oz (½ cup) WATER CHESTNUTS, DRAINED AND FINELY CHOPPED

25 g/1 oz DRIED SHRIMPS, SOAKED AND DRAINED, OR CANNED SHRIMPS, FINELY CHOPPED

3 SPRING ONIONS, FINELY CHOPPED

1 SLICE FRESH ROOT GINGER, PEELED AND FINELY CHOPPED

PINCH OF CHINESE FIVE SPICES

2.5 ml/½ tsp SALT

7.5 ml/½ tbsp SUGAR

30 ml/ 2 tbsp DARK SOY SAUCE

30 ml/2 tbsp RICE WINE, DRY SHERRY OR GIN

1 CHINESE CABBAGE

45 ml/3 tbsp GROUNDNUT (PEANUT) OIL

225 ml/8 fl oz (1 cup) GOOD CHICKEN STOCK, PREFERABLY HOMEMADE (p. 183)

In a food processor with the steel blade process the pork to a paste. (The colder the pork, the easier this is. Even having it slightly frozen is a help.) Add the water chestnuts, shrimps, onions, ginger and five spices and blend for a few seconds. Scrape out into a clean bowl then mix in thoroughly the salt, sugar, soy sauce and rice wine. Wet your hands and shape the mixture into 4 large balls. Refrigerate until ready to cook.

Wash the cabbage well and shake off the surplus water, cut it in 4 lengthways and pat dry.

In a wok or heavy-based deep pan, heat the oil until smoking hot. Carefully add the cabbage quarters and stir fry until soft (only takes a few minutes). Lower the heat slightly, place the pork balls on top of the cabbage, pour over the chicken stock, cover and simmer for 20-30 minutes. Heat a serving plate, carefully remove the pork balls to the plate and set aside. Lay the cabbage out on the plate, place the balls on top and pour any juices over the dish. Serve with plain steamed rice. *Serves 4.*

Bacon Roly Poly

*Here is some old-fashioned stodge – simple but very tasty. You can either wrap the roll in
2 thicknesses of heavily floured muslin, or you can butter a double layer of foil and enclose the
roll so as to stop too much water seeping into it. In either case don't wrap too tightly, as you must
allow for the roll to swell during cooking.*

1 THICK SLICE BREAD, CRUSTS REMOVED

275 g/10 oz (2 cups) SELF-RAISING FLOUR

5 ml/1 tsp BAKING POWDER

2.5 ml/½ tsp SALT

100 g/4 oz (1 cup) SHREDDED BEEF SUET

ABOUT 225 ml/8 fl oz (1 cup) WATER

500 g/18 oz LEAN BACON

2 SLICES HAM

½ ONION, FINELY CHOPPED

8 GRINDINGS BLACK PEPPER

2.5 ml/½ tsp DRIED THYME

Turn the bread into crumbs in a food processor fitted with the steel blade and place in a
large mixing bowl. Sift the flour, baking powder and salt onto the crumbs and add the
shredded suet. Mix together with either a blunt knife or a metal spoon, and gradually add
enough water to make a soft but non-sticky dough. Lightly flour a work surface and roll the
dough out into an oblong (it will have to fit into a large saucepan comfortably so that you
can boil it). Chop the bacon and the ham into fairly small pieces and scatter them over the
rolled-out dough to within 2.5 cm/1 inch of the edges. Evenly scatter over this the onion,
pepper and thyme. Moisten round the edge of the dough with water and start rolling it up
with the shortest side towards you, as for a Swiss roll. Try and trap as much air in it as you
can, so as to let it expand in the cooking, thus keeping it lighter than if you rolled it up very
tightly. Pinch the ends and the long edge to seal and wrap up in either the floured muslin or
the buttered double foil, as described above. Carefully drop into a large saucepan of
simmering water, cover and simmer for 1½ hours. The water doesn't have to come more
than half way up the sides of the roll, but keep it simmering, and check occasionally in case
you need to replenish the water. If you do have to add some, make sure it is boiling water, so
as not to stop the cooking process. If the saucepan has a heavy lid, you shouldn't have too
much evaporation. Another precaution is to place an old up-turned plate in the bottom of
the saucepan to stop the roll touching the bottom of the pan itself. Alternatively, you can
place it in the top of a steamer and increase the cooking time to 2 hours.

Carefully remove the roll, take off the foil or muslin and serve cut into thick slices. Serve
with a green vegetable and possibly an onion gravy or an onion sauce. *Serves 4 to 6.*

Simple Herbed Pork Chops

*This very simple yet tasty dish stretches pork chops somewhat because of the thick layer of crumbs.
You can use normal pork chops that still contain the bone, but trim off the rind and a good
proportion of the fat first. Alternatively, buy already trimmed and boned pork medallions. Serve
with steamed spinach that has had a little butter, nutmeg and salt and pepper added to it, and you
have an easy meal that you can prepare in advance.
The amount of Parmesan is minimal – it is there to give a golden appearance to the crumbs when
they are cooked.
No sauce or gravy is required with these, but you might like to serve horseradish sauce or a fruit
chutney on the side.*

4 PORK CHOPS, TRIMMED, OR PORK MEDALLIONS

4 THICK SLICES FRESH BREAD, CRUSTS REMOVED

30 ml/2 tbsp FRESHLY GRATED PARMESAN CHEESE

5 ml/1 tsp DRIED THYME

5 ml/1 tsp DRIED SAGE

SEVERAL STALKS FRESH PARSLEY, COARSELY CHOPPED

2 SPRING ONIONS, COARSELY CHOPPED

ABOUT 2.5 ml/½ tsp SALT

ABOUT 2.5 ml/½ tsp FRESHLY GROUND BLACK PEPPER

PLAIN FLOUR FOR DUSTING

2 EGGS, BEATEN WITH 5 ml/1 tsp OIL AND 5 ml/1 tsp WATER

30 ml/2 tbsp GROUNDNUT (PEANUT) OIL

50 g/2 oz BUTTER

Pat the chops or medallions dry with kitchen paper. Break the bread slices into pieces and
turn them into crumbs in a food processor fitted with the steel blade, by dropping them a
few at a time through the feed tube while the motor is running. When they are relatively
fine, switch off. Add the Parmesan cheese, thyme, sage, parsley, spring onions, salt and
pepper. Process for a few seconds to mix everything together, then tip on to a large plate.

Dredge each pork chop with flour, shake off the excess and dip into the beaten egg
mixture. Hold for a while to drain off some of the egg, then drop onto the breadcrumbs.
Turn over and press down into the crumbs firmly to get a thick layer adhering to the pork.
Turn over and press the first side into the crumbs again. When you have put on a thickish
coating, place on another clean plate. Proceed with the remaining pork, cover with
kitchen paper and keep in the fridge until ready to cook or cook straight away. Heat the oil
and butter, preferably in a non-stick frying pan. Gently fry the coated chops over moderate
heat for about 5 minutes on either side until golden brown. *Serves 4.*

Chicken Breasts Stuffed with Leeks

This is one of those dishes that can be made in advance to get rid of the fiddly bits, then chilled, to be reheated later and just finished off with a sauce. Make the filling and stuff the breasts, then cover and chill overnight if need be. Next morning fry the breasts and then poach them till they are just cooked, leave to cool and then reheat with a little of the juices. Make the sauce just before serving.

6 CHICKEN BREASTS

25 g/1 oz BUTTER

3 to 4 LARGE LEEKS, THINLY SLICED AND WASHED

3. 75 ml/¾ tsp DRY TARRAGON

EXTRA 25 g/1 oz BUTTER

65 ml/2½ fl oz (⅓ cup) DRY WHITE WINE OR DRY VERMOUTH

150 ml/5 fl oz (⅔ cup) CHICKEN STOCK, PREFERABLY HOMEMADE (p. 183)

175 ml/6 fl oz (¾ cup) SINGLE (LIGHT) CREAM

FINELY GRATED RIND OF ½ LEMON

15 ml/1 tbsp LEMON JUICE

Remove any skin and bone from the chicken breasts. From the thickest side of the breast, using a sharp-pointed knife, carefully cut a long pocket going through nearly to the other side, but not separating each piece into 2. Melt the butter in a non-stick pan and cook the thinly sliced leeks over low heat together with the tarragon until soft. It's best to cover them with a lid at first and then remove it when the leeks are nearly cooked to allow the moisture to evaporate. Leave to cool. Stuff 30-45 ml/2-3 tbsp of the cooked leeks into the cut pocket of each chicken breast, cover with cling film and chill until firm. Melt the next 25 g/1 oz butter in the cleaned-out non-stick pan and fry the stuffed chicken breasts gently on each side until lightly browned, being careful when you turn them not to lose the leek filling. Don't overcrowd the pan – do several at a time, not all together. When you have browned them all, return them all to the pan and add the wine or vermouth and the chicken stock. Simmer gently, covered, for 7 minutes, carefully turn them over and simmer for a further 4 minutes. At this stage you can leave them to cool completely in the pan juices and leave in a cool place for up to 6 hours.

Remove the breasts with a slotted spoon to another dish that has a cover and spoon a little of the juices over them. Reheat in a 180C/350F/Gas 4 oven for about 15 to 20 minutes, until thoroughly heated through. Remove with a slotted spoon to a plate and keep warm while you make the sauce.

Boil the pan juices down by half over a fairly high heat, add the cream and any juices that have exuded from the warm chicken and boil down to about 100 ml/4 fl oz (½ cup). Stir in the rind and lemon juice, check for seasoning and serve the chicken breasts on warm plates with the sauce spooned over them. This is really nice served simply with fresh green vegetables and plain boiled small potatoes. *Serves 6.*

Fried Chicken with Lemon Sauce

The quantities we give here are for 2 people. It is easiest cooked in a wok, as you don't need as much oil. Failing that a heavy-based casserole will do, but add extra oil.

2 CHICKEN BREASTS

1.25 ml/¼ tsp SALT

1 EGG WHITE, LIGHTLY BEATEN

7.5 ml/1½ tbsp CORNFLOUR

GROUNDNUT (PEANUT) OIL

TOMATO SLICES AND CUCUMBER SLICES (OPTIONAL), TO GARNISH

Sauce

2.5 ml/½ tsp GRATED LEMON RIND

30 ml/2 tbsp LEMON JUICE

30 ml/2 tbsp SUGAR

15 ml/1 tbsp WORCESTERSHIRE SAUCE

15 ml/1 tbsp TOMATO SAUCE

350 ml/12 fl oz (¾ cup) CHICKEN STOCK, PREFERABLY HOMEMADE (p. 183)

1.25 ml/¼ tsp SALT

15 ml/1 tbsp CORNFLOUR

Remove the skin and any bones from the chicken, cut into bite-sized pieces and place in a bowl. Add the salt, lightly beaten egg white and the cornflour, then mix with a spoon to coat the pieces. Heat about 5 cm/2 inches of groundnut oil in a wok and fry the chicken pieces, a few at a time, about 3 to 4 minutes for each batch, until they are browned. Don't overcrowd them as you want to keep them separate and not clogged together. Remove with a slotted spoon or wire strainer and place in a heatproof dish lined with crumpled kitchen paper. Keep warm while you make the sauce.

Place the sauce ingredients in a small saucepan over moderate heat until thick and bubbling, whisking all the time so that you achieve a smooth sauce. Place the drained chicken on a warm serving dish and pour the sauce over. Garnish, if you wish, with sliced tomato and cucumber, and serve with plain rice to which you have added a hint of soy and sesame oil over the top to flavour it. *Serves 2.*

Chicken Maryland

Fried bananas go well with this dish, as do fried pineapple rings. We must admit we have altered this recipe from the true Maryland and slipped a little into Southern Fried Chicken – still, we're sure you won't mind!

1 LARGE ROASTING CHICKEN, CUT INTO SERVING PORTIONS, OR GOOD FRESH CHICKEN PIECES

125 g/4 oz PLAIN FLOUR

AT LEAST 2.5 ml/½ tsp PAPRIKA

SALT

1 EGG

125 g/4 oz DRIED BREADCRUMBS

125 g/4 oz BUTTER

225 ml/8 fl oz (1 cup) MILK

Pat the chicken portions dry with kitchen paper. Have a flat dish ready to hold the prepared chicken. In a small bowl, mix together the flour, paprika and about 2.5 ml/½ tsp salt. In another bowl, whisk the egg together with a little water.

Place on separate flat plates the flour, the egg and the breadcrumbs. Roll each chicken portion in the flour, then in the egg and lastly in the breadcrumbs. Place on the clean plate, lightly cover with cling film and chill for an hour.

In a heavy-based frying pan melt the butter over moderate heat, and fry the chicken pieces until golden brown all over. Lower the heat, cover and cook for about 30 minutes, turning several times. Remove to a heated plate and keep warm.

Shake the leftover flour into the pan, gradually add the milk and stir until thickened (you may need a little extra flour). Pour over chicken and serve.

Note: we like to add a few shakes of Tabasco sauce and a couple of spoonfuls of bourbon – the sauce curdles slightly, but tastes divine!

If frying bananas as well you will need more of the flour, eggs etc. Cut the bananas in half crossways, dip in a little lemon juice and proceed as for chicken. You will probably need a little extra butter as well. Do the same for pineapple rings. We usually use a fresh frying pan for this, as the chicken is cooking in the other. *Serves 4.*

Southern Fried Chicken

This dish was cooked for us in America by a Southern gentleman. You may have to collect the bacon dripping over a period of weeks. If there isn't sufficient, use unsalted butter to make up the difference – not as nice, mind you. The bourbon is important as well. We don't like to give plugs, but it has to be either Jim Beam or Jack Daniels – the blend of herbs is just right, and some bourbons are far too sweet.

750 ml/1¼ pints (3 cups) MILK

8 CHICKEN PIECES

15 ml/1 tbsp TABASCO SAUCE

PLAIN FLOUR FOR DUSTING

450 g/1 lb (2 cups) BACON DRIPPING

50 ml/2 fl oz (¼ cup) BOURBON

2.5 ml/½ tsp SALT

Pour milk into a large bowl that will hold all the chicken pieces comfortably, place the chicken pieces in and add more milk if necessary to cover completely. Add the Tabasco and stir well to mix. Marinate the chicken in this overnight, turning the pieces every now and then. Drain each piece well, but do not pat dry, and dip in flour until well coated. Dip in the milk again and re-flour, place on a plate and let rest for about 5 minutes.

In a large, heavy-based frying pan, heat the bacon dripping and fry the chicken portions about 20 minutes until golden brown and cooked through. Remove from pan, place on a serving plate and keep aside in a warm oven. Pour off most of the bacon fat, leaving just enough to cover the base of the pan.

Stir the milk well (some of the flour from the chicken may have sunk to the bottom), add about half to the pan (throw the rest away), stir constantly until it thickens, add the bourbon and 2.5 ml/½ tsp salt. Pour into a serving bowl and let your guests help themselves. This is a very rich dish, so a salad is ideal to go with it *Serves 4.*

Country Chicken Pie

On a chilly night when you have guests over, why not consider a pie that has practically everything in it, can be made ahead earlier in the day and then baked to perfection with a glorious golden crust. Make either 1 very large pie or 2 smaller pies, so that you have enough to feed anything up to 8 people, with nothing else needed. To serve more people, serve with creamy mashed potatoes and perhaps a green vegetable.

Pie

1 LARGE CHICKEN

1 ONION, 1 CARROT, 1 STALK CELERY AND A FEW SPRIGS FRESH PARSLEY FOR STOCK

50 g/2 oz BUTTER

1 LARGE ONION, FINELY CHOPPED

3 STALKS CELERY, THINLY SLICED

3 CARROTS, CHOPPED INTO LARGE DICE

8 MUSHROOMS, QUARTERED

175 g/6 oz (1 cup) COOKED PEAS

4 HARD-BOILED EGGS, QUARTERED

2.5 ml/½ tsp DRIED MIXED HERBS

SALT AND FRESHLY GROUND BLACK PEPPER

ABOUT 500 g/18 oz PACKET PUFF OR FLAKY PASTRY, THAWED IF FROZEN

1 EGG, BEATEN WITH 5 ml/1 tsp WATER AND PINCH OF SALT, TO GLAZE

Sauce

25 g/1 oz BUTTER

30 ml/2 tbsp PLAIN FLOUR

100 ml/4 fl oz (½ cup) CHICKEN STOCK, PREFERABLY HOMEMADE (p. 183)

100 ml/4 fl oz (½ cup) MILK

15 ml/1 tbsp BRANDY

45 ml/3 tbsp MEDIUM-DRY SHERRY

Put the chicken in a large casserole with the onion, carrot, celery and parsley for stock, and add enough water to just cover the chicken. Bring to the boil, then lower the heat, cover and simmer gently about 45 minutes, until just cooked. Remove chicken and, when cool enough to handle, remove all the meat and put to one side. Put all the bones and skin back into the casserole and continue to simmer for another 30 minutes, then strain and reserve the stock. Cut the meat into pieces, not too small. If you do this ahead, cover the meat with cling film when cold and keep in the fridge. When the strained stock is cold place this in the fridge also, and remove the fat when chilled.

To make the filling, melt 50 g/2 oz of butter in a heavy-based casserole, add the chopped onion, sliced celery and diced carrots and sauté gently with the lid on for 10 minutes, stirring occasionally so as to not let them brown. Add the mushrooms and simmer a further 3 minutes, again with the lid on, then remove from heat and stir in the peas.

To make the sauce, melt the butter in a heavy-based saucepan and stir in the flour. Add the chicken stock and milk and whisk while cooking over moderate heat until the sauce boils and thickens. Add the brandy and sherry and check for seasoning.

Put the filling in a large pie dish, together with the chicken, moisten with a little of the finished sauce and stir the rest of the sauce in gradually. Distribute the quartered eggs over the top, then sprinkle on the dried herbs and a little salt and freshly ground black pepper. Roll out the pastry and place over the top and decorate with leaves made from pastry scraps. Make a steam hole in the centre of the pastry and brush the pie with the egg glaze. Place in the fridge while you heat the oven to 200C/400F/Gas 6. Bake the pie 25 to 35 minutes, until golden brown.

As this is a piecrust top only, serve as follows. Cut a wedge of crust for 1 serving and place aside on a heated plate. Spoon out the filling directly under this first crust onto a second heated serving plate. Cut the next wedge of crust and place on top of that serving of filling. Proceed until you come to the last serving and then place the first piece of crust that you reserved on the last serving of filling. The crust will not be too cold, and the heat of the serving plate and filling will quickly bring the crust back to heat. This way, after all the time you have spent decorating and baking the crust to a golden perfection, it will not be smothered by the filling. *Serves 8 to 12.*

Stuffed Chicken, Italian Style

For this dish it is better to use 2 smallish chickens, just large enough that when cut in half they will serve 4 people. We have found it much better than stuffing 1 large bird. The stuffing should be made in advance so that it has time to cool down before it is put inside the birds. If you have an aversion to olive oil, use a lighter-flavoured one such as groundnut (peanut) or safflower, but the end result won't have the same flavour.
A sauce is not really needed, but should you want to make one, mix together 10 ml/2 tsp cornflour with 100 ml/4 fl oz (½ cup) dissolved chicken stock cube and deglaze the pan with this, adding also just a few spoonfuls of dry vermouth.

2 CHICKENS, ABOUT 750g/1½ lb EACH

30 ml/2 tbsp OLIVE OIL

50 g/2 oz BUTTER

1 LARGE ONION, FINELY CHOPPED

CHOPPED LIVER AND HEART, IF PACKAGED WITH THE CHICKENS

100 g/4 oz (½ cup) HAM, FINELY CHOPPED (BACON IS TOO STRONG)

3 SLICES STALE BREAD, TURNED INTO COARSE CRUMBS

SALT AND FRESHLY GROUND BLACK PEPPER

25 g/1 oz (¼ cup) PARMESAN CHEESE, GRATED

100 ml/4 fl oz (½ cup) CHICKEN STOCK, PREFERABLY HOMEMADE (p. 183)

2.5 ml/½ tsp DRIED OREGANO

50 g/2 oz BUTTER

Wash the chickens and pat dry inside and out with kitchen paper. Heat 30 ml/2 tbsp oil and the 50 g/2 oz butter in a large, heavy-based frying pan and cook the onion over moderate heat about 8 minutes until soft and golden. Add the chopped liver and heart, if using, plus the ham and the coarse breadcrumbs. Fry, stirring, until the crumbs are lightly browned over moderate heat. Add a little salt and pepper, the Parmesan and the stock. Cook all together for a couple of minutes, then leave to cool completely. Stir in the oregano. Divide the mixture between the 2 chickens and secure with fine skewers. Dot the tops with the remaining 50 g/2 oz butter and roast at 170C/325F/Gas 3 for about 1¼ to 1½ hours, or until the juices run clear when you prick one of the thighs. (All stuffed birds take longer to cook than ones that contain no stuffing.) Baste the chickens every now and again to keep them moist. Remove from the oven, leave to rest for 5 minutes, then cut the chickens in half through the back and breastbones and serve. Served with some steamed courgettes and perhaps grilled tomatoes, this makes a very good dinner or luncheon. *Serves 4.*

Deep-fried Chicken with Dark Rum

This Spanish-style dish is very nice for a light meal, accompanied by a green salad.

100 ml/4 fl oz (½ cup) FRESH LIME JUICE, PLUS A LITTLE EXTRA FOR SERVING

50 ml/2 fl oz (¼ cup) LIGHT SOY SAUCE

30 ml/2 tbsp DARK RUM

4 CLOVES GARLIC, FINELY CHOPPED

1 CHICKEN, ABOUT 2 kg/4½ lb, OR CHICKEN PIECES

SALT AND FRESHLY GROUND BLACK PEPPER

PLAIN FLOUR FOR DUSTING

450 ml/¾ pint (2 cups) VEGETABLE OIL (NOT OLIVE)

In a large ceramic or glass bowl, combine the lime juice, soy sauce, rum and garlic, and mix well. Cut chicken into about 8 portions, place in the marinade, mix well to coat, cover and refrigerate for at least 4 hours or better still overnight. Turn often.

When ready to cook, drain pieces of chicken, pepper and salt them, then dust with flour. In a deep-fat fryer or deep, heavy-based pan, heat the oil until hot. Flick a drop of water into the oil – if it hisses like mad, it's hot! Carefully place a few pieces of chicken in the hot oil and fry about 10 minutes until golden brown. Remove to a heated platter covered with crinkled kitchen paper to drain. Let the oil recover its heat and fry the other pieces. Sprinkle with more fresh lime juice and serve with pepper and salt. *Serves 4.*

Chinese-style Orange Chicken

1 CHICKEN, ABOUT 1.5 kg/3 lb 5 oz

1 LARGE ORANGE

30 ml/2 tbsp LIGHT SOY SAUCE

45 ml/3 tbsp HONEY

SALT AND FRESHLY GROUND BLACK PEPPER

50 g/2 oz BUTTER OR MARGARINE

10 ml/2 tsp CORNFLOUR

15 ml/1 tbsp WATER

100 ml/4 fl oz (½ cup) ORANGE JUICE

10 ml/2 tsp LIGHT SOY SAUCE

45 ml/3 tbsp GRAND MARNIER

PINCH OF CHINESE FIVE SPICES (OPTIONAL)

Place a large sheet of foil in an ovenproof dish, turn foil up round the edges (you are going to enclose the chicken). Place chicken in the centre of the foil. Cut ends from orange and cut in thick slices, cut slices in half, place on top and round sides of the chicken. Mix the 30 ml/2 tbsp soy sauce and honey together and gently pour all over the chicken, sprinkle with salt and pepper and dot with the butter. Fold foil over chicken to completely enclose it. Bake in a 200-230C/400-450F/Gas 6-8 oven for 10 minutes, then reduce heat to 170C/325F/Gas 3 and cook for 1½ hours. Carefully remove chicken to a heated serving dish and reserve juices for the sauce.

To make sauce, blend cornflour with water in a small saucepan. Add combined orange juice, soy sauce, salt and pepper, Chinese five spices and reserved liquid from the chicken, then mix well. Place saucepan over moderate heat and stir until it boils and thickens slightly. Stir in Grand Marnier and serve at once. *Serves 4.*

Quick Microwave Chicken Breasts with Mushroom Cream Sauce

This recipe is very simple and quick if you are in a hurry and you want to serve an elegant main course. Make a mixed green salad and a lemony dressing, have ready some fruit and cheese, such as fresh pears with Camembert or brie, and you have virtually nothing to do. Make a simple Béchamel Sauce (p. 186) enriched with cream, and tip in some button mushrooms (fresh or canned), plus a couple of spoonfuls of sherry.

8 CHICKEN BREASTS, SKINNED AND BONED

25 g/1 oz BUTTER

SALT AND FRESHLY GROUND BLACK PEPPER

5 ml/1 tsp FINELY GRATED ORANGE RIND

Place the chicken breasts in a single layer in a microwaveproof casserole. Melt the butter in the microwave together with a little salt and pepper and the orange rind. Brush this over the chicken breasts and cook, covered loosely with a sheet of kitchen paper, at 70% for 8 to 10 minutes, until just cooked through. Make the sauce (p. 186) and tip in the mushrooms. Heat and pour over the drained chicken breasts, return to the microwave and warm for 2 to 3 minutes at 80%. Serve on heated plates with the sauce and mushrooms spooned over. Small plain new potatoes are nice with this.

Note: microwaves vary, ours has many power settings. If yours only has Low, Medium, and High, proceed as follows: cook the chicken breasts on High for 3 minutes, then on Medium for about 8 minutes or until cooked through, reheat with the sauce on High for 2 minutes or until just starting to bubble. *Serves 4.*

Roast Stuffed Chicken

As this is to serve half a chicken per person, choose medium-sized roasting birds. The dish is very rich, with its accompanying sauce, so have something very simple to start with, such as a portion of smoked eel or trout served with horseradish sauce. No potatoes with the meal, as the flavourful stuffing provides the starch. Perhaps some Tomatoes Stuffed with Pea Purée (p. 129) to accompany it, and a salad and fresh fruit to finish off the meal, or perhaps Rose Cream with Frozen Fruit (p. 171).

The joy of this meal is in its relative simplicity. The smoked eel or trout is simply served with toast and horseradish sauce, so there is virtually no preparation. The chicken can be stuffed and made ready for the oven earlier in the day. The basting of the chicken during cooking and the final making of the sauce are not too time consuming. If you are going to make the rose-flavoured cream, that can be done a day ahead. All in all, a meal that is very elegant, has a lot of flavour, but doesn't require you to panic when it comes to finally putting it all together. A crisp dry white wine, well chilled, perhaps a Burgundy or Chablis, will complement the richness of the chicken.

2 CHICKENS, ABOUT 1.1 kg/2½ lb EACH

100 g/4 oz BUTTER, SOFTENED

3 SPRING ONIONS, FINELY CHOPPED

45 ml/3 tbsp FINELY CHOPPED FRESH PARSLEY

10 ml/2 tsp DIJON MUSTARD

5 ml/1 tsp DRIED TARRAGON

SALT AND FRESHLY GROUND BLACK PEPPER

175 g/6 oz (3 cups) FRESH BREADCRUMBS

5 ml/1 tsp DRIED THYME

60 g/2⅓ oz BUTTER

1 SMALL ONION, FINELY CHOPPED

2 RASHERS BACON, RINDED, OR 2 SLICES HAM, FINELY CHOPPED

30 ml/2 tbsp FINELY CHOPPED FRESH PARSLEY

1 EGG, SIZE 1, BEATEN

225 ml/8 fl oz (1 cup) DRY WHITE WINE

100 ml/4 fl oz (½ cup) WATER OR DRY VERMOUTH

5 ml/1 tsp CRUMBLED CHICKEN STOCK CUBE

15 ml/1 tbsp CORNFLOUR

100 ml/4 fl oz (½ cup) CHICKEN STOCK, PREFERABLY HOMEMADE (p. 183)

100 ml/4 fl oz (½ cup) SINGLE (LIGHT) CREAM

Rinse the chickens inside and out under cold running water, remove any necks and giblets and also the excess fat. Pat dry. With either your fingers or a teaspoon, rounded side up, loosen the skin from the meat all over the breast area and also over the legs as much as possible. Be careful not to break the skin. The part that usually gives the most difficulty is on the ridge of the breastbone, where the skin is very firmly attached. To help get this away, carefully cut the anchoring membrane away between the skin and the flesh to start releasing the skin by using a pair of scissors.

Make the flavoured butter that you will stuff under the loosened skin. Beat together the softened butter, spring onions, parsley, mustard, tarragon and a little salt and pepper until well combined. (Alternatively, place all these ingredients in a food processor fitted with the steel blade and process until well combined.) Divide the mixture in half and carefully, with your fingers, spread the butter as evenly as possible under the loosened skin of the chickens. Should you not be able to do this evenly, don't worry too much, as it will melt out over the breast meat when you start cooking them. As you are working with fat against a slippery surface you might like to try placing the flavoured butter in the fridge for about 30 minutes, until it has hardened somewhat, and then put little chunks under the loosened skin, being careful not to break the skin. The end result before cooking looks as though it has warts like a frog, but that won't put you off, we're sure. Set aside in a cool place while you make the stuffing.

Place the breadcrumbs in a large bowl, and sprinkle in the thyme and some salt and pepper, not too much. Melt the 60 g/2⅓ oz butter in a heavy-based frying pan and sauté the onion and the bacon or ham. Cook for about 5 minutes until the onion is soft and tip into the breadcrumbs. Add the parsley and the beaten egg and mix together. Divide this stuffing in half and fill the cavities of the chickens equally.

When the chickens are stuffed, secure with small metal skewers and tie the legs together with kitchen string. Bend the wings so the wing tips are underneath the back of the birds. Place in a baking tin just large enough to hold them comfortably, pour round them the wine, water or vermouth and sprinkle in the crumbled chicken stock cube. Roast in a preheated oven at 180C/350F/Gas 4 for 1½ hours, basting frequently with the pan juices. The top skin where you have stuffed the butter will go quite brown. (It looks as though it has burnt, but we have never found this to actually happen. If you're worried, cover the tops loosely with a piece of foil in the last half hour of cooking, but really you don't have to.) When the chickens are cooked, remove from the baking tin, place carefully on a warmed serving dish, and keep warm while you make the sauce.

Place the baking tin on top of the oven and boil down the liquid in it until you are left with about 225 ml/8 fl oz (1 cup). Mix the cornflour with the chicken stock, pour into the pan and continue boiling while whisking briskly, until the sauce thickens. Add the cream and bring back to the boil, whisking all the time to prevent lumps. Check for seasoning and pour into a warm sauceboat or jug.

Remove the skewers and strings from the chickens and cut in half with the aid of a pair of poultry shears or kitchen scissors through the length of the breastbones and along the back. Place, cut side down, on warm serving plates, being careful not to disturb the stuffing, and spoon a little sauce over each half. Serve with the extra sauce in a sauceboat at the table. *Serves 4.*

Tandoori Murgh

This is a delicious way to do chicken and looks spectacular when served up with the Salat. If you are in the millionaire class use saffron threads (at the time of writing, they cost more per weight than pure gold). If down to your last million, use saffron powder. The Cold Cucumber Relish (p. 94) is a nice accompaniment.

5ml/1 tsp SAFFRON THREADS OR POWDER

37.5 ml/2½ tbsp BOILING WATER

2 CHICKENS, ABOUT 1.5 kg/3 lb 5 oz EACH

15 ml/1 tbsp SALT

90 ml/6 tbsp FRESH LEMON JUICE

7.5 ml/1½ tsp CORIANDER SEEDS

5 ml/1 tsp CUMIN SEEDS

2.5 cm/1 inch PIECE FRESH ROOT GINGER, PEELED AND COARSELY CHOPPED

2 CLOVES GARLIC, ROUGHLY CHOPPED

225 g/8 oz (1 cup) PLAIN YOGHURT

2.5 ml/½ tsp RED FOOD COLOURING

1.25 ml/¼ tsp CAYENNE PEPPER

25 ml/5 tsp GHEE OR VEGETABLE OIL

SALAT INGREDIENTS (p. 93)

If using saffron threads, soak in a bowl with the boiling water for 5 minutes. If using powder, just mix with the water. Pat the chickens dry inside and out and truss up securely with string. With a sharp knife, cut 2 slits in the thighs and breasts of the birds – about 1 cm/½ inch deep and 2.5 cm/1 inch long. Mix the salt and lemon juice together and rub well into the chickens, making sure you get it into the slits. Place the birds in a dish, side by side, pour over the saffron liquid and leave to stand at room temperature for 30 minutes. Baste with the liquid every now and again.

Sprinkle the coriander and cumin seeds in a small pan and toast over moderate heat for 2-3 minutes, shaking the pan constantly. Place the seeds in the bowl of an electric blender, add the ginger, garlic and 22.5 ml/1½ tbsp of the yoghurt, and blend on high speed until the mixture forms a paste. Scrape the paste into a mixing bowl, stir in the remaining yoghurt, food colouring and the cayenne pepper. This is called masala. Spread the masala evenly over the chickens, underneath as well. Put back in the dish, cover with the lid or foil and marinate, for 12 hours if unrefrigerated, or 24 hours in the fridge.

Preheat oven to 220C/425F/Gas 7. Place the chickens side by side on a rack in a shallow baking dish and pour any liquid remaining from the marinade over them. Coat each chicken with 12.5 ml/2½ tsp ghee. Roast, uncovered, in the centre of the oven for 15 minutes, then reduce heat to 190C/375F/Gas 5 and cook undisturbed for 1 hour. With a very sharp pointed knife lightly prick the thigh of a chicken – the juice that runs out should be pale yellow. If slightly pink, cook another 5-10 minutes. Just watch this carefully, as birds which are plumper and more tender may cook more quickly. Remove birds from oven, cut trussing strings, and let them rest for 5 minutes.

These cook beautifully on a rotisserie barbecue, as long as it has a cover. If doing it this way, proceed with the recipe, but don't truss the birds – place them on the spit, adjust the prongs and then truss the legs and wings. Use the marinade to baste the birds during cooking, but make sure they don't *burn*!

When ready to serve, cut each chicken into 8 pieces, then either place attractively on top of the Salat or arrange the Salat around the chicken. *Serves 6-8.*

Salat
(Mixed Vegetable Salad)

2 LARGE ONIONS

2 LARGE FIRM TOMATOES

24 RADISHES, TRIMMED AND WASHED

2 LEMONS, CUT LENGTHWAYS INTO QUARTERS

3 HOT GREEN CHILLIES, CUT LENGTHWAYS AND SEEDED, OR 1 GREEN PEPPER, CORED, SEEDED AND CUT INTO STRIPS

45 ml/3 tbsp FRESH LEMON JUICE

5 ml/1 tsp SALT

FRESHLY GROUND BLACK PEPPER

GARAM MASALA (OPTIONAL)

Peel the onions, cut in half lengthways, then cut lengthways into paper thin slices. Cut tomatoes crossways into thin slices. If you are going to serve the chicken on the Salat, spread the thinly sliced onion over the serving plate, arrange the tomato slices in a ring round the edge. Arrange the radishes, lemon wedges and chillies decoratively round the tomatoes – sprinkle the vegetables evenly with the lemon juice, salt and plenty of ground black pepper.

Usually when the finished dish is about to be presented, the chicken is sprinkled with a little garam masala. *Serves 6-8.*

Cold Cucumber Relish

1 LARGE CUCUMBER

750 ml/1¼ pints (3 cups) PLAIN YOGHURT

30 ml/2 tbsp FINELY CHOPPED FRESH MINT

40 g/1½ oz (⅓ cup) ONION, FINELY CHOPPED (RED IF THEY ARE AVAILABLE)

7.5 ml/1½ tsp SALT

Peel the cucumber, cut in half lengthways, and run a spoon down the inside to remove the seeds. Chop coarsely. In a bowl which you can take to the table, mix all the ingredients together, cover and refrigerate overnight – must be served cold! *Serves 6-8.*

Chicken Livers with Ham and Sage

Although chicken livers can be rather rich, in this dish the richness is cut down somewhat by the addition of the sage leaves. Fresh sage is best when it is available, but you can use dried. A very simple thing to have as an after-theatre supper, with crisp chilled wine and some cheese and fruit or a simple fruit dessert.

450 g/1 lb CHICKEN LIVERS, THAWED IF FROZEN

4 SLICES BREAD, CRUSTS REMOVED

ABOUT 50 g/2 oz BUTTER

30 g/1¼ oz EXTRA BUTTER

SALT AND FRESHLY GROUND BLACK PEPPER

2 SLICES HAM, CUT INTO THIN STRIPS

8 to 12 FRESH SAGE LEAVES, FINELY CHOPPED, OR 5 ml/1 tsp DRIED

30 ml/2 tbsp MARSALA

Stiffen the chicken livers by soaking them in boiling water for a few minutes. Drain and trim, then cut into 3 pieces if they are very large. Cut the crustless bread into triangles and fry until golden in the first amount of butter. (You may, instead, brush both sides of the triangles of bread with melted butter, place them on a baking tray and bake at 200C/400F/Gas 6 for 10 to 15 minutes, until golden, turning once during that time. These are then less fatty than if they are fried.) Keep to one side in a warm oven while you cook the livers.

Melt the second amount of butter over moderate heat in a heavy-based frying pan and add the livers, some salt and pepper, the ham and the sage. Stir all together and cook the livers for about 5 minutes. Do not overcook them or they will become too tough. Transfer

livers for about 5 minutes. Do not overcook them or they will become too tough. Transfer to the top of the fried bread, on heated plates, using a slotted spoon. Add the Marsala to the juices in the pan, raise the heat and boil, scraping the bits from the bottom of the pan. Stir well and after about 1 minute spoon this resulting sauce over the livers. *Serves 4.*

Lamb Cutlets in Phyllo

This dish relies, as do many, on the cutlets being of first grade quality. Rosemary has a very good affinity with lamb. If you cannot get ground dried rosemary, grind the dried rosemary spikes in a pestle and mortar so that you end up with a fairly fine ground powder, rather than woody spikes, which can be unpleasant to chew and can get lodged between your teeth.
Allow 1 cutlet per person; if you are not serving any accompanying vegetables, just a green salad afterwards, you might like to allow 2 per person, in which case just double the rest of the ingredients.

4 GOOD LAMB CUTLETS

15 ml/1 tbsp BUTTER

1 ONION, FINELY CHOPPED

4 LARGE MUSHROOMS, SLICED

2.5 ml/½ tsp POWDERED ROSEMARY, OR 5 ml/1 tsp DRIED, GROUND

30 ml/2 tbsp MEDIUM-DRY SHERRY

A LITTLE SALT AND FRESHLY GROUND BLACK PEPPER

12 SHEETS PHYLLO PASTRY, THAWED IF FROZEN

ABOUT 100 g/4 oz BUTTER, MELTED

Quickly sear the cutlets in the butter over high heat, no longer than 5 minutes altogether for each cutlet. Set aside to cool. In the same pan, sauté the onion over a moderate heat, about 5 minutes until soft, then add the sliced mushrooms. Add the rosemary, sherry, a little salt and a few grindings of black pepper. Stir all together for 3 minutes, remove from the heat and leave to cool. Take 3 sheets of phyllo per cutlet and brush some melted butter between them. Place each cooled cutlet on the corner of 3 buttered sheets, then divide the cooled mushroom mixture and place a quarter of it on the meat portion of each cutlet. Wrap the cutlet and filling in the phyllo sheets, as you would a parcel, but try and keep some of the end of the bone exposed so that you can present the cooked cutlet with a cutlet frill on that portion of bone. Place on a lightly buttered baking sheet and brush the finished parcels with a little cold water. This stops the pastry from getting too brown before the filling is heated, and also helps stop it rising into large blisters. Cook at 220C/425F/Gas 7 in a preheated oven for about 20 minutes, until well browned. *Serves 4.*

Crumbed Lamb Cutlets with Apricot Sauce

This is a superb way to do lamb cutlets and can be prepared in advance, ready for cooking. Fresh asparagus or a green salad would go well with it.

8 LAMB CUTLETS

4 SLICES BREAD TURNED INTO CRUMBS

50 g/2 oz (½ cup) GROUND ALMONDS

2 EGGS

30 ml/2 tbsp WATER

5 ml/1 tsp VEGETABLE OIL

PLAIN FLOUR

50 g/2 oz BUTTER

45 ml/3 tbsp VEGETABLE OIL

Sauce

40 g/1½ oz BUTTER

1 ONION, FINELY CHOPPED

10 ml/2 tsp CURRY POWDER

30 ml/2 tbsp WHITE WINE VINEGAR

350 ml/12 fl oz (1½ cups) CHICKEN STOCK, PREFERABLY HOMEMADE (p. 183)

5 ml/1 tsp LIGHT SOY SAUCE

75 g/3 oz (½ cup) READY-TO-EAT DRIED APRICOTS

10 ml/2 tsp SUGAR

SALT AND FRESHLY GROUND BLACK PEPPER

Trim the fat from the cutlets and pound thinly. Combine the fresh breadcrumbs and ground almonds and place on a double layer of kitchen paper. Mix together the eggs, water and oil and put on a large plate. Dip the cutlets in flour, shake off excess, then dip into the egg mixture, shake off excess and then place on the crumb mixture. Cover both sides with the crumbs, pressing well in, then place on a clean plate. Refrigerate until ready to cook.

To make the sauce, melt 40 g/1½ oz butter in a heavy-based pan and sauté the onion until soft. Add the curry powder and cook for about a minute. Add the rest of the ingredients and simmer for 10 minutes. Cool, and purée in a food processor, half at a time; return to the saucepan and simmer gently to reheat while cooking the cutlets. Check seasoning and serve in a heated sauceboat.

Melt 50 g/2 oz butter and oil in a heavy-based pan and cook the cutlets gently about 6 minutes per side, until golden brown on each side. *Serves 4.*

Chilled Cream of Parsley Soup

Hot Courgette and Carrot Salad with Gorgonzola and Cashews

Fish Fillets Steamed with Sesame Oil

Lion's Head Stew

Baked Rabbit with Port

Vegetable Custards

Herb Jellies

'H & H' Tia Maria Chocolate Mousse Cake

Boiled Leg of Lamb with Caper Sauce

There are so many old-fashioned dishes that no longer appear on our tables – more's the pity in many cases. This recipe will evoke childhood memories for some. The perfect accompaniment is scrubbed new potatoes, cooked till just tender. You will need a large piece of muslin big enough to completely encase the lamb when doubled.

10 ml/2 tsp EACH DRIED HERBS, SUCH AS THYME, CRUMBLED BAY LEAVES, MARJORAM, PERHAPS A LITTLE ROSEMARY

1 LEG OF LAMB, ABOUT 2.5 kg/5½ lb

1 CLOVE GARLIC (OPTIONAL)

100 ml/4 fl oz (½ cup) SINGLE (LIGHT) CREAM

40 g/1½ oz BUTTER

60 g/2⅓ oz PLAIN FLOUR

30 ml/2 tbsp CAPERS, WELL DRAINED

Fold a large piece of muslin in half and lay flat on the work surface. Sprinkle the herbs over and place lamb on top. You can, if you wish, cut a pocket close to the bone at either end and insert a peeled clove of garlic. Wrap up and sew tightly so that it will not unwind during cooking. Cover with water in a large pan, bring to the boil, lower the heat, cover and simmer for 80 minutes per 1 kg/2¼ lb (about 3½ hours for 2.5 kg/5½ lb). Skim the froth several times during cooking.

Remove the lamb from the stock, retaining the stock. Unwrap the meat and wash off the herbs with some of the stock, place on a heated serving plate and keep warm while you make the sauce.

In a heavy-based saucepan, bring the cream and 450 ml/¾ pint (2 cups) of the reserved stock to boil. Work the butter and flour together (beurre manié) and add bit by bit, whisking all the time until the sauce thickens. Add the whole capers (chop them if you prefer the sauce more pungent), stir and reheat for just a few minutes.

To serve, cut the lamb into nice thick slices and ladle over the sauce. Put the leftover lamb back in the stock and keep warm for second helpings! *Serves 6-8.*

Boned Leg of Lamb with Lemon Stuffing

Ask the butcher to bone the leg for you. You will need to have a piece from the shank end weighing about 1.5 kg/3 lb 5 oz after the bone has been removed. The stuffing is not intended to add much extra bulk to the finished dish, but rather to add flavour to the meat itself during the cooking time. This dish goes well with plain boiled potatoes glazed in a little butter, and green beans.

2 THICK SLICES BREAD, CRUSTS REMOVED

JUICE AND FINELY GRATED RIND OF 1 LEMON

30 ml/2 tbsp FINELY CHOPPED FRESH PARSLEY

3 CLOVES GARLIC, CRUSHED

1 SMALL ONION, FINELY CHOPPED

5 ml/1 tsp DRIED MIXED HERBS

5 ml/1 tsp DRIED ROSEMARY

2.5 ml/½ tsp SALT

6 GRINDINGS FRESH BLACK PEPPER

8 JUNIPER BERRIES, CRUSHED

1 EGG, BEATEN

BONED LEG OF LAMB (AS ABOVE)

50 g/2 oz BUTTER, SOFTENED

Sauce

15 ml/1 tbsp CORNFLOUR

5 ml/1 tsp CRUMBLED BEEF STOCK CUBE

10 ml/2 tsp TOMATO PURÉE (PASTE)

225 ml/8 fl oz (1 cup) WATER

100 ml/4 fl oz (½ cup) DRY WHITE WINE

JUICE OF ½ LEMON, OR TO TASTE

SALT AND FRESHLY GROUND BLACK PEPPER, TO TASTE

Break up the bread and drop through the feed tube of a food processor fitted with the steel blade, with the motor running, to make the crumbs. Tip into a mixing bowl and add the juice and rind of the lemon, parsley, garlic, onion, mixed herbs, rosemary, salt and pepper and the juniper berries. Mix well and add the beaten egg to bind it all together. Cover with cling film and leave in the fridge to chill and firm, and let the flavours meld together.

When ready to cook the lamb stuff it with the breadcrumb mixture and sew up both ends to hold in the stuffing, using fine string and close stitches. Place the lamb in a roasting pan and spread the softened butter over the top. Preheat the oven to 200C/400F/Gas 6 and roast the prepared lamb for 15 minutes; reduce the heat to 170C/325F/Gas 3 and roast, basting occasionally, for a further 1¼ to 1½ hours. Remove the lamb to a serving dish and keep warm while you make the sauce.

In a jug, mix together the cornflour, beef cube and tomato purée, then gradually whisk in the water. (You can use vegetable cooking water if you wish, but check the seasoning so that you don't end up with an oversalted sauce.) Now add the wine and lemon juice. Place the roasting pan over moderate heat on top of the oven and pour in the sauce liquids. (During the cooking, some of the stuffing may have oozed from the lamb – don't worry about it as it adds flavour.) Raise the heat and whisk the sauce together until it starts to boil. Lower the heat and continue to whisk to avoid any lumps, until it has reduced and thickened. Check for seasoning and strain, if you wish, into a warm sauceboat. Remove the lamb and cut away the string. Carve into slices and serve on warmed plates. Spoon a little of the sauce over each serving and serve the rest separately. *Serves* 6.

Marinated Leg of Lamb with Anchovies

Mark in the margin of this recipe: 'To do ahead'. It's one that must be prepared the day before. The taste is really terrific. The sauce can be rather salty, but that's its charm. The idea was to try and recreate the taste of sheep which have been grazing on salty grasses by the sea, as in Normandy.

1 LEG OF LAMB, ABOUT 1.5 kg/3 lb 5 oz

2 LARGE CLOVES GARLIC

100 ml/4 fl oz (½ cup) OLIVE OIL

225 ml/8 fl oz (1 cup) DRY WHITE WINE

1 ONION, FINELY SLICED

1 CARROT, FINELY SLICED

4 WHOLE CLOVES

2 WHOLE PICKLED CUCUMBERS

2 STALKS CELERY

5 ml/1 tsp DRIED TARRAGON

FRESHLY GROUND BLACK PEPPER

6 ANCHOVY FILLETS, WELL DRAINED

2 RASHERS STREAKY BACON

Remove much of the skin and fat from the lamb. (You don't have to cut it all off, just most of it.) You need a good sharp knife. Place the meat on some kitchen paper to stop it slipping round too much, and stop you cutting yourself. Peel the garlic cloves, cut them in half lengthways, and insert a piece in either end of the leg close to the bone, making a deep stab with your sharp knife so that you can get the garlic slivers in at least 2.5 cm/1 inch. Stab the lamb carefully with the knife on 2 opposite sides and insert the other 2 slivers of garlic, again at least 2.5 cm/1 inch. If you have friends who don't like garlic, don't tell them about it, but make sure, when you are carving the lamb, that you remove the garlic before serving the slices. (Don't, however, try to disguise the fact that there is garlic present to those people who are allergic to it.) Now mix the oil, wine, the onion and carrot. When these have all been well stirred together in a large china or glass bowl, add the whole cloves and the skinned lamb. Cover with cling film and refrigerate for at least 24 hours, turning the lamb over 6 times to baste it. You can leave it for up to 36 hours, but certainly no longer. The more you turn it the better the flavours will penetrate, and the wine will have a slight tenderising effect.

When you are ready to cook the lamb, preheat the oven to 200C/400F/Gas 6. Place the meat in a roasting pan with the sliced onions and carrots around it (taken from the marinade liquid with a slotted spoon). At this point the choice is up to you. We like to dump the remaining oil and wine into the pan as well. This means the end sauce is a bit on the oily side, but we don't mind that. You might like to add only about 90 ml/6 tbsp of the oil and wine mixture on your first try. Thinly slice the pickled cucumbers and the celery, and place some on the lamb and the rest round it with the other vegetables. Sprinkle the tarragon over the top of the lamb, and a few grindings of black pepper. Lay the anchovies across the top, and finally cover with the bacon. If the bacon is in long strips, cut it in pieces and place over the top to protect and add flavour to as much of the lamb's surface as possible. Cook, basting often, for 1 hour (or work the time out at 40 minutes per 1 kg/ 2¼ lb), depending on the size of the piece of lamb you have chosen). Keep it pink.

When the lamb is cooked, remove it from the oven, scrape all the bits off the top into the roasting pan, and keep the meat warm for 10 minutes or so before carving while you prepare the sauce. You can do this 2 ways:

1. Transfer all the solids and juices to a sieve over a bowl and press down hard with the back of a wooden spoon to extract all the juices from them. Return the juices to the roasting pan, add a little extra white wine and simmer, scraping up any brown bits from the bottom of the roasting pan as you stir. Spoon the resulting juices or sauce over the sliced lamb. There won't be much, just enough to moisten and flavour the meat – in other words, it's a concentrate.

2. Just scrape off the solids from the top of the lamb when you remove it after it has cooked, add a little bit of white wine to the pan, and boil it up for a couple of minutes, trying to break up the bacon into little bits, which should be crispy anyway, and pour the whole jolly lot into a warm sauceboat. Spoon some over the slices of lamb, lumps of vegetables and all. This second method is the way we like it – rustic, but full of flavour.

We do not carve in the traditional manner, which is down through the meat in a perpendicular fashion to the bone. We prefer to carve across the joint from the thick to the shank end, which means 2 people can get the outside portions from either side, and 2 get the rarer pink portions from nearer the bone. Since one of us likes the outside bits and the other likes the bloodier portions, this method suits us very well.

We think the best thing is to place several carved slices on each plate, pour the sauce over and serve it with small plain boiled potatoes and a simple green salad to follow. *Serves 4 to 6.*

Lamb in Puff Pastry with Sauce

Although the piece of lamb needed for this recipe is rather expensive, the meat that is not used can be turned into a stew for another occasion. As an alternative, you can use fillet of lamb if you are lucky enough to be able to buy it. The piece we have specified is the very tasty and tender 'eye' portion of the piece of lamb that you get noisettes from. You need practically all the fat and bone removed. If you cannot manage this, ask your butcher to prepare it for you.

This recipe can also be prepared with pork tenderloins – make sure you remove any sinew from them before you cook them. Use dried sage instead of rosemary. Sear the meat in the initial stage after removing it from the oil for 2 minutes, rather than 1.

It is rather nice to serve this dish without any accompanying vegetables, but with a salad before or after.

2.5 ml/½ tsp DRIED ROSEMARY, CRUSHED

2.5 ml/½ tsp DRIED THYME

2 'EYE' PORTIONS FROM LOIN OF LAMB

100 ml/4 fl oz (½ cup) OLIVE OIL

500 g/18 oz FRESH SPINACH

FRESHLY GRATED NUTMEG

SALT AND FRESHLY GROUND BLACK PEPPER

250 g/9 oz MUSHROOMS

30 ml/2 tbsp UNSALTED BUTTER

30 ml/2 tbsp FINELY CHOPPED SHALLOTS OR ONION

50 ml/2 fl oz (¼ cup) DRY WHITE WINE

SALT AND FRESHLY GROUND BLACK PEPPER

ABOUT 500 g/18 oz PUFF OR FLAKY PASTRY, THAWED IF FROZEN

1 EGG, BEATEN

Sauce

30 ml/2 tbsp UNSALTED BUTTER

30 ml/2 tbsp FINELY CHOPPED SHALLOTS OR ONION

100 ml/4 fl oz (½ cup) SERCIAL MADEIRA OR DRY SHERRY

750 ml/1¼ pints (3 cups) BROWN STOCK OR CANNED BEEF CONSOMMÉ, OR DISSOLVED STOCK CUBES

30 ml/2 tbsp SINGLE (LIGHT) CREAM

30 g/1¼ oz UNSALTED BUTTER, CUBED

Sprinkle the rosemary and thyme over the 2 pieces of lamb and rub the herbs into them. Lay the lamb in a long, shallow dish and pour over the olive oil. Marinate, covered, in the fridge for 12 hours or overnight, turning them several times.

Heat a heavy-based or non-stick frying pan and remove the lamb from the oil, letting the excess drip off. Sear all over in the pan to seal the lamb and brown it slightly for no longer than a minute; transfer to a plate and leave the lamb to cool.

Wash the spinach thoroughly to remove all grit, and tear away the stalks. Cook in a pan over moderate heat, with only the water that clings to the leaves, for a few minutes, until it has wilted. Alternatively, place in a covered, glass microwaveproof dish and microwave at High for 4 minutes, or until wilted. When the spinach has cooled sufficiently to handle, squeeze out the excess water between 2 plates. Purée the spinach in a food processor, or chop it very finely by hand. Place the purée in a bowl and season with freshly grated nutmeg and salt and pepper, then leave to cool.

Finely chop the cleaned mushrooms in a food processor, or by hand. Melt the 30 ml/ 2 tbsp butter in a heavy-based frying pan. Add the mushrooms and the finely chopped shallots or onion, and cook over moderate heat, stirring all the time, for about 2 minutes. Add the dry white wine and continue to cook, stirring all the time, until it has evaporated. Transfer to a bowl and cool. Season with a little salt and pepper.

Roll out the pastry thinly, about 3 mm/⅛ inch, and cut into 2 rectangles, each 4 times the width of the lamb and about 5 cm/2 inch longer to allow for 'tuck-ins'. Place the rectangles with the shortest sides towards you. Divide the spinach purée and spread across the centre of each rectangle, to about the width of the lamb. Divide the mushroom mixture and spread on top of the purée. Place a piece of lamb on the mushrooms and brush round the edges of the pastry with some water. Roll up the pastry to enclose, pinching the long seam together, then turn up the ends to seal. Place on a lightly buttered baking sheet, with the seam side down. Brush with the beaten egg and make a steam hole in the centre. Chill for 10 minutes while you preheat the oven to 200C/400F/Gas 6. Bake in the middle of the oven for 20 minutes, until nice and brown.

In a large enamel or stainless steel saucepan, melt 30 ml/2 tbsp unsalted butter for the sauce and add the finely chopped shallots or onion. Cook, stirring over moderate heat, until softened. Now add the Sercial Madeira or sherry and reduce over high heat until it has almost evaporated. Add 750 ml/1¼ pints (3 cups) brown stock and boil to reduce to about 175 ml/6 fl oz (¾ cup) skimming any froth if necessary. Add the cream and simmer for a further 2 minutes. Remove the pan from the heat and swirl in the butter, bit by bit. Season the sauce if needed and strain through a fine sieve into a heated sauceboat. Let the lamb rest for five minutes on a cutting board, then cut each package into 4 thick slices. Place 2 slices on each plate, side by side, then pour a little of the sauce round the meat and serve the rest separately. *Serves 4.*

GAME

No, you won't find Bear Burgers or Possum Pie here, just venison, duck, pheasant and rabbit – tame game, that can be fairly readily purchased in a lot of stores. There are lots of books that specialise in game, and go the gamut from camels' feet in aspic to buffalo breasts, rolled and stuffed, but unless you are the type that loves toting a gun these few examples should be sufficient for your needs.

A nice plump duck from your butcher or poulterer (not many in existence nowadays) is usually the best proposition for that special dinner or party. The wild ducks that are brought down from the skies by intrepid shooters during the season are usually so full of lead you need an extra bowl to spit the shot into, rather like disposing of the stones from olives.

Wild game needs to be fatted in some way. With small birds, this is done by laying strips or sheets of thinly sliced pork fat or not too strongly flavoured bacon rashers over it. A larger cut of meat, such as a haunch of venison, is larded with fatty strips. In most cases (naturally there are exceptions to every rule), young game is cooked very quickly, and older birds or portions are cooked slowly in a liquid for a fairly long time.

Hedgehog covered in clay and cooked on an open fire has never been something that we could try, having over the years rescued many of them from the swimming pool with the aid of a large sieve, dried them out a little, fed them a saucer of warm milk and sent them on their merry way to eradicate pests from the lettuce rows.

In recipes in older books, rabbit is usually required to be soaked overnight in cold water and a touch of vinegar. This is really meant for rabbit caught in the field, and the soaking does take away some of that gamey flavour and also helps to blanch the meat slightly. Any meat that has a slight aroma is given this treatment to rid it of that smell, but no meat, whatever it is, should be used if it does have an off odour.

Duck with Green Peppercorn Sauce

Only top-quality, young, meaty duck can be used for this, as it is not casseroled. As with all recipes that contain green peppercorns, we suggest that you take them from their container and rinse them under running water before adding them to the sauce. This is cooked at a fairly high heat, so it is advisable to take the duck from the roasting pan half way through the cooking time, drain off the fat from the pan, then replace the duck and cook till tender. This stops the fat burning and also decreases the spatter in the oven somewhat. As commercial stock tends to be somewhat oversalted, you might be well advised to use unsalted butter if you are using stock cubes for this recipe. Once you get to the end of a sauce like this, there is very little you can do if it is oversalted.

1 LARGE DUCK, ENOUGH FOR 2

SALT AND FRESHLY GROUND BLACK PEPPER

100 ml/4 fl oz (½ cup) HOT WATER

100 ml/4 fl oz (½ cup) SERCIAL MADEIRA OR DRY SHERRY

300 ml/½ pint (1¼ cups) CHICKEN STOCK, PREFERABLY HOMEMADE (p. 183)

10 ml/2 tsp CORNFLOUR

30 ml/2 tbsp WATER

30 ml/2 tbsp GREEN PEPPERCORNS, DRAINED

50 g/2 oz BUTTER, CUBED

Trim the loose fat from around the cavity of the duck, and prick it all over with a skewer or the tines of a sharp fork. Rinse it and pat dry inside and out with kitchen paper. Sprinkle both inside and out with a little salt and pepper. Place it breast side up in a roasting pan and add the giblets (if any supplied). Pour the hot water over the duck and bake in a preheated oven at 200C/400F/Gas 6 for 45 minutes. Take the duck out of the pan (you might have to ease it off the bottom, where it will have stuck, with a fish slice). Pour off the fat from the pan, place the duck back into it, still breast side up, and continue roasting for a further 45 minutes, or until it is well browned and cooked through. Transfer the duck to another dish and keep warm and again tip any fat from the roasting pan.

Deglaze the pan on top of the oven with the Madeira and the chicken stock, scraping up any brown bits from the base of the pan. Reduce this liquid over high heat by half and tip into a small saucepan. Mix the cornflour and water together, add to the sauce and simmer for 2 minutes, whisking to ensure that it remains lump free. Stir in the peppercorns, check for seasoning and bring back to simmering point. Remove the pan from the heat and swirl in the butter cubes bit by bit. This will not only thicken the sauce slightly, but will also enrich it. Cut the duck in half through the back and breastbone, pour over the sauce and serve. *Serves 2.*

Roast Duck with Mandarin Liqueur Sauce

There are ducks and ducks. We have tried to eat our way through lots of tough ones, and frankly, we turn down ones that have been shot in the wild unless we want to make a good duck stock or soup. We have found our own supply of specially reared ducks for the table. No one is going to know from where we get them, enough to say that they have sufficient breast meat to serve 4 people. We stress the importance of having a good young duckling from a reliable supplier, as there is nothing worse than going to the trouble of making a gorgeous sauce only to find that the duck meat is tough.

A GOOD MEATY DUCK, OR 2 SMALL ONES, TO SERVE 4 PEOPLE

75 g/3 oz BUTTER, MELTED

40 g/1½ oz (⅓ cup) PLAIN FLOUR

450 ml/¾ pint (2 cups) WATER

225 ml/8 fl oz (1 cup) DRY WHITE WINE

50 ml/2 fl oz (¼ cup) TAWNY PORT

100 ml/4 fl oz (½ cup) MANDARIN LIQUEUR OR OTHER ORANGE-FLAVOUR LIQUEUR

50 ml/2 fl oz (¼ cup) COGNAC

65 ml/2½ fl oz (⅓ cup) FRESH ORANGE JUICE

JUICE OF ½ LEMON

SALT AND FRESHLY GROUND BLACK PEPPER

2 BAY LEAVES

2.5 ml/½ tsp DRIED THYME

Wash the duck or ducks inside and out and pat dry. Tie the legs together to keep them from splaying out when cooking. If the ducks look very fatty, prick them all over with a sharp fork to allow the maximum fat to exude while they are roasting. Brush with some of the melted butter and cook, breast side up, on a wire rack in a large roasting pan at 190C/375F/ Gas 5 for 20 minutes. Turn over, brush with a little more butter and continue to roast for another 20 minutes. Return to breast side up and continue to roast for another 20 minutes. Remove the ducks from the oven, drain out any liquid from the cavity into the roasting pan and put the ducks to one side.

Take out the rack and drain off all the fat from the pan into another small container. Put the roasting pan on top of the oven over moderate heat until the residue has turned golden – don't let it burn. This will be the juices not the fat. Add just under 100 ml/4 fl oz (½ cup) of the reserved fat, remove the pan from the heat and sprinkle on the flour. Stir with a wooden spoon until well combined and then return the pan to the oven top. Keep stirring the flour and the fat together over a fairly high heat until the flour starts to turn a deep golden colour, but don't let it burn. The colour you achieve now will enhance the final colour and flavour of the finished sauce. Add the water, wine, port, liqueur, Cognac, orange and lemon juices, previously all mixed together, and stir until the sauce boils and thickens. Add some salt and pepper, bay leaves and thyme, and stir until all mixed together. Place the duck or ducks into either 2 casseroles or 1 large one, pour over the hot sauce, cover, and bake at 180C/350F/Gas 4 for about 1½ hours, or until the duck is tender. Baste at least 4 or 5 times during the cooking. You will find it easier to baste the duck if you have a bulb baster. To baste with a spoon is not easy, as you haven't sufficient space to dip the spoon down by the side of the duck to scoop up the sauce. If you buy a bulb baster, get a stainless steel one, and ask at the same time for an extra rubber bulb, as these wear out first.

The sauce will evaporate somewhat, but if there is still a lot, remove the cooked duck from the casserole and drain any liquids from the cavities into the pan. Place on a plate and keep warm while you reduce the sauce over high heat, stirring all the time, until it has thickened enough to coat the back of a spoon fairly thickly. Either cut all the meat off the duck and spoon the sauce over, or if you have 2 small ones, cut in half lengthways through the back and breast and serve one half per person with the sauce poured over. For some reason, even if you pour a lot of the sauce over the duck, and it looks as if it is floating in the stuff, there will be none left over by the time you have eaten the meat. *Serves 4.*

Steamed Duck with Oranges and Onions

For this Chinese dish the duck is cut into small pieces and fried, then steamed till tender. You don't require all of the duck, just the meatier parts, the breast and legs. The back and wings, which have practically no meat on them, can be used to make a duck stock for another occasion. Cutting the carcass isn't easy – we suggest you use a good pair of sturdy poultry shears to remove the back and wings, then a sharp cleaver to cut the duck into bite-sized pieces. To fry the duck, either use a wok with a lid or a deep-fat fryer with a lid. The lid stops the duck pieces spattering too much. The frying helps to eliminate some of the excess duck fat. You will need a steamer to finish off the dish.

1 DUCK, ABOUT 2 kg/4½ lb

45 ml/3 tbsp LIGHT SOY SAUCE

175 ml/6 fl oz (¾ cup) WATER

30 ml/2 tbsp TOMATO SAUCE

22.5 ml/1½ tbsp SUGAR

7.5 ml/1½ tsp SALT

1.25 ml/¼ tsp GROUND WHITE PEPPER

3 ORANGES, PEELED AND SEGMENTED

22.5 ml/1½ tbsp RICE WINE, DRY SHERRY OR GIN

1 LARGE ONION, HALVED AND THINLY SLICED

3 CLOVES GARLIC, CRUSHED

1 litre/1¾ pints (4 cups) GROUNDNUT (PEANUT) OIL

15 ml/1 tbsp CORNFLOUR

30 ml/2 tbsp WATER

FRESH ORANGE SLICES, TO GARNISH

Prepare the duck breast and legs as described and cut into bite-sized pieces. Place in a bowl and add the soy sauce, turn with a spoon to coat, and marinate for 15 minutes, turning the pieces once or twice during that time. Meanwhile, in a small bowl, combine the water, tomato sauce, sugar, salt and pepper. Place the oranges in a bowl with the rice wine, sherry or gin, and leave to one side also. Mix the sliced onion and garlic together in another bowl.

Heat the oil in a wok or a deep-fat fryer and fry the duck pieces in several batches. When first you put the pieces in, cover with the lid to prevent excess spattering, then remove the lid to fry them until golden – about 3 minutes, depending on the heat of the oil. With a skimmer or slotted spoon, transfer each batch of browned duck pieces to kitchen paper to drain. Carefully pour off the oil into an ovenproof bowl. Place 30 ml/2 tbsp of this oil back into the wok and heat until it is very hot. Add the onion and garlic and stir fry for 1 minute, until it releases its fragrance. Add the orange and liquid and toss the mixture until combined, then add the tomato sauce mixture. Bring to a boil while stirring, then remove from the heat.

Put the drained duck into an ovenproof bowl and pour the contents of the wok over it. Cover the bowl with foil to seal, and steam in a steamer for 1 hour, making sure that the water does not boil dry. Remove the cooked duck to a warm serving dish with tongs, and keep warm. Remove any fat that may have accumulated on the remaining sauce and tip that sauce into another small pan. Mix the cornflour and water together and add to the sauce. Gently bring to the boil, stirring, and simmer for about 1 minute, or until it has thickened slightly. Pour over the duck pieces and serve, garnished if you wish with fresh orange slices, as part of a Chinese meal. *Serves 6.*

Baked Rabbit with Port

After you have tried this once, you might wish to sharpen the sauce just before serving. If you do, we recommend that you use 5-10 ml/1-2 tsp wine vinegar or even raspberry vinegar, which we find gives a better flavour than lemon juice.

1 RABBIT, CUT INTO SERVING PIECES

30 ml/2 tbsp SOFT BROWN SUGAR

2 ONIONS, FINELY CHOPPED

100 g/4 oz BUTTER, MELTED

100 ml/4 fl oz (½ cup) PORT

225 ml/8 fl oz (1 cup) CHICKEN STOCK

30 ml/2 tbsp REDCURRANT JELLY

Take a piece of foil large enough to encase the rabbit pieces. Place it in a shallow ovenproof dish. Lay the rabbit pieces on the foil and rub on the soft brown sugar. Sprinkle the onions evenly over the rabbit, and drizzle over all the melted butter. Close the foil over the rabbit to seal it and cook in a preheated oven at 200C/400F/Gas 6 for 1¼ hours.

Remove the dish from the oven, and very carefully fold back the foil to expose the rabbit. Be careful that the steam doesn't burn you. Carefully pour the port over the rabbit pieces, return to the oven, and cook, uncovered, for another 15 minutes. Place the cooked rabbit pieces on a warm serving dish and keep warm while you make the sauce.

Strain the juices from the pan into a heavy-based saucepan and add the chicken stock and redcurrant jelly. Boil rapidly, uncovered, until it has reduced and is fairly thick and shiny. Carefully check seasoning at this stage, as nothing was added to the rabbit while cooking. Accompany with plain steamed or boiled potatoes, and a green vegetable. Serve the sauce separately in a warm sauceboat. *Serves 4.*

Rabbit in Lemon-flavoured Raisin Sauce

Choose enough rabbit pieces for 4 people, about 2 pieces per person. Although it isn't really necessary to soak rabbit in water (unless of course it is wild rabbit), the action of the lemon juice in the water does help flavour it for this particular recipe. So it is best to start this a day ahead to allow for the soaking. If you haven't any beurre manié on hand mix 30 ml/2 tbsp plain flour with about 22.5 ml/1 ½ tbsp butter till combined.

ABOUT 1.5 kg/3 lb 5 oz RABBIT PIECES

50 ml/2 fl oz (¼ cup) LEMON JUICE

SALT AND FRESHLY GROUND BLACK PEPPER

50 ml/2 fl oz (¼ cup) OIL, OLIVE OR A BLANDER ONE, IF YOU PREFER

2 CLOVES GARLIC, CRUSHED

30 ml/2 tbsp FINELY CHOPPED FRESH PARSLEY

30 ml/2 tbsp FINELY GRATED LEMON RIND

5 ml/1 tsp DRIED SAGE

3 BAY LEAVES

300 ml/½ pint (1¼ cups) DRY WHITE WINE

300 ml/½ pint (1¼ cups) SINGLE (LIGHT) CREAM

BEURRE MANIÉ (see above)

50 g/2 oz (⅓ cup) SULTANAS

1.25 ml/¼ tsp WHITE WINE VINEGAR

1 OR 2 ONIONS, COARSELY CHOPPED (OPTIONAL)

Place the rabbit pieces, the lemon juice and enough water to cover in a glass dish, cover and place in the fridge for up to 24 hours. Drain and pat dry, and sprinkle with a little salt and pepper. In a large, heavy-based saucepan or flameproof casserole with a lid, heat the oil and the garlic together. After a minute, add the rabbit pieces and sauté until golden on all sides; do this a few pieces at a time so as to make it easier to manoeuvre them. Transfer the cooked pieces to a plate while you brown the remainder. When they have all been browned, put them back in the pan or casserole and sprinkle over the parsley, lemon rind and sage. Add the bay leaves and pour in the white wine. Bring the wine to the boil and stir round the rabbit pieces with a wooden spoon, trying to scrape up any residue bits from the bottom of the casserole. Lower the heat and in a separate, small saucepan heat the cream. When the cream starts to boil, pour it over the rabbit pieces, stir for about 2 minutes to get everything mixed together and then add the beurre manié, bit by bit, to thicken. Add the sultanas and the wine vinegar. Simmer the rabbit gently, covered, 50 to 60 minutes, until tender.

You can add 1 or 2 coarsely chopped, sautéed onions to this if you wish. The taste naturally is fairly sharp but not too much so, as the cream tends to soften the bite somewhat. Serve with simple vegetables and noodles, rice, or boiled potatoes. *Serves 4.*

Rabbit with Mustard Sauce

As with all recipes for rabbit, this also works well with chicken pieces. Buy either a whole rabbit or pieces. In the case of the latter, try to buy the backs and the back legs, as there isn't much meat on the front ones nor on the flap parts which constitute the ribs. Dijon mustard is the best, but you can use some of the grainier mustards that are about. Serve this delicious rabbit over rice or plain noodles.

45 ml/3 tbsp VEGETABLE OIL, SUCH AS CORN

1.5 kg/3 lb 5 oz RABBIT PIECES

A LITTLE SALT AND FRESHLY GROUND BLACK PEPPER

1 CLOVE GARLIC, CRUSHED

3.75 ml/ ¾ tsp DRIED ROSEMARY, CRUSHED

2.5 ml/½ tsp OREGANO

1.25 ml/¼ tsp DRIED TARRAGON

1.25 ml/¼ tsp DRIED SAGE

30 ml/2 tbsp PLAIN FLOUR

3 ONIONS, HALVED

450 ml/¾ pint (2 cups) DRY WHITE WINE, OR HALF WINE, HALF DRY VERMOUTH

22.5 ml/1½ tbsp DIJON MUSTARD

225 ml/8 fl oz (1 cup) SINGLE (LIGHT) CREAM

30 ml/2 tbsp FINELY CHOPPED FRESH PARSLEY OR CORIANDER

In a heavy-based flameproof casserole with a tight-fitting lid, heat the oil. Add the rabbit pieces, lightly season with salt and pepper, and brown on all sides for about 10 minutes. It is easiest if you do this a few pieces at a time. When the pieces are all cooked, return them to the casserole and add the garlic, rosemary, oregano, tarragon, sage and flour. Turn the pieces over to coat them with this mixture and then add the onion halves and the wine, or wine and vermouth. Stir everything round to mix together, cover and simmer gently, rearranging the rabbit pieces occasionally, 50 to 60 minutes, until tender. Remove the rabbit pieces and the onions to an ovenproof serving dish, cover and keep warm in the oven. Bring the cooking liquid to the boil and add the mustard and the cream. Simmer, stirring, until the sauce thickens. Check for seasoning. Spoon about 100 ml/4 fl oz (½ cup) of this sauce over the cooked rabbit and onions and sprinkle with the parsley or coriander. Serve the rest of the sauce separately in a warm bowl or sauceboat so that it can be poured over the rice or noodles. Green vegetables and carrots can be served on a separate side plate, or you can have a mixed green salad to go with this. *Serves 4.*

Simple Rabbit Casserole

The good thing about rabbit, particularly when bred for the table, is the fact that it can be cooked and later reheated without falling apart. This makes it ideal to use when you are expecting company. It shouldn't dry out too much either if it is gently cooked in a stock. Most recipes that call for chicken pieces can be replaced with jointed rabbit, but you have to add 15-25 per cent more cooking time.

1 RABBIT, JOINTED

SALT AND FRESHLY GROUND BLACK PEPPER

PLAIN FLOUR FOR DUSTING

30 g/1 ¼ oz BUTTER

2 ONIONS, COARSELY CHOPPED

2 RASHERS STREAKY BACON, FINELY CHOPPED

30 ml/2 tbsp BRANDY

100 ml/4 fl oz (½ cup) DRY WHITE WINE

225 ml/8 fl oz (1 cup) CHICKEN STOCK

5 ml/1 tsp MIXED DRIED HERBS (HERBES DE PROVENCE ARE IDEAL)

BEURRE MANIÉ OR CORNFLOUR AND WATER, TO THICKEN (OPTIONAL)

Rinse the rabbit in cold water and pat dry with kitchen paper. Sprinkle over each piece some salt and freshly ground black pepper, and dust the pieces with flour, shaking off any surplus. In a large, heavy-based flameproof casserole, melt the butter and add the chopped onions. Cook them over moderate heat until softened and starting to turn golden, then add the chopped bacon. Continue to cook for 5 minutes, then remove the onions and bacon to a plate with a slotted spoon. Sauté the rabbit pieces, a few at a time, over fairly high heat in the casserole, until both sides are coloured slightly. (Don't overcrowd the pan when you do this, and don't be tempted to add more butter either. What you are doing is virtually dry frying the rabbit, just to seal it slightly and give it a little colour.) Transfer to the plate with the onions and bacon.

Now, keeping the heat fairly high, add the brandy, wait for 30 seconds, then add the wine and the chicken stock (in this instance it is perfectly acceptable to use chicken stock cubes). Replace the rabbit portions, onions and bacon, and sprinkle over the mixed herbs. Cover and simmer very gently over a low heat for 1 to 1½ hours, until tender, depending on the size and age of the rabbit. Remove rabbit to a serving dish and keep warm. Thicken the liquid with beurre manié or some cornflour dissolved in a little cold water, if desired. Personally we prefer not to thicken it, but to spoon a little over the meat when serving and strain the remainder to make up part of the stock for a vegetable soup.

If made in advance, up to a day, cool completely and place in the fridge. Reheat either on top of the oven, very gently, or in a moderate oven. Alternatively, transfer the whole thing to a microwaveproof casserole and reheat in the microwave for about 10 to 12 minutes (if taken straight from the fridge). Whichever method you use to reheat, you must stir the contents round once or twice during the reheating process. We prefer the microwave for this. *Serves 4.*

Roast Stuffed Pheasant

We are very fond of pheasant. It can be a bit chewy, but we think the taste is worth this possibility. As pheasants seem to come in more or less a standard size and weight, the cooking time remains constant at 1 hour. The candied oranges we suggest for the Roasted Venison with Bread Sauce (p. 119) are excellent with this too.

250 g/9 oz PORK SAUSAGEMEAT

1 APPLE, PEELED, CORED AND FINELY CHOPPED

4 SPRIGS FRESH PARSLEY, FINELY CHOPPED

SALT AND FRESHLY GROUND BLACK PEPPER

1 EGG

1 ROASTING PHEASANT, ABOUT 1 kg/2¼ lb

2 LONG RASHERS STREAKY BACON

60 g/2⅓ oz BUTTER

175 ml/6 fl oz (1 wine glass) MEDIUM-DRY SHERRY

15 ml/1 tbsp REDCURRANT JELLY

JUICE OF ½ LEMON

4 SLICES OF FRIED BREAD, TO SERVE

In a large bowl mix well together the sausagemeat, chopped apple, parsley, salt and pepper. When evenly mixed, lightly beat the egg and mix in well to bind the ingredients. Stuff the bird with this mixture. If there is any left over, dampen your hands, roll into tiny balls (about the size of a walnut), and bake with the roast. Wrap the bacon rashers round the bird, place in an ovenproof dish, cover with the butter, and roast in a preheated oven at 160C/325F/Gas 3 for 1 hour. After 45 minutes, drain off any fat and pour over the sherry. Add the redcurrant jelly, lemon juice, salt and pepper. Baste the bird with this several times before cooking time is up. To serve, cut the bird in half down the breastbone, then cut across into halves again. Serve on fried bread and pour the sauce over.

If you are lucky enough to get the heart and liver as well, sauté them slowly in butter until soft, chop them, then mash them with the yolk of a hard-boiled egg and some salt and pepper. Spread this on the pieces of fried bread. If you didn't get these spare parts with your bird, buy a little liverwurst and use this instead. Little boiled, buttered new potatoes are ideal with this. *Serves 4.*

Terrine of Pheasant

This is a delicious terrine. If you can't get pheasant, use duck or chicken.

1 PHEASANT

1 SMALL ONION, SLICED

2 SMALL CARROTS, SLICED

2 to 3 SPRIGS FRESH PARSLEY

1 BAY LEAF

SALT

PINCH OF FRESH THYME

45 ml/3 tbsp MADEIRA

45 ml/3 tbsp COGNAC

250 g/9 oz LEAN PORK

750 g/1½ lb SALT PORK

1 EGG, LIGHTLY BEATEN

1 CLOVE GARLIC, CRUSHED

FRESHLY GROUND BLACK PEPPER

2 LONG RASHERS BACON

1 BAY LEAF

MADEIRA ASPIC (p. 115, OPTIONAL)

Split the bird open and remove the breasts. Cut these into long, narrow strips. In a large, non-metal bowl, gently mix the breast strips, sliced onion, carrots, parsley, bay leaf, salt, pinch of thyme, Madeira and Cognac. Cover and refrigerate for 2-3 hours (don't forget to stir every now and then). Remove the marinated breasts and put aside. Strain the marinade; discard the vegetables but keep the juice.

Cut the remaining flesh from the bird and cut the pork into chunks. In a food processor with the steel blade, chop the meat until fine (the colder the meat the easier this is to do). Add the beaten egg, garlic, ½ teaspoon salt, a few grinds of pepper and the reserved marinade. Blend until very smooth.

Place a bay leaf in the bottom of a terrine. Line the terrine with bacon, making sure there are long 'hang-overs' (to fold back later). Spread a third of the meat mixture over the bottom and place half the marinated strips of breast in. Cover with another third of the blended mixture, then place on the rest of the breast strips and cover with the last of the blended meat. Turn back the bacon 'hang-overs' (if not long enough to cover the top of the terrine, lay another rasher of bacon on top). Cover with lid and put the terrine into a baking dish, fill with hot water to half way up the terrine. Preheat oven to 170C/325F/

Gas 3. Place the pan in the centre of the oven and cook for 1½ hours.

Remove from the pan of water and place the terrine on a board, cover with a folded piece of aluminium foil, weight with 2 or 3 small cans (such as baked beans) just to compress the filling. When cold, uncover and run a knife carefully round the inside of the terrine (usually you will find the filling has shrunk), invert onto a plate and unmould. You can eat it at this stage, though it's best left a day.

If you want to go further and coat it with aspic, wash out the terrine, place the terrine (the name refers to the container as well as the cooked dish) back in, bottom side up. Pour in the Madeira Aspic, cooled, but not set, and re-chill. To unmould, dip the terrine quickly into very hot water to loosen the aspic, turn out and chill again. *Serves 6 to 8.*

Madeira Aspic

BONES OF PHEASANT CARCASS

1 CALF'S FOOT, OR 2 PIG'S TROTTERS

1 ONION, SLICED

2 CARROTS, SLICED

2 STALKS CELERY, CUT UP

1.7 litres/3 pints (8 cups) WATER

SALT AND FRESHLY GROUND BLACK PEPPER

1 SPRIG FRESH PARSLEY

1 SPRIG FRESH THYME

1 BAY LEAF

125 g/4 oz MINCED BEEF

5 ml/1 tsp DRIED TARRAGON

1 EGG WHITE

60 ml/4 tbsp MADEIRA

In a large pan, add the carcass, calf's foot, onion, carrots, celery, water, salt and pepper, parsley, thyme and bay leaf. Bring to the boil and simmer gently for 4 hours, skimming the scum off from time to time. Strain, cool, then skim off the fat.

Clean the pan and add the minced beef and 5 ml/1 tsp tarragon. Lightly beat the egg white and mix in. Pour in the cooled stock, mix well and gently bring back to the boil, stirring all the time. Now lower the heat and simmer for 15 minutes. Strain through a damp tea towel and cool, then stir in the Madeira. When starting to set, pour into the terrine.

There are excellent prepared aspic powders on the market that will save you all this trouble (not as nice as the real thing, of course). You can substitute 60 ml/4 tbsp Madeira for an equal amount of water if you use a powder.

Venison Ragoût

Venison is game and therefore is usually fairly fatless so ensure some fat is added, either fatty bacon or lard. When making a ragoût such as this stir it during cooking to make sure the meat is kept moist.

1.5-2 kg/3 lb 5oz-4½ lb VENISON, PREFERABLY LEG

600 ml/1 pint (2½ cups) FULL-BODIED DRY RED WINE

2 LARGE CARROTS, SLICED

1 LARGE ONION, SLICED

1 BUNCH CELERY, CHOPPED

1 LEEK, WHITE PART ONLY, CHOPPED

24 JUNIPER BERRIES, CRUSHED

30 ml/2 tbsp OLIVE OIL

175 g/6 oz (¾ cup) WATER

65 ml/2½ fl oz (⅓ cup) GIN

10 ml/2 tsp SALT

5 ml/1 tsp DRIED MARJORAM

GOOD GRIND BLACK PEPPER

2 BAY LEAVES, CRUSHED

PLAIN FLOUR FOR DUSTING

50 g/2 oz LARD

350 ml/12 fl oz (1½ cups) BROWN STOCK OR CANNED CONSOMMÉ

2.5 ml/½ tsp RED WINE VINEGAR

Bone the leg and cut the meat into 4 cm/1½ inch cubes. In a large bowl, combine all the ingredients down to and including the bay leaves to make a marinade. Add the venison and cover with cling film. Marinate for at least 6 hours, tossing the meat round from time to time. Remove the meat and pat dry with kitchen paper. Season and dust with flour.

In a large frying pan, melt the lard and fry the meat a few pieces at a time until lightly browned. Transfer the browned venison to a large, heavy-based flameproof casserole. Drain the marinade through a sieve into a bowl, and when the vegetables are fairly dry, sauté them in the frying pan until lightly browned, then add to the casserole. Add the strained marinade liquid to the frying pan, plus the stock. Bring to the boil over high heat, stirring all the time, for 3 minutes. Pour over the venison and vegetables in the casserole until just covered; add the reserved leg bone if you have it. Bring the casserole to simmering point on top of the oven and transfer to the oven preheated to 170C/325F/Gas 3. Cook for 1½ to 2 hours or until tender, basting well every 30 minutes. Remove the bone and stir in the red wine vinegar. Serve with the plainest of vegetables. *Serves 6.*

Venison Meat Loaf

*The Prune Sauce is an optional extra. Its sharp, sweet taste is a fantastic complement
to the venison.*

500 g/18 oz VENISON, CUT INTO STRIPS

4 SLICES BREAD, CRUSTS REMOVED AND THEN CRUMBED

2 SLICES STREAKY BACON, RINDED AND CHOPPED

1 ONION, FINELY CHOPPED

SALT AND FRESHLY GROUND BLACK PEPPER

5 ml/1 tsp MIXED DRIED HERBS

1 EGG

30 ml/2 tbsp BRANDY

75 g/3 oz BUTTER

Mince the venison or process it with the steel blade of a food processor (not too fine, you
want some texture). Place in a large bowl with the breadcrumbs, bacon, onion, salt and
pepper and herbs, and mix thoroughly. Lightly beat the egg with the brandy and mix this in
very well. Shape mixture into a loaf with moist hands. Preheat the oven to 170C/325F/
Gas 3. Melt the butter in a roasting pan, and place the loaf carefully in. Cook for 1 hour,
basting with the butter and juices regularly.

While this is cooking make the Prune Sauce.

Prune Sauce

250 g/9 oz PITTED PRUNES

RIND OF ½ LEMON, CUT INTO THIN STRIPS

1.25 ml/¼ tsp GROUND CLOVES

1.25 ml/¼ tsp GROUND CINNAMON

40-50 g/1½-2 oz (¼ cup) SUGAR

50 ml/2 fl oz (¼ cup) CIDER VINEGAR

In a heavy-based saucepan, stew the prunes, lemon rind, cinnamon, cloves with a little
water, till very soft. When cooked, stir in the sugar and cider vinegar and cook a minute or
so, until the sugar has dissolved.

Slice the loaf and serve the sauce separately. *Serves 4.*

Roasted Venison with Bread Sauce

Father Christmas may not approve of this dish, but we certainly do! The Candied Orange Slices are easy to do and make a delicious addition.

1 HAUNCH VENISON, 3 kg/6 lb 10oz

8 LONG RASHERS STREAKY BACON

2 LARGE SPRIGS FRESH ROSEMARY

350 ml/12 fl oz (1½ cups) CLARET

2.5 ml/½ tsp GROUND GINGER

2.5 ml/½ tsp GROUND CINNAMON

2 WHOLE CLOVES

5 ml/1 tsp SUGAR

SALT AND FRESHLY GROUND BLACK PEPPER

30 ml/2 tbsp FRESH BREADCRUMBS

60 g/2⅓ oz BUTTER

5 ml/1 tsp VINEGAR

Wrap the haunch in the bacon strips. If they are nice and long they will go right round. Place the sprigs of rosemary in a large ovenproof dish and place the venison on top. Pour the claret round (not over), and sprinkle onto the claret the ginger, cinnamon, cloves and sugar; swirl round to mix. Season well with salt and pepper. Place a piece of greaseproof paper on top.

Preheat the oven to 160C/325F/Gas 3 and roast for 50 minutes per 1 kg/2¼ lb – in this instance 2½ hours. Watch the cooking and occasionally baste with the pan juices. *Very important*: when the claret starts to evaporate, pour in 225 ml/8 fl oz (1 cup) warm water and keep basting. If it evaporates further, add another 225 ml/8 fl oz (1 cup) water. Don't be concerned if there is quite a lot of liquid at the end, as you want these pan juices for the gravy.

At the end of the cooking time, remove the venison to a carving board to rest. Strain the pan juices into a heavy-based saucepan, heat over moderate heat, then stir in the breadcrumbs, bring to the boil and add the butter and vinegar, stir well and keep on a low heat or pour into a heated sauceboat and hold in the oven until ready for use.

Remove the bacon from the roast, place on a plate and keep in the oven to serve with the meat. Carve the roast (we cut it across, thereby giving some well cooked slices and the inner slightly pink slices). Try this with roasted sweet potatoes and fresh green peas cooked with a little mint, drained and buttered, Candied Orange Slices, and redcurrant jelly. *Serves 10.*

Game Sausages with Bread Sauce

Prepare as for Roasted Venison with Bread Sauce and bake for 1 hour at moderate temperature. Fifteen minutes before the end of the hour remove the bacon to allow sausages to brown on top. Keep bacon on a heated plate and proceed with the sauce . . . super!

Candied Orange Slices

400 g/14 oz (2 cups) GRANULATED SUGAR

225 ml/8 fl oz (1 cup) WATER

30 ml/2 tbsp LEMON JUICE

3-4 LARGE SEEDLESS ORANGES

In a large, heavy-based frying pan, combine sugar, water and lemon juice. Bring to a boil and simmer for about 5 minutes, until the sugar has dissolved . . . make sure you stir it several times. Wash the oranges (don't peel) and cut into fairly thick rings. Carefully place these in the simmering sugar mixture, in a single layer if possible. Simmer gently for about half an hour, turning the slices from time to time. The sugar water should have become quite thick and the orange slices slightly shrivelled and caramelized. Leave in the pan to cool. Arrange on an attractive plate, pour the sauce over and serve with the venison.

VEGETABLES AND SALADS

One cannot overstress the importance of vegetables and fruit to our wellbeing – but they must be fresh. We are strong believers in 'big is not beautiful'. To our taste, young, freshly picked vegetables are supreme, they need less cooking and often no peeling (a lot of goodness lies just under the skin). New little potatoes or baby carrots need only a scrub to smarten them up. Because they require less cooking, young vegetables retain their goodness and vitamins.

In the bad old days, vegetables for a Sunday roast were usually prepared in the early morning, then soaked in a large bowl of water (supposedly to keep them fresh), then roasted or boiled later on for lunch. Soaking vegetables in water leaches out most of the vitamins, so we prepare them just before cooking.

If we can avoid it we don't cook vegetables in water at all. Steaming, of course, is perfect – you can control crispness and maintain colour. A stacked steamer is a great investment. Try little potatoes, asparagus, baby carrots, courgettes or beans steamed, then just tossed in a little butter and dusted with fresh herbs.

The microwave cooks vegetables magnificently. Prepare the vegetables, place in a covered bowl with a tiny amount of water (just enough to create some steam), and then cook – no vitamins are poured down the sink, and the microwave preserves the colour.

The old manner of preparing vegetables ahead, popping them in a saucepan, covering them with cold water and a couple of teaspoons of salt, then boiling them like mad till the mushy stage has been reached is no longer acceptable. Everything has gone, including the texture of what you were cooking. If you are going to boil vegetables, bring the water to the boil and add a little sugar in the case of vegetables such as beans to sweeten them up – but never add salt! Place the vegetables in the rolling boiling water and cook till just tender, drain and serve; add the salt at table. Actually, tossing in butter (unless it's unsalted) should give you sufficient salt taste. To boil potatoes, drop them into boiling, unsalted water, bring back to the boil and boil for a few minutes, then turn them off, cover with a lid, and leave till just tender. Gently prick with a sharp pointed knife now and again, till the desired stage is reached . . . saves on electricity or gas and also stops some of the flourier varieties breaking up.

To sauté vegetables, heat the butter and oil and cook as quickly as possible. (We very rarely sauté in straight butter, as the addition of a little oil makes it possible to obtain a hotter temperature without burning.)

Many modern writers on dietary requirements advise that a high proportion of vegetable intake should be raw. This of course is where salads come into their own. We usually make dressing with good oil and lemon juice, which we prefer to vinegar as the end result is not so sharp.

Once when we were staying with friends in Miami we went to a restaurant that was famous for its salads and particularly the dressings. The waiter came and introduced himself and explained that there were 5 kinds of lettuce in the salad that was being served that night and that the dressing contained 24 different herbs and spices along with lemon juice and honey. Always interested in new combinations, we asked him to name the lettuce and the herbs and spices. The waiter hesitated and said, 'Good evening, my name is Carl and the salad tonight contains 5 kinds of lettuce and is served with a dressing that contains 24 different herbs and spices along with lemon and honey'. We never found out what they were, and we could only surmise that he was a sort of wind-up doll where you pulled the ring and string attached to his back that gave out the programmed message. . . . One thing though, the salad was fresh and the service was terrific.

Rösti Potatoes

To cook or not to cook, that is the question with this type of potato pancake. When making the uncooked version you have to have a thin layer of potatoes, otherwise there is always the possibility of not having the centre cooked through when the outside is brown and crusty. We feel that a thicker pancake using cooked potatoes is preferable. A non-stick surface in the pan you use is a great advantage, and clarified butter or ghee is best, but failing that you can use some butter and a non-flavoured oil so that the butter doesn't burn too quickly before the dish is cooked. You can also decide whether you want to peel the potatoes after you have boiled them. We like them with the skins left on, but if the potatoes are really old, it may be best to peel them before grating – it all depends on their quality and condition. If in doubt peel them after they have cooled in the fridge.

4 MEDIUM TO LARGE POTATOES

3 SPRING ONIONS, FINELY CHOPPED

GOOD PINCH OF DRIED BASIL

2.5 ml/½ tsp SALT

8 GRINDINGS FRESH BLACK PEPPER

CLARIFIED BUTTER OR GHEE, OR MIXTURE OF OIL AND BUTTER

Scrub the potatoes well and cook in plenty of lightly salted water. Bring to the boil, and boil gently for 10 minutes. (They won't be quite cooked through by this time, but will have cooked sufficiently for this recipe.) Drain, top with cold water to cool them quickly, drain again after 5 minutes and place in the fridge to chill thoroughly. Peel them, if you wish. Coarsely grate them either by hand with a grater, or in the food processor with the grating disc. Transfer the grated potatoes to a large bowl and carefully mix in the finely chopped spring onions, basil, salt and pepper. Stir gently to mix. (Don't beat them to death as if you were trying to make mashed potatoes.)

Heat about 50 g/2 oz (¼ cup) clarified butter (or other fat) in a moderate-sized frying pan. Carefully spoon in the potatoes and pat down firmly with a palette knife or fish slice to even out the thickness.

Fry over moderate heat until you can smell the nuttiness that they give off when browned. It will take about 7 minutes for the underneath to turn golden brown and crispy. Run a knife or palette knife round the edge to release the 'cake' and also check the underneath, and very carefully invert the 'cake' onto a large plate. Heat some extra clarified butter in the pan and gently slide the 'cake' back into it. (Be very careful not to splash hot butter or oil on yourself.) Now cook the underside over moderate heat until crispy. When cooked, cut into wedges and serve. Good with a main course, or alternatively it is nice to serve for breakfast with grilled bacon or sausages, or for lunch with grilled lamb chops. *Serves 4.*

Mushroom and Blue Cheese Salad

When you add cheese to salad you are adding protein and therefore making it suitable to serve on its own as a light lunch or as a starter. Marinated mushrooms combined with blue cheese and walnuts is a combination that is very Californian. We have always been impressed by the variety of combinations that come from that area.

50 ml/2 fl oz (¼ cup) OLIVE OR GROUNDNUT (PEANUT) OIL

15 ml/1 tbsp CHOPPED FRESH BASIL LEAVES

2.5 ml/½ tsp SALT

1.25 ml/¼ tsp GROUND BLACK PEPPER

1.25 ml/¼ tsp PAPRIKA

10 ml/2 tsp DIJON MUSTARD

15 ml/1 tbsp WHITE WINE OR CIDER VINEGAR

JUICE OF ½ LEMON

250 g/9 oz BUTTON MUSHROOMS, SLICED

4 SPRING ONIONS, THINLY SLICED

1 LARGE HEAD LETTUCE, WASHED AND TORN INTO PIECES

ABOUT 100 g/4 oz (¾ cup) WALNUTS, COARSELY CHOPPED

125 g/4 oz BLUE CHEESE, COARSELY CRUMBLED

12 CHERRY TOMATOES, HALVED (OR EQUIVALENT CHOPPED TOMATOES)

In a large bowl, whisk together the oil, basil, salt, pepper, paprika, mustard, vinegar and lemon juice until it emulsifies. Add the sliced mushrooms and spring onions and marinate at room temperature, turning occasionally, for at least an hour. Place the dried torn lettuce in a large salad bowl, pour over the dressing and mushrooms, add the walnuts and cheese and carefully toss all together so that the dressing coats the lettuce. Serve straight away. *Serves 4.*

Waldorf Salad

This salad is superb, whether served as a light luncheon by itself or as a starter. The essential ingredient is the walnuts – make sure they are very fresh, otherwise the salad becomes bitter.

2 RED DELICIOUS APPLES, WASHED, POLISHED, CORED AND DICED

2 GRANNY SMITH APPLES, WASHED, POLISHED, CORED AND DICED

15 ml/1 tbsp LEMON JUICE

15 ml/1 tbsp ORANGE JUICE

4 STALKS CELERY, TOPPED AND TAILED, WASHED, PEELED WITH A VEGETABLE PEELER, THEN DICED

30 ml/2 tbsp RAISINS, SOAKED IN HOT WATER FOR 10 MINUTES, THEN WELL DRAINED

250 g/9 oz (1½ cups) WALNUTS, COARSELY CHOPPED

DRESSING (see below)

2 SMALL HEADS CRISP LETTUCE, SUCH AS ICEBERG

15 ml/1 tbsp GRATED ORANGE RIND

In a large bowl, toss together the diced apples with the lemon and orange juices (apart from adding taste, the juice stops the apples from discolouring). Add the celery, drained raisins and the walnuts and toss again. Pour over the dressing and toss very well.

Wash and dry the lettuce and break into a salad bowl, pour over the apple mixture, dust with grated orange rind and toss when ready to serve. You can, if you prefer, break the lettuce into leaves and use as cups and fill with the salad. *Serves 6.*

Dressing

1 WHOLE EGG AND 1 EGG YOLK, AT ROOM TEMPERATURE

1.25 ml/¼ tsp DIJON MUSTARD

1.25 ml/¼ tsp CURRY POWDER

2.5 ml/½ tsp SALT

15 ml/1 tbsp FRESH LEMON JUICE

50 ml/2 fl oz (¼ cup) WALNUT OIL

175 ml/6 fl oz (¾ cup) VEGETABLE OIL, NOT OLIVE

50 ml/2 fl oz (¼ cup) WHIPPING CREAM, SOFTLY WHIPPED, NOT SWEETENED

In a food processor with the steel blade, process the egg and yolk, mustard, curry powder, salt and lemon juice, for a few seconds, until well amalgamated. Through the feed tube, with the motor running, slowly pour in the oils and blend for about 1 minute or until mixture is smooth and creamy. Scrape into a clean bowl and fold in the whipped cream. Cover with cling film and refrigerate until ready to use. Just gently re-fold before using in case it may have settled slightly.

Indian-style Cabbage

This is ideal to accompany a curry and we suggest it to go with our recipe for Prawn Curry (p. 47). Slightly Anglicized though it is, it tastes delicious and certainly makes a change. Freshly grated coconut is preferred for flavour, but you can use desiccated.

30 ml/2 tbsp GROUNDNUT (PEANUT) OIL

7.5 ml/1½ tsp BROWN MUSTARD SEEDS

2 GREEN CHILLIES, FRESH OR CANNED, SEEDED AND CHOPPED

1 SMALL ONION, THINLY SLICED

5 ml/1 tsp CURRY POWDER

2.5 ml/½ tsp TURMERIC

1.25 ml/¼ tsp GROUND CARDAMOM

½ LARGE CABBAGE, SHREDDED

1.25 ml/¼ tsp SUGAR

5 ml/1 tsp SALT

SCANT 50 ml/2 fl oz (¼ cup) WATER

45 ml/3 tbsp SHREDDED COCONUT

Heat the oil in the large saucepan, add the mustard seeds, cover with the lid and leave to heat through for 2 minutes. Add the chillies, onion, curry, turmeric and cardamom and continue cooking over moderate heat for another 4 to 5 minutes to release the flavour of the spices. Add the shredded cabbage and cook, stirring, for another minute or so. Now add the sugar, salt and water, cover the saucepan and cook for about 8 to 10 minutes, until the cabbage is just soft, but still retains some crunch. Remove the lid and turn up the heat to evaporate the excess moisture. Keep stirring so that it doesn't catch and burn. Stir in the coconut and serve straight away. *Serves 4.*

Crisp-skinned Stuffed Potatoes

So much nicer than those things done in metal foil . . . yuk! You may prefer to use sour cream instead of butter and cream. Instead of chives you could use finely chopped onion, chopped peppers, fresh herbs or finely chopped, lightly sautéed bacon. Also you may wish to dust with Parmesan cheese just before finishing off under the grill.

5 LARGE POTATOES, WELL SCRUBBED BUT NOT PEELED

15 ml/1 tbsp BUTTER

15 ml/1 tbsp SINGLE (LIGHT) CREAM

SALT AND FRESHLY GROUND BLACK PEPPER

6 to 8 LONG SPEARS CHIVES

Prick the whole washed potatoes in several places. Preheat the oven to 200C/400F/Gas 6 and place the potatoes on the centre rack. Bake for about 1 hour, or until potatoes feel soft when gently squeezed. Remove from oven and let cool enough to handle. Cut potatoes in half lengthways, and carefully scoop flesh into a bowl . . . be careful not to pierce the skin. Mash the potato flesh with butter, cream and salt and pepper to taste. Finely chop chives and mix in; set aside. (You are only going to stuff 8 halves; the extra potato was to give extra filling, so they are piled up a bit. If you have ever dug a hole and then put the soil back, you will know there is never enough.)

There are 2 methods now to crisp the skins: either deep fry them or bake them. Frying is cheaper than baking, unless you are using the oven for something else at the same time.

To fry. In a heavy-based pan, heat about 5 cm/2 inches vegetable oil over high heat until it starts to smoke a little. Flick a dot of water into the oil: if it hisses and foams, the oil is hot enough. Fry the potato skins, a few at a time, a minute or so, until golden brown and crisp. Remove with a slotted spoon and drain on kitchen paper.

To bake. Brush skins inside and out with melted butter, about 65 ml/2½ fl oz (⅓ cup), place cut side up on a baking sheet. Preheat oven to 270C/475F/Gas 9 and cook 10 to 12 minutes, until crisp. Remove skins from oven and turn on the grill.

Fill the 8 halves with potato mixture, slightly mounded. Brush with a little melted butter, then lightly fork the top into lines, pop under the grill and cook until lightly golden (watch they don't burn). *Serves 4 to 8.*

Courgettes with Rosemary

This is made in a trice. It is so simple and the taste goes well with most chicken dishes or pork chops.

8 COURGETTES

5 ml/1 tsp SALT

5 ml/1 tsp DRIED ROSEMARY

25 g/1 oz BUTTER

FRESHLY GROUND BLACK PEPPER

Trim the ends from the courgettes, wipe them clean and grate them using either a hand grater or the grating disc of a food processor. Tip half into a colander and sprinkle with half the salt, top with the remaining grated courgettes and the remaining salt; leave to drain for 30 minutes. Press out the moisture with either the back of your hand or the back of a large serving spoon. Grind the rosemary in a pestle and mortar and reduce it to a powder. (This is important – rosemary spikes in the courgettes don't make for pleasant eating.) Melt the butter in a fairly large saucepan and add the pounded rosemary. Add the grated courgettes and stir over moderate heat. Cover with a lid and cook, stirring once or twice, for about 7 minutes. Sprinkle on some pepper, stir and serve immediately. *Serves 4.*

Brussels Sprouts in Walnut Cream Sauce

Brussels sprouts should be a nice bright green, and the leaves tightly together (not open and floppy) and of uniform size. If they have yellowed or spotted leaves, don't buy them. As with all vegetables, big is not beautiful – young, tender and fresh vegetables are a must. Steaming Brussels sprouts is really the best way to cook them, as it retains their colour and they don't get waterlogged and mushy. You can try macadamias, almonds or cashews in place of the walnuts in this recipe.

750 g/1½ lb SMALL BRUSSELS SPROUTS

45 ml/3 tbsp UNSALTED BUTTER

45 ml/3 tbsp PLAIN FLOUR

450 ml/¾ pint (2 cups) SINGLE (LIGHT) CREAM, SCALDED

2 BAY LEAVES

1 CLOVE GARLIC, FINELY CHOPPED

100 g/4 oz (1 cup) WALNUTS, FINELY CHOPPED

45 ml/3 tbsp FRESHLY GRATED PARMESAN CHEESE

65 ml/2½ fl oz (⅓ cup) MILK

65 ml/2½ fl oz (⅓ cup) SINGLE (LIGHT) CREAM

SALT AND GROUND WHITE PEPPER

Remove any imperfect outside leaves from the sprouts, trim the stalks and cut a cross in the stalk base (this allows the heat to penetrate the centre of the vegetable more quickly). Place sprouts in a steamer with a tight-fitting lid and steam for 10 to 12 minutes, until just tender crisp. Check with the tip of a sharp knife – please do not overcook. (Don't forget to allow enough water in the base of the steamer; you don't want the bottom to burn out of it.) Remove sprouts to a heated serving dish and keep warm.

For the sauce, melt the butter in a medium-sized, heavy-based pan and add the flour. Cook, stirring over a moderate heat, for 3 minutes. Remove the pan from the heat and pour in the scalded cream, whisking to prevent lumps. Place back on the heat and continue whisking until it thickens. Add bay leaves and garlic and continue to cook over a low heat for another 3 minutes. Whisk in the walnuts and the Parmesan cheese, and slowly whisk in the milk and remaining cream. Bring just to boiling point, still whisking, remove from the heat and add salt and white pepper to taste. Cover and let stand off the heat for 5 minutes. Remove bay leaves just before pouring over the sprouts. *Serves 6 to 8.*

Tomatoes Stuffed with Pea Purée

These are colourful and simple to prepare. They can be made in advance and cooked just before they are served. They go well with most meats, and are very good to serve with Roast Stuffed Chicken (p. 90).

8 FIRM TOMATOES

SALT AND FRESHLY GROUND BLACK PEPPER

1 SMALL PACKET FROZEN PEAS

30 ml/2 tbsp BUTTER

50 ml/2 fl oz (¼ cup) SINGLE (LIGHT) CREAM

Remove the cores from the tomatoes, and carefully remove the seeds with a small spoon, making hollowed-out cups. Sprinkle the inside of each cup with a little salt and turn upside down. Leave to drain for 20 minutes.

Meanwhile, cook the peas according to packet instructions and drain well. Place the cooked and drained peas in the bowl of a food processor fitted with the steel blade, add the butter and process until smooth. With the motor still running, pour in the cream through the feed tube. Switch off the motor, season the purée with a little salt and pepper, then spoon it equally between the tomato cups. To heat through, place the tomatoes in a circle on a microwaveproof plate, cover with a sheet of kitchen paper and microwave on High for about 4 minutes or until warmed through (do not overmicrowave or they may disintegrate when you try to transfer them to the serving plates). Alternatively, place in a lightly buttered ovenproof dish, close together so that they do not fall over, cover with a sheet of lightly buttered foil and bake at 180C/350F/Gas 4 for 15 to 20 minutes. *Serves 4 to 8.*

Cheesy New Potatoes

New potatoes boiled in their skins are the best to use in this dish; old ones that you peel and cut into smaller portions can work, but not as well. However, you can pick out small, older potatoes, peel them thinly and cook them carefully. In this instance, rather than boiling them for 20 minutes, put them in boiling salted water, simmer for 5 minutes, turn off the heat, place a lid on the pan and leave them to cook slowly in their residual heat until they are just cooked. As the water isn't continually boiling they are less likely to break up. Alternatively, you can steam them until they are just cooked. We advise using mozzarella as it melts beautifully, but you can use other cheeses – finely grated Cheddar, or crumbled blue cheese, if you wish. If the latter, use only 75 g/3 oz (½ cup) crumbled, otherwise the flavour becomes too overpowering.

12 NEW POTATOES

30 g/1¼ oz UNSALTED BUTTER

1 ONION, FINELY CHOPPED

2 LARGE TOMATOES, PEELED AND SEEDED

100 ml/4 fl oz (½ cup) SINGLE (LIGHT) CREAM

15 ml/1 tbsp FINELY CHOPPED FRESH PARSLEY

2.5 ml/½ tsp DRIED OREGANO

2.5 ml/½ tsp GROUND CUMIN

2.5 ml/½ tsp SALT

8 GRINDINGS BLACK PEPPER

ABOUT 100 g/4 oz (1 cup) MOZZARELLA CHEESE, GRATED

Wash and thoroughly scrub the potatoes, then cook until just tender. Drain them, place in a serving dish and keep warm. In a large frying pan, melt the butter and add the onion. Cook over moderate heat about 5 minutes, until soft but not browned. Coarsely chop the peeled tomatoes, add to the onions and continue to cook, stirring, for another 5 minutes. Stir in the cream, parsley, oregano, cumin and the salt and pepper. Keep stirring and add the grated cheese. When this has melted and the sauce is hot, pour over the potatoes and serve at once. *Serves 4.*

Baked Sweet Potatoes with Orange Butter

This is a variant of the old plain jacket potato, using red or yellow sweet potatoes. It puts them into the haute cuisine class, and they really are scrumptious. It's best to pick over the potatoes when you are buying them and try for large ones so that you serve 1 per person. Should you only be able to buy small ones, choose 2 per person and cut down on the cooking time accordingly. You may substitute 15 ml/1 tbsp liqueur for 15 ml/1 tbsp of juice . . . gorgeous.

175 g/6 oz BUTTER, SOFTENED

45ml/3 tbsp GRATED ORANGE RIND

45 ml/3 tbsp ORANGE JUICE

6 LARGE RED OR YELLOW SWEET POTATOES

GROUNDNUT (PEANUT) OIL

SALT

In a bowl, cream the softened butter with the orange rind until light and fluffy. Gradually beat the juice into this little by little until well combined. Transfer to a serving dish and keep at room temperature – do not refrigerate. Scrub the potatoes and pat dry. Mix a little groundnut oil in the palm of your hand with a small amount of salt and rub over the skins of the sweet potatoes. Place on a baking tray and bake in a preheated oven at 200C/400F/ Gas 6 for 20 minutes. Prick tops with a fork and continue to bake for a further 30 to 40 minutes, until soft when squeezed. Using an oven glove, roll the potatoes back and forth lightly on a board to lightly mash the interior. Slit deeply lengthways but not right through. Open them slightly and dollop in the orange butter. (These can be prepared with the oil and salt and microwaved at High. Be sure to prick them with a fork beforehand so that they will not burst.)

This is a superb vegetable to serve with grilled pork chops or pork sausages. *Serves 6.*

Salami Salad and Croûtes

We made this salad many years ago on television and were delighted when the crew gave it the thumbs up sign. Later, when we wanted to make it again, could we find the recipe? Not on your life. In vain we hunted high and low. Just before writing this book we found it tucked away. We hope you like it as much as we do. It is in 4 parts: the salad, the dressing, the croûtes and the mayonnaise. Instead of potatoes, you can use large pasta shells or macaroni, about 300 g/11 oz dry weight. Cook and drain according to packet directions; use when cool.

Salad

1 kg/2¼ lb POTATOES

250 g/9 oz GREEN VEGETABLES, SUCH AS BEANS, COURGETTES OR CAULIFLOWER

1 LARGE RED PEPPER

6 SPRING ONIONS

250 g/9 oz SLICED SALAMI
(MIX UP THE VARIETIES, IF YOU WISH)

Scrub the potatoes well and gently cook them in their jackets until tender. Cool, remove the skins and cut into medium-sized cubes. Cook the vegetables until tender-crisp, refresh in cold water and drain. Cut into attractive shapes, for example, cut the beans into diagonal pieces, the courgettes into diagonal slices, and the cauliflower into florets. Core, seed and thinly slice the red pepper and cut the spring onions into diagonal slices also. Place all this together with the salami in a serving bowl and keep to one side while you make the dressing.

Dressing

50 g/2oz CAN ANCHOVY FILLETS AND THEIR OIL

100 g/4 oz (½ cup) MAYONNAISE (OPPOSITE)

5 ml/1 tsp WORCESTERSHIRE SAUCE

60 ml/4 tbsp GROUNDNUT (PEANUT) OIL

15 ml/1 tbsp CIDER VINEGAR

45 ml/3 tbsp FINELY CHOPPED FRESH PARSLEY

SEVERAL GRINDINGS BLACK PEPPER

SALT, IF YOU MUST, BUT THE ANCHOVIES WILL PROBABLY BE SUFFICIENT

Mash the anchovies and mix in all the other ingredients, whisk together in a bowl, then pour over the salad ingredients. Gently spoon them all together with the dressing to coat and cover with cling film. Chill for at least an hour.

Croûtes

While the salad and dressing are chilling, make the croûtes.

1 FRENCH LOAF

75 g/3 oz BUTTER, MELTED

30 ml/2 tbsp FINELY CHOPPED FRESH PARSLEY

15 ml/1 tbsp FINELY SNIPPED FRESH CHIVES

2.5 ml/½ tsp DRIED MARJORAM

2 CLOVES GARLIC, CRUSHED

Cut the bread into thin diagonal slices. Mix all the other ingredients into the melted butter and brush over both sides of the bread. Bake on a baking sheet at 180C/350F/Gas 4 about 10 minutes (best to do this on a rack near the top of the oven), until golden. Serve with the tossed chilled salad.

Mayonnaise

You can use commercial mayonnaise for the salad dressing, but we like to serve extra at the table to spoon over the salad, so we prefer to make our own, which isn't quite as vinegary as the bought kind. The choice of oils is up to you, but in this instance we feel that a strong oil only, such as olive, can be too overpowering.

2 EGGS, SIZE 1, AT ROOM TEMPERATURE

5 ml/1 tsp DIJON MUSTARD

2.5 ml/½ tsp SALT

A LITTLE GROUND WHITE PEPPER, OR, IF YOU DON'T MIND THE SPECKS, BLACK PEPPER

JUICE OF 1 LEMON, OR 10 ml/2 tsp CIDER VINEGAR

ABOUT 350 ml/12 fl oz (1½ cups) OIL, MIX OLIVE AND SAFFLOWER OR GROUNDNUT (PEANUT) AND CORN OIL

To make this in a food processor, use the plastic blade. Break in the eggs, which must be at room temperature. Add the mustard, salt and pepper. Switch on the processor and leave it to run until the eggs start to thicken. Add half the lemon juice and very gradually drizzle in the oil. The same principle applies if you are making it by hand with a whisk – don't rush the oil, drizzle it onto the beaten eggs slowly until the eggs start to thicken. Once this happens, add more lemon juice to taste and increase the flow of the oil. Check for final seasoning, cover and keep to one side (do not put it in the fridge).

Note: if the mayonnaise doesn't thicken enough, which sometimes happens, remove the mixture to a jug from the food processor. Clean out the container and blade and dry thoroughly. Place back onto the motor and break in a fresh egg yolk. Start the motor running, and when the yolk has thickened slightly, gently start pouring back the mixture from the jug. This same procedure applies if you have added too much oil too quickly and the mayonnaise curdles. It has happened to us on many occasions – don't despair if it happens to you the first time. The use of whole eggs tends to give you a lighter sauce, but if you wish you can use 1 whole egg and 2 egg yolks, to give you a richer flavour.

This salad is an excellent lunch dish. *Serves 4.*

Tomato and Onion Pie

This is one of our favourites, especially with a roast. It's based on a Mrs Beeton special. To really get the full flavour you need to make this when there are plenty of beautiful, sun-ripened tomatoes available, although hot-house ones work, too.

2 LARGE ONIONS

50 g/2 oz BUTTER

1 kg/2¼ lb FAT RED RIPE TOMATOES

175 g/6 oz (3 cups) FRESHLY MADE BREADCRUMBS (ABOUT 6 SLICES)

SALT AND FRESHLY GROUND BLACK PEPPER

EXTRA 50 g/2 oz BUTTER, TO DOT THE TOP

Peel the onions, place them in a heatproof bowl, cover with boiling water and leave to stand for 2 hours. This leaches out some of the 'fire' and tends to sweeten them. Drain and cut into slices, then separate into rings. Melt the butter in a heavy-based frying pan and cook the onion rings until lightly golden, stirring often.

Lightly butter a fairly large, ovenproof pie dish. Slice the tomatoes thickly, removing the cores first, and layer in the dish with the onions and breadcrumbs, starting with tomatoes, onions, breadcrumbs, and ending up with a thickish layer of breadcrumbs. Sprinkle each layer with a little salt and freshly ground black pepper. Cut the extra butter into bits and dot over the top of the last layer of crumbs. Bake at 180C/350F/Gas 4 for 45 to 55 minutes, or until the top is golden brown. An extra touch (not Mrs Beeton's) is to sprinkle each tomato layer with a little dried basil and sugar. *Serves 6.*

Baby Squash Stuffed with Guacamole

Avocado is usually served cold, which is fine when they are perfectly ripe and in the best of condition – but what if they are past their best? Here is a recipe for them to be served hot in combination with baby squash. Once you de-seed them, there is not a great deal of flesh left, hence the stuffing. These are ideal to serve with chops, roast lamb, chicken, or even as a first course on its own. If you fancy a hot flavour, then add some hot chilli sauce or chilli powder when blending the filling.

4 SMALL BABY SQUASH OR PUMPKINS

2 RIPE AVOCADOS, PEELED AND COARSELY CHOPPED

2 LARGE TOMATOES, PEELED, SEEDED AND COARSELY CHOPPED

2 SPRING ONIONS, CHOPPED

5 ml/1 tsp SALT

FRESHLY GROUND BLACK PEPPER

45 ml/3 tbsp LEMON JUICE

1 GREEN PEPPER, CORED, SEEDED AND CHOPPED

DASH OF TABASCO SAUCE

1 EXTRA TOMATO

8 BLACK OLIVES

Wipe the squash and place in a microwaveproof dish with 100 ml/4 fl oz (½ cup) water. Poke several holes with a skewer to stop the skins bursting, and microwave on High for 10 to 12 minutes, turning twice, until they start to soften. Alternatively, steam them until just tender. (Timing naturally depends on type, size and age, but do not allow them to overcook and become mushy, as you will be cooking them again when you have filled them.) Remove and leave to cool slightly so that you can handle them easily.

In the meantime, prepare the filling. Mash the avocados in a large bowl together with all the other ingredients, except the extra tomato and the olives (this will give you a somewhat chunky filling), or place in a food processor fitted with the steel blade and blend until smooth and creamy.

Slice the squash in half lengthways. Scoop out any seeds and discard. Now scoop out the remaining flesh, being careful not to pierce the sides of the squash. Place the flesh in a bowl, mash with a fork and add the guacamole filling to it; mix well. Divide the mixture equally and re-stuff back into the squash shells. Cut a large extra tomato into 4 thick slices and cut these slices in half. Place 2 halves on the top of each squash, butterfly fashion, and place a stoned black olive in the centre. Before serving reheat in an oven, covered with a piece of lightly buttered foil, or microwave until just heated through.

Note: these may be made ahead, in which case let them come back to room temperature after taking from the fridge and reheat for about 10 minutes at 180C/350F/Gas 4 in an oven, or about 3 minutes on High in a microwave. *Serves 4.*

Chicken Salad 'Lorraine' with Peanut Cream Sauce

As a main course salad or part of a larger buffet meal in the warmer weather, this dish take a lot of beating, for looks as well as taste. We named it for Lorraine Downes, who was Miss Universe 1983, and was a guest on our show.

2 CHICKENS

CARROT, ONION, BAY LEAF, 1 SPRIG FRESH THYME

12 CORIANDER SEEDS AND 12 BLACK PEPPERCORNS

½ LEMON

250 g/9 oz DRIED TAGLIATELLE

30 ml/2 tbsp GROUNDNUT (PEANUT) OIL

2 SMALL MELONS OF CONTRASTING COLOUR, SUCH AS CANTALOUPE AND HONEYDEW

SPRING ONIONS, FINELY CHOPPED (OPTIONAL)

Dressing

65 g/2½ oz (⅔ cup) SMOOTH PEANUT BUTTER

30 ml/2 tbsp LIGHT SOY SAUCE

2 CLOVES GARLIC, CRUSHED

5 cm/2 inch PIECE FRESH ROOT GINGER, GRATED

15 ml/1 tbsp CASTER SUGAR

15 ml/1 tbsp LEMON JUICE

2 DASHES TABASCO SAUCE

ABOUT 100 ml/4 fl oz (½ cup) SINGLE (LIGHT) CREAM

Place chickens in a large pan and just cover with water. Add sliced carrot, onion, bay leaf and thyme. Tie the coriander, peppercorns and lemon in a piece of muslin and add. Simmer about 40 minutes, until just tender. Cool in liquid, remove chickens, and strain the liquid into a bowl. Measure out 450 ml/¾ pint (2 cups) stock and boil down until you have 65 ml/2½ fl oz (⅓ cup) for the peanut sauce. When the chickens are cool enough to handle, remove skin, and cut into slices or bite-sized pieces; set aside.

Boil the noodles in the remaining strained chicken stock (possibly made up with a little extra water) according to packet directions – about 7 to 8 minutes. Drain – reserving the liquid – into a bowl. Into the drained noodles mix 30 ml/2 tbsp groundnut oil. Keep to one side to cool. You can now place all the skin and bones from the chicken, together with the liquid from the noodles, in a large saucepan, and reduce it for stock for another use.

Peel and seed the melons, and cut into wedges. Cover, and chill until needed. Place all the dressing ingredients, including the reduced stock, but not the cream, in a food processor or blender and blend until smooth. Tip into a bowl and thin with the cream until it is of a pouring consistency. Place the noodles on a serving plate and arrange the chicken slices and melon slices decoratively on them. Drizzle a little of the sauce over, and scatter over chopped spring onions, if desired. Serve the remaining sauce separately. *Serves 6 to 8.*

Ginger Ribboned Carrots

4 LARGISH CARROTS

10 ml/2 tsp CRUMBLED CHICKEN STOCK CUBE

30 ml/2 tbsp HONEY

2.5 ml/½ tsp GROUND GINGER

30 ml/2 tbsp BUTTER

Peel the carrots thinly with a vegetable peeler. Shave off ribbons of carrot with the peeler, trying to get the length of the carrot in 1 sweep. Press fairly hard with the peeler and rotate the carrot after several shavings are cut from the same place. (You won't be able to use all the carrot, especially the central woody portion, as you cannot hold it in your hand and keep cutting.) Bring a pan of water to the boil; add the chicken stock cube and toss in the carrots. Return to boiling point, and boil for 3 to 5 minutes, until just tender. Tip into a colander or sieve and rinse under running cold water; drain and place in a serving dish. *Note:* if you want to reheat later in a microwave, make sure the dish is microwaveproof. At this stage, you can hold these covered in cling film and keep in the fridge until you finish them off.

Drizzle the honey over the carrots, sprinkle on the ginger, then dot with butter. Either microwave for 3 or 4 minutes, stirring the carrots round half way through to coat with the butter, or cover with some buttered foil and heat in the oven. *Serves 4.*

A Javanese Bahmi

To devise tasty recipes that cater for vegetarians without making meat eaters feel deprived can sometimes be a problem. This dish can be made with or without meat. Without meat, it is still very satisfying, so that even the most carnivorous of friends should not feel left out. The red pepper sauce is hot . . . you will either love it, or drink the well dry. Sambal oelek can be purchased in most Chinese or Asian supermarkets, as well as some delicatessens. For the oven baking, we transfer the ingredients to a large, heavy paella dish, so that the Bahmi can come straight from the oven to the table. Even though it contains noodles, this dish goes well with steamed rice, plus chilled, peeled and seeded cucumbers cut into fingers, and lime wedges.

500 g/18 oz TAGLIATELLE OR OTHER NOODLES

45 ml/3 tbsp LIGHT SOY SAUCE

6.25 ml/1¼ tsp SALT

2.5 ml/½ tsp ANCHOVY PASTE

ABOUT 900 g/2 lb (4 cups) RAW CHICKEN, PORK OR BEEF (OPTIONAL), CHOPPED

15 ml/1 tbsp GROUNDNUT (PEANUT) OIL

30 g/ 1¼ oz BUTTER

2 ONIONS, SLICED

4 CLOVES GARLIC, SQUEEZED

350 g/12 oz (3 cups) CELERY, THINLY SLICED

7.5 ml/1½ tsp RED PEPPER SAUCE (SAMBAL OELEK)

1 SMALL CABBAGE, COARSELY CHOPPED

275 g/11 oz (2 cups) MANGE-TOUT, TIPS AND STRINGS REMOVED

2 LARGE TOMATOES, SKINNED AND CHOPPED

30 g/1¼ oz BUTTER

2 EGGS, SIZE 1, LIGHTLY BEATEN

Boil the noodles according to package instructions, drain and keep to one side. In a small bowl, mix together the soy sauce, salt and anchovy paste. If using the meat, mix these ingredients in a larger bowl, then add the meat and mix well.

In a large, heavy-based flameproof casserole, heat the oil and butter and add the onions, squeezed garlic, celery and red pepper sauce. Stir fry over high heat about 3 minutes until the vegetables are just tender crisp. Stir in soy sauce mixture (with meat if used), and cook for another 5 minutes, or until the meat has lost its raw appearance. Add drained noodles, cabbage and mange-tout, mix gently and cook for another 3 minutes. Remove from oven top and stir in the tomatoes. Cook, uncovered, in the oven at 150C/300F/Gas 2 for 15 minutes, stirring once or twice during that time. Remove, leave to cool completely, cover with cling film and refrigerate for 24 hours.

To reheat and serve, cook in a preheated oven at 150C/300F/Gas 2 for 35 to 40 minutes, until piping hot, stirring several times during that period. While this is reheating, melt the butter in a large frying pan and tip in the beaten eggs; tilt the pan quickly to disperse the liquid egg over the base. Cook gently until the egg is set, slide onto a cutting board and slice into 1 cm/½ inch ribbons. Arrange on the heated Bahmi in a lattice fashion just before serving. *Serves 6*

Beetroot and Orange

Beetroot is not often used except for salads, yet the colour makes it so good to serve as a hot vegetable, especially to accompany a pale meat. This recipe calls for fresh beetroot, but you can use whole baby ones that have been canned in water or brine; do not use ones that have been canned in a vinegar solution. Make sure that the glaze has thickened slightly before you add the beetroots, as you don't want to turn them into a mush.

25 g/1 oz UNSALTED BUTTER

30 ml/2 tbsp ORANGE MARMALADE

50 ml/2 fl oz (¼ cup) FRESH ORANGE JUICE

500 g/18 oz COOKED BEETROOTS

Using a heavy-based saucepan, melt the butter with the marmalade; then add the orange juice and bring to the boil. Lower the heat and simmer for about 2 minutes. Dice the beetroots and add. Simmer very gently, stirring from time to time, until most of the liquid has evaporated and has glazed the beetroots. *Serves 4 to 6.*

To cook fresh beetroots. Firstly choose small beetroots of a similar size so that they will cook quickly. Trim off the green stalks fairly close to the beetroots, but do not cut into the beetroots, or they will bleed during cooking and lose their rich colour. Place the beetroot in a large saucepan and cover with cold water. Add to the pan 3 cloves of peeled garlic, 8 whole black peppercorns, 2 bay leaves and 2.5 ml/½ tsp salt. Gradually bring to the boil, cover, lower the heat and gently simmer, about 15 minutes, until just cooked, depending on the size and freshness. Test by inserting a skewer into them; you should meet some resistance, about that of boiled new potatoes. When cooked, drain and run under cold water to cool. Cut off the stem close to the beet and slip off the skins under running water so as not to discolour your hands. Place in a glass bowl, cool, cover with cling film and keep in the fridge until ready to use.

Pumpkin Salad

This is a delightful change from potato salad. For a change we like to add a little cayenne pepper and a chopped apple. The pumpkin mustn't be overcooked. Steam or microwave the cubes till just tender or cook them in water. To boil them, cover the cubes with water, bring to the boil, lower the heat, cover and cook for 5 minutes. Remove from the heat and let stand, covered, till tender; look in the pan now and again and test with the point of a knife.

1 kg/2¼ lb PUMPKIN, PEELED AND CUBED

75g/3 oz (¾ cup) WALNUTS, CHOPPED

6 SPRING ONIONS, CHOPPED, INCLUDING SOME GREEN

30 ml/2 tbsp (¼ cup) FINELY CHOPPED PARSLEY

SALT AND FINELY GROUND BLACK PEPPER, TO TASTE

1 STALK CELERY, THINLY SLICED

225 g/8 oz (1 cup) MAYONNAISE, PREFERABLY HOMEMADE (p. 186)

Having cooked the pumpkin until *just* tender, drain and refresh in cold water (this not only maintains the colour, but stops the pumpkin cooking in its own heat). Place in a colander lined with kitchen paper to drain thoroughly. Now place in a serving bowl, cover and chill until ready to serve. Add all the ingredients, except mayonnaise, and toss gently, until well combined. Pour in the mayonnaise and toss gently again. *Serves 6.*

Orange Baked Parsnips

Some people have an aversion to parsnips, but this recipe will change their opinion. Choose small, young parsnips rather than large ones, which tend to have a 'woody' interior. The dish may be assembled in advance, except for the butter, covered with cling film and kept in the fridge till ready to bake.

12 SMALL PARSNIPS

225 g/8 oz (1 cup) CANNED CRUSHED PINEAPPLE, WELL DRAINED

100 ml/4 fl oz (½ cup) FRESH ORANGE JUICE

30 ml/2 tbsp BROWN SUGAR

GRATED RIND OF 1 ORANGE

FEW GRATINGS NUTMEG

5 ml/1 tsp FINELY CHOPPED FRESH ROOT GINGER

50 g/2 oz BUTTER

Thinly peel the parsnips and trim both ends, leaving the parsnips whole. Bring a large saucepan of lightly salted water to the boil and pop in the parsnips. Cook about 10 minutes, until just tender – do not overcook. Mix the crushed pineapple, orange juice, brown sugar, orange rind, nutmeg and chopped ginger together. Drain the parsnips and split them in half lengthways. Place them in an ovenproof dish large enough to accommodate them in a single layer. Spoon the pineapple mixture over them equally and dot with the butter. Bake, uncovered, for 30 minutes at 175C/340F/Gas 3½. *Serves 4 to 6.*

Cabbage and Cheese

This will make non cabbage-eaters eat cabbage – it really is delicious, and a breeze to cook. It's excellent with corned beef or even frankfurters.

1 MEDIUM-SIZED CABBAGE, OR ½ LARGE ONE, WASHED AND SHREDDED

125 ml/4 oz FULL-FAT SOFT CHEESE, CUT INTO CUBES

30 ml/2 tbsp MILK

2.5 ml/½ tsp SALT

2.5 ml/½ tsp CELERY OR CARAWAY SEEDS

SEVERAL GRINDINGS BLACK PEPPER

PAPRIKA FOR DUSTING

Microwave version. Place the shredded cabbage in a large, microwaveproof casserole with a lid. Add 30 ml/2 tbsp water, cover and cook on High for 7 to 9 minutes, or until just tender; stir several times during the cooking time. Add the remaining ingredients, with the exception of the paprika, and cook again on High for another minute. Remove from oven, remove the lid carefully and stir the cabbage gently to distribute the cheese. Serve, dusted with paprika.

Oven-top version. Simmer the shredded cabbage with 450 ml/¾ pint (2 cups) water in a large, covered saucepan until just tender, stirring occasionally; do not overcook. Drain thoroughly, return to the pan and keep warm over a low heat. Place the cubed cheese, milk, salt, celery seeds and pepper in a small, separate pan, and stir over low heat until the cheese has melted. Pour over the cabbage and mix gently. Serve, dusted with paprika. *Serves 6.*

Fresh Green Salad with Fresh Herbs

A really fresh green salad is still hard to beat. We like a combination of lettuces or lettuce and spinach. There are many varieties of lettuce on the market now, such as cos, iceberg and butterhead, so try some combinations for change! Almost any fresh herbs you have to hand will enhance a green salad – except basil and rosemary, which are a bit too pungent and better used on their own. The lettuce should be washed quickly in water, dried very well (this allows the dressing to adhere to the leaves more readily), placed in a polythene bag and refrigerated on the day required. Lettuce for a salad should be torn, never cut with a knife, as the metal tends to turn the cut edges brown and unattractive.

LETTUCE LEAVES OR COMBINATION OF LETTUCE AND SPINACH

SEVERAL SPRIGS FRESH THYME, LEAVES REMOVED FROM STALKS

ABOUT 8 SPRIGS FRESH CORIANDER OR PARSLEY

6 CHIVES, SNIPPED

3 SPRIGS APPLE MINT, OR OTHER COMBINATIONS OF HERBS AS AVAILABLE

5 ml/1 tsp SALAD OIL (NOT OLIVE OIL)

50 g/2 oz (⅓ cup) PINE NUTS

Dressing

1.25 ml/¼ tsp SUGAR

1 CLOVE GARLIC, CRUSHED (IF GARLIC CHIVES NOT USED)

1.25 ml/¼ tsp SALT

FEW GRINDS BLACK PEPPER

65 ml/2½ fl oz (⅓ cup) VEGETABLE OIL, OR HALF SALAD, HALF GOOD OLIVE OIL

JUICE OF 1½ LEMONS

In a bowl, assemble the torn lettuce leaves and whatever herbs you intend using. Set aside. In a small, heavy-based frying pan, heat the 5 ml/1 tsp oil. When oil is moderately hot, tip in the pine nuts and stir until golden brown; drain on kitchen paper.

To make the dressing, mix the sugar, garlic, salt and pepper together until the sugar is well crushed. Add the oil and whisk with a wire whisk or fork until well blended. Add the lemon juice last and whisk until the dressing has turned opaque (this means the ingredients have been amalgamated).

Just before serving, add the pine nuts, the dressing and toss. *Serves 4.*

Tomato, Carrot and Orange Salad

This salad relies totally on the freshness of the ingredients for its flavour. It is very good to serve before a thick steak or something robust, such as Burgundy Beef (p. 70) or venison. For the dressing you might like to try the various flavoured vinegars that are now on the market instead of red wine vinegar. Raspberry vinegar is a lovely alternative.

Salad

4 LARGE, RIPE, FIRM TOMATOES

2 ORANGES

4 SMALL CARROTS

LETTUCE LEAVES

Dressing

150 ml/5 fl oz (⅔ cup) GROUNDNUT (PEANUT) OIL

JUICE AND FINELY GRATED RIND OF 1 ORANGE

15 ml/1 tbsp RED WINE VINEGAR

5 ml/1 tsp DIJON MUSTARD

5 ml/1 tsp CASTER SUGAR

SALT AND FRESHLY GROUND BLACK PEPPER

Skin and seed the tomatoes, then cut them into wedges. Peel the oranges thickly so as to remove all the pith, then cut into segments. Peel carrots and grate or julienne them in a food processor or by hand. Line 4 individual bowls with some washed lettuce leaves and arrange the tomato wedges, orange segments and carrot attractively on them. Whisk all the salad dressing ingredients together. Pour a little over each salad just before serving and pass the remainder separately. *Serves 4.*

Vegetable Custards

This is a very adaptable recipe. You can use puréed asparagus, cauliflower with 15 ml/1 tbsp of grated Parmesan cheese added, grated and well-drained courgettes, sautéed onions or mushrooms, broccoli, well-drained spinach, pumpkin – practically anything. You may find that when you turn them out a slight separation occurs between the custard and the vegetable; no matter – they will look attractive and taste delicious.

Should you make these in advance, take out of the oven after 20 minutes and leave to one side. To reheat, replace the water in the ovenproof dish with boiling water and pop into the oven for about 15 minutes to heat through.

350 g/12 oz (1½ cups) COOKED VEGETABLES

225 ml/8 fl oz (1 cup) CHICKEN STOCK, WARM, PREFERABLY HOMEMADE (p. 183)

100 ml/4 fl oz (½ cup) SINGLE (LIGHT) CREAM

4 EGGS, SIZE 1

1.25 ml/¼ tsp SALT

8 GRINDINGS BLACK PEPPER

4 GRATINGS NUTMEG

Purée the chosen vegetable in a food processor fitted with a steel blade and add the other ingredients; blend for about 20 seconds. Spoon the mixture into 4 well-buttered 225 ml/ 8 fl oz (1 cup) moulds and cover each with a square of buttered foil, pressing down round the sides. Place in an ovenproof dish and fill to half way up the moulds with hot water. Bake at 170C/325F/Gas 3 for about 25 minutes, or until when tested with a thin skewer it comes out clean. Remove from oven and allow to stand for a few minutes to set; run a knife round the edge to loosen and tip onto a serving dish. *Makes 4.*

PASTA AND SAUCES, RICE DISHES AND... TWO BREADS

Years ago, pasta dishes consisted of macaroni cheese (the ideal thing for the budget) and tinned spaghetti in tomato sauce. These days a wide variety of types and shapes of pasta is available, but we still fall back on our own simple, homemade version, which is truly superb. Because we make ours from standard flour and not the strong flours that most commercial pasta is made from, we do stress that you should cook it for only a very short time.

From the traditional spaghetti with homemade tomato or meat sauce, to the more elaborate concoctions like lasagne, pastas supply a very satisfying meal that is not too heavy on the pocket.

Rice is a valuable staple that is often overlooked. It can be simply cooked and with some herbs and a little butter stirred in, goes very well with many main course dishes as well as the familiar curry. We now have many varieties of rice on the market, plus prepared packaged products that can be a boon to the person putting together a meal in a hurry who wants a change from potatoes.

The sauces that we mention in this section are easy to prepare and not too costly, with the exception of one, Truffle Sauce – we include it in case you strike it lucky and are given some truffles, either fresh or canned.

We have included 2 homemade breads as they are simple to make and excellent to accompany soups, pâtés or starters. Ideal for mopping up those superb sauces, they act the same way as pasta and rice in helping to pad out a meal and blunt the appetite.

Homemade Pasta and Simple Sauces

The virtues of homemade pasta are three-fold; it's delicious, relatively simple to make and inexpensive. Even the simple dressings or sauces that you use with it are quick to prepare and not usually costly. (Mind you, in Italy it gets rather expensive when they coat the pasta with slices or shavings of truffles.) With a simple, hand-cranked pasta machine making it is very easy, but even if you make it entirely by hand it is one of those jobs that give you great satisfaction. Most pasta recipes call for special strong flours, and although these are available, this recipe is for a simple flour pasta that you can make easily using plain flour. We will describe 2 methods: firstly the one by hand, strong arms being an essential requirement, and secondly by manual machine (much easier). There are electric machines available, and also machines that make and produce the end result automatically.

A word about Parmesan cheese, an essential ingredient in 2 sauce recipes given here. We prefer for taste and texture to prepare our own rather than buy it already grated. Take the quantity of Parmesan required in one piece, cut into small, thinnish slices and gradually drop through the feed tube of a food processor fitted with the steel blade while the motor is running. Keep chopping with a mixture of continuous and occasionally on-off motions until the cheese has the appearance of fine granules. It is much more economical to do it this way, and has a better flavour. Any left over can be wrapped tightly in foil and frozen for up to 1 month without too much loss of flavour.

200-225 g/7-8 oz (about 1½ cups) PLAIN FLOUR, PLUS EXTRA FOR ROLLING

2 EGGS, SIZE 1

10 ml/2 tsp OIL (FLAVOUR IS NOT IMPORTANT IN THIS INSTANCE, AS YOU DON'T TASTE IT IN THE END RESULT)

5 ml/1 tsp SALT

FEW DROPS WATER

15 ml/1 tbsp OIL FOR COOKING

By hand. Place the flour in a large mixing bowl and make a well in the centre. Add the eggs, oil and salt, and with a fork start mixing the dough together. When it starts to form a ball and is dry enough to handle, continue to mix with your hands, add just a few drops of water if needed, to gather it together into a ball (you do not want it to be too wet). Now knead the dough on a lightly floured surface for 10 minutes, adding extra flour if needed to keep it from sticking to the surface. When it has been kneaded into a smooth, elastic dough, place in a polythene bag and leave to rest for 15 minutes. (By this time you will need a rest also.)

Divide the dough in 2 and roll each piece out very thinly. You will need a long, thin rolling pin for this (they are available). Keep the second half of the dough in the bag while you do the first. The dough should be thin enough that you could read the printing of a book through it. To make fettucine, dust the surface of the dough lightly with flour and leave for 5 to 10 minutes for it to dry out slightly, certainly not long enough for it to become brittle – the time depends on the heat of the working area and the humidity. Roll it up fairly tightly, as for a Swiss roll, and then with a very sharp, heavy knife cut it into slices about half the thickness of a finger. Unroll straight away and hang over the back of a chair on dry tea-towels, or over pieces of dowelling (racks can be made or bought for this purpose). To cook, bring a large pan of well salted water to the boil, add about 15 ml/1 tbsp oil to help prevent it boiling over, and cook the pasta for about 3 minutes. As this is a very soft dough, it cooks much more quickly than commercial pasta.

By machine. (This recipe is not suitable for automatic machines.) Place the flour, eggs, oil and salt into the bowl of a food processor fitted with the steel blade, cover with the lid and switch on. After 30 seconds switch off, then proceed to mix using the pulse switch with an on-off motion. Add tiny amounts of water until the pasta starts to 'ball'. Tip out onto a floured surface and knead just a little until you have a ball of dough, place in a polythene bag and leave to rest for 15 minutes.

Assemble your pasta machine (manual) and divide the dough into 6 to 8 pieces. Setting the rollers to their widest, start rolling dough through the rollers, folding in half each time and dusting with some flour occasionally to prevent sticking. Do this about 10 times, or until the dough is smooth and elastic and has lost any crumbly appearance. (This takes the place of lengthy hand-kneading.) Do this with each piece of dough and set aside on a lightly floured surface lightly covered with a dry tea-towel. Now take each piece and re-roll twice more through the widest setting, then reduce the setting to half its maximum number and roll through once again; by this time the length of the dough has extended. Set to the second-thinnest setting. (Most machines number from 1, the widest setting, to about 7 or 10, the thinnest setting, so you should try 6 or 9, according to your machine.) As this is a soft and slightly fragile dough, don't go to the thinnest setting. Place on dry tea-towels after you have rolled it thin and leave until you have finished with all your dough before proceeding to cut it up with the machine on the fettucine cutters. Hang to dry as in the hand method before cooking or to store for a few days. This is not the type of pasta that keeps for a long time, so plan to use within 2 to 3 days. Cook as for handmade version.

The next 5 recipes suggest simple ways of dressing and serving this creation:

Garlic, Parsley and Oil

100 ml/4 fl oz (½ cup) OLIVE OIL

4 to 6 CLOVES GARLIC

15 g/½ oz (½ cup) FINELY CHOPPED FRESH PARSLEY

FRESHLY GRATED PARMESAN CHEESE

Place the oil in a small saucepan and crush the garlic into it. Place over a low heat and warm slightly so that the garlic infuses the oil with its flavour. Do not let it get too hot (will take about 5 minutes). Meanwhile, cook and drain the pasta and tip it into a warm serving dish. Pour over the oil and garlic and mix in. Place into individual heated bowls and sprinkle with parsley. Pass the Parmesan cheese separately. *Serves 4 to 6.*

Crab and Artichoke Heart Sauce

2 MEDIUM ONIONS, FINELY SLICED

45 ml/3 tbsp OIL

200 g/7 oz CAN ARTICHOKE HEARTS

2 CLOVES GARLIC, CRUSHED

300 ml/½ pint (1¼ cups) MILK

175 g/6 oz (1½ cups) MILD CHEDDAR, GRATED

SALT AND FRESHLY GROUND BLACK PEPPER

170 g/6 oz CAN CRAB MEAT

50 ml/2 fl oz (¼ cup) MEDIUM-DRY SHERRY

500 g/18 oz HOMEMADE NOODLES

FINELY CHOPPED FRESH PARSLEY

Place the onions in a saucepan with the oil. Simmer them gently with the lid on, until soft but not browned. Drain the artichoke hearts, cut in half and add to the onions together with the garlic, milk, cheese and a little seasoning. Cook slowly, stirring all the time, until the cheese has melted. (Do not be tempted to do this over a very high heat or the cheese will exude its fat and spoil the sauce. Should this happen, remove from the heat and mix together 10 ml/2 tsp cornflour with 50 ml/2 fl oz (¼ cup) water, pour into the sauce and stir until thickened.) Drain and flake the crab meat and add together with the sherry to the cheese sauce; warm through gently.

Cook and drain the pasta, tip into a warm serving bowl, pour over the sauce and mix carefully. Serve sprinkled with the finely chopped parsley. *Serves 4.*

With Butter and Cream

125 g/4 oz UNSALTED BUTTER, SOFTENED

50 ml/2 fl oz (¼ cup) SINGLE (LIGHT) CREAM

175 g/6 oz (½ cup) PARMESAN CHEESE, FRESHLY GRATED

EXTRA PARMESAN CHEESE AND FRESHLY GROUND BLACK PEPPER, TO FINISH

Beat the butter in a bowl with a wooden spoon until creamy; gradually beat in the cream bit by bit, until incorporated. Fold in the Parmesan. Cook and drain the fettucine and place in a warm serving bowl, spoon on the creamy butter mixture and mix well. Serve with additional cheese and lots of freshly ground black pepper. *Serves 4 to 6.*

Truffle Sauce

The Italians use white truffles, shaved very thin, with pasta, and it is quite expensive. You can use black truffles if you wish. At first we were not going to give the recipe, then we thought, why not, you may get lucky and find someone rich has given you some and you don't know how to use them. It is not worth making this expensive sauce and serving it over just any pasta, or pasta that might be old and horrid. Either make your own or buy it from someone that you know makes it from the best ingredients.

125 g/4 oz TRUFFLES, FRESH OR TINNED, CHOPPED

3 ANCHOVY FILLETS, WELL DRAINED

15 ml/1 tbsp FINELY CHOPPED FRESH PARSLEY

SCANT 100 ml/4 fl oz (⅜ cup) GOOD OLIVE OIL

2 CLOVES GARLIC, HALVED

60 ml/4 tbsp TOMATO PURÉE (PASTE)

225 ml/8 fl oz (1 cup) WARM WATER

SALT, TO TASTE

ABOUT 500 g/18 oz HOMEMADE NOODLES, COOKED AND DRAINED

Place the chopped truffles in a mortar with the anchovy fillets and pound them to a paste, then work in the chopped parsley. You can do this in a blender if you wish, but there is much more satisfaction in doing it in a mortar with a pestle – somehow it seems so decadent to mash up truffles. Meanwhile, warm the oil together with the cut garlic (don't let it get too hot), take it off the heat and let the garlic steep in it for about 6 minutes to imbue the oil with the fragrance. Remove the pieces of garlic and add the pounded truffle mixture to the oil. Dilute the purée with the warm water and add this to the oil and truffle mixture. Add salt if needed, stir until just below boiling point and serve over the cooked drained pasta. Good luck to you all, rich devils . . . *Serves 4.*

Chicken Liver and Mushroom Sauce

500 g/18 oz CHICKEN LIVERS

500 g/18 oz BUTTON MUSHROOMS

25 g/1 oz (1 cup) FINELY CHOPPED FRESH PARSLEY

2 CLOVES GARLIC, CRUSHED

90 ml/6 tbsp OLIVE OR GROUNDNUT (PEANUT) OIL

ABOUT 500 g/18 oz HOMEMADE NOODLES

100 g/4 oz BUTTER, MELTED

Trim and check the chicken livers, place in a bowl and pour over enough boiling water to cover them. Leave for 5 minutes, then drain. Slice the mushrooms either by hand or with the slicing disc of a food processor and set aside. Place the livers, chopped parsley and garlic in a food processor fitted with the steel blade and chop with an on-off motion (do not over-chop and turn them into a paste). Place 45 ml/3 tbsp oil into a non-stick frying pan and cook the livers until they lose their raw colour, then push to one side. Add the remaining oil and tip in the sliced mushrooms; cook all together for about another 3 minutes. Cook and drain the pasta, tip into a warm serving bowl, pour over the melted butter, then the sauce and mix together. Rich and very satisfying. *Serves 4 to 6.*

Steamed Rice

There are many methods of cooking rice; this is very easy. A basic thing to remember is that 200 g/oz (1 cup) raw rice yields three times as much when cooked. Try a wedge of lemon in the first boiling water – keeps the rice nice and white.

WATER

15 ml/1 tbsp SALT

400 g/14 oz (2 cups) LONG-GRAINED RICE

In large pan, bring about 4 litres/7 pints water to the boil; add the salt. On a good rolling boil sprinkle in the rice; try to keep the water boiling all the time to prevent the rice sticking on the bottom. Boil, uncovered, for 10 minutes. Tip into a colander, drain, rinse thoroughly in hot water and shake well. Bring some more water to the boil in the same pan. Place the colander on top of the pan, over the water, not in it; cover with a tea towel and then the lid, then steam for 15 minutes. It should be fluffy and dry. Check every now and again to make sure the water hasn't boiled away. *Makes 6-8 servings.*

To cook rice in the microwave. In a large glass or ceramic bowl (not metal), microwave 200 g/7 oz (1 cup) washed rice and 950 ml/1 ¼ pints (3 cups) water on full power for 15 minutes (we fork it up half way through) . . . done!

Spaghetti Carbonara

You might call this the 'bacon and egg' dish of Italian cooking. It is very quick to prepare – don't linger when you are adding the eggs to make the sauce, or you will end up with 'scrambled carbonara' instead of a creamy sauce. The spaghetti must be cooked just al dente, and must be very hot when you serve it, so that the egg mixture cooks just slightly when the whole is mixed together.

30 g/1¼ oz BUTTER

30 ml/2 tbsp OLIVE OIL

3 RASHERS BACON, RINDED AND DICED

2 SLICES HAM, CUT INTO THIN STRIPS

3 EGGS, SIZE 1

75 g/3 oz (⅔ cup) PARMESAN CHEESE, OR
40 g/1½ oz (⅓ cup) PARMESAN AND 40 g/1½ oz (⅓ cup) ROMANO CHEESE

ABOUT 500 g/18 oz SPAGHETTI

FINELY CHOPPED FRESH PARSLEY, TO SERVE

In a medium-sized saucepan, heat together the butter and the oil over moderate heat. Cook the bacon and the ham until the bacon starts to brown slightly. While this is cooking, beat the eggs together and the cheese until well mixed, using a whisk. Assuming that you have cooked the spaghetti, drain it and place in a hot serving bowl. Take the bacon and ham off the heat, and immediately stir in all the egg and cheese mixture. Stir rapidly to mix and pour over the hot spaghetti. Mix all together and the heat of the spaghetti will cook the egg mixture slightly. Dust with extra cheese if desired and also very finely chopped parsley. *Serves 4 to 6.*

Risotto with Chicken Liver Sauce

A risotto is a good basis for many dishes; it can be served on its own as a simple luncheon dish, or as a side dish, or even added to, as in this case, to make a substantial meal. It is best to try and buy Italian rice for this as the texture of the end result is better and slightly drier. Should you not use Italian rice, called arborio, use long-grained rice rather than the softer, shorter, fatter-grained types with which you make a rice pudding. Good homemade stock enhances the flavour of the end result, although in this instance commercial stock is quite acceptable. The stock used depends on what you are adding after the risotto has cooked. In this case use chicken stock to go with the livers.

Basic Risotto

25 g/1 oz BUTTER

30 ml/2 tbsp OLIVE OIL

1 SMALL ONION, FINELY CHOPPED

1 SMALL CLOVE GARLIC, CRUSHED

200 g/7 oz (1 cup) RICE, WASHED AND THOROUGHLY DRAINED

825 ml/28 fl oz (3½ cups) HOT STOCK, CHICKEN OR BEEF, PREFERABLY HOMEMADE
(pp. 182, 183)

25 g/1 oz BUTTER

25 g/1 oz (¼ cup) PARMESAN CHEESE, GRATED

SALT AND FRESHLY GROUND BLACK PEPPER

EXTRA PARMESAN CHEESE, TO SERVE (OPTIONAL)

In a heavy-based saucepan with a tight-fitting lid, heat the butter and oil together over moderate heat. Add the onion and cook until it is pale gold, then stir in the crushed garlic. Add the drained rice and continue to stir while cooking, until it is well coated with the butter and oil and takes on a pale golden hue. Add 225 ml/8 fl oz (1 cup) of the heated stock, cover the pan and cook over gentle heat until the liquid has been absorbed. Pour in the remaining heated stock, cover and simmer gently, stirring occasionally, until the stock has been absorbed and the rice is cooked. This will take about 20 minutes. Stir in the extra butter and the Parmesan and serve at once. Add additional salt and pepper to taste at the table, plus extra Parmesan, if you require it. *Serves 4.*

Chicken Liver Sauce

You will probably find it easier to prepare the chicken livers if you place them in a small basin and cover them with boiling water to stiffen them slightly before cleaning and cutting into pieces. Just steep them for about 5 minutes in the hot water, drain, and proceed when they have cooled down enough to allow you to handle them easily.

1 ONION, FINELY CHOPPED

25 g/1 oz BUTTER

8 CHICKEN LIVERS, THAWED IF FROZEN, CLEANED AND CHOPPED

SMALL STRIP LEMON RIND

6 MUSHROOMS, SLICED

45 ml/3 tbsp CHICKEN STOCK

30 ml/2 tbsp DRY VERMOUTH OR DRY MADEIRA

SALT AND FRESHLY GROUND BLACK PEPPER

PARMESAN CHEESE, TO SERVE (OPTIONAL)

Sauté the onion in the butter until it turns pale gold. Add the prepared livers, the lemon rind and the sliced mushrooms and cook over moderate heat for about 3 minutes, stirring once or twice. Add the stock and vermouth or Madeira, cover the pan and simmer gently for 10 minutes. Remove the lemon rind and check for seasoning. Serve over the cooked risotto and pass the Parmesan separately. *Serves 4.*

Macaroni Cheese

There is so much you can do with this Macaroni Cheese – throw in virtually anything you fancy and you get an interesting dish. The recipe has a German influence, because of the sausage and the mustard. You could go Italian with tomatoes, basil and Parmesan. If you want to extend the dish, serve some lightly boiled cabbage with it, drained and tossed in a little melted butter. Please don't cook the cabbage till it has the consistency of a well used floor mop!

250 g/9 oz ELBOW MACARONI

BOILING SALTED WATER

375 g/13 oz GARLIC SAUSAGE OR POLISH SAUSAGE, THINLY SLICED

60 ml/4 tbsp BUTTER

2 LARGE ONIONS, CHOPPED

GENEROUS 25 g/1 oz (¼ cup) PLAIN FLOUR

450 ml/¾ pint (2 cups) MILK

20 ml/4 tsp PREPARED GERMAN MUSTARD

2.5 ml/½ tsp CARAWAY SEEDS

2.5 ml/½ tsp SALT

ABOUT 1.25 ml/¼ tsp FRESHLY GROUND BLACK PEPPER

350 g/12 oz (3 cups) EMMENTHAL CHEESE, SHREDDED

Cook the macaroni in boiling salted water according to packet instructions, drain and rinse in warm water, then drain again.

In a heavy-based frying pan over medium heat, brown the sausage slices in 15 ml/1 tbsp of the butter. Remove from the pan with a slotted spoon and set aside. In the same pan cook the onions in the rest of the butter, until lightly golden. Stir in the flour, mix well, then slowly stir in the milk to make a nice thick sauce. Cook for about 3 minutes, stirring all the time. Remove from the heat and stir in the mustard, caraway seeds, salt and pepper and the macaroni. Stir until well mixed.

Butter an ovenproof dish and place half the macaroni mixture in it. Arrange half the sausage over this and top with half the cheese . . . add the rest of the macaroni, then the sausage, ending with a cheese topping. Cover with cling film and refrigerate overnight.

Preheat oven to 190C/375F/Gas 5. Place dish in the centre of the oven and cook for about 35 minutes, or until the dish is bubbly and the cheese is lightly browned. *Serves 6.*

Risotto with Salami

55 g/21 oz (3 cups) RICE

30 ml/2 tbsp BUTTER

37.5 ml/2½ tbsp OLIVE OIL

1 ONION, FINELY CHOPPED

500 g/18 oz SALAMI, PEELED AND CHOPPED COARSELY (WE USE PEPPERONI – VERY HOT)

2 CLOVES GARLIC, FINELY CHOPPED

15 ml/1 tbsp FINELY CHOPPED FRESH BASIL, OR 7.5 ml/1½ tsp DRIED

15 ml/1 tbsp FINELY CHOPPED FRESH CORIANDER OR PARSLEY

525 g/21 oz (3 cups) RICE

1.5 litres/2½ pints (6 cups) CHICKEN STOCK

2 x 230 g cans PLUM TOMATOES, CHOPPED WITH JUICE RESERVED

75 g/3 oz (¾ cup) PARMESAN CHEESE, FRESHLY GRATED

45 ml/3 tbsp BUTTER, CUBED

SALT AND FRESHLY GROUND BLACK PEPPER

Wash the rice well, until the water is clear; tip into a sieve and let dry. In a very large, heavy-based saucepan, heat butter and oil over moderate heat. Add onion, salami, garlic, basil and coriander or parsley and sauté about 10 minutes, until onions are transparent, stirring now and then. Tip drained rice into onion mixture and stir for 5 minutes to make sure all the rice is well covered with the mixture. Heat the chicken stock. Add 225 ml/8 fl oz (1 cup) to the rice, stir and cook, uncovered, about 10 minutes, until the stock has been absorbed. Add the tomatoes and their juice and stir until this liquid has been absorbed. Now add the remaining chicken stock, 225 ml/8 fl oz (1 cup) at a time, waiting until each addition has been absorbed by the rice. When the final addition of stock has been absorbed the rice should be done. It mustn't be mushy, just tender. If not quite tender enough for your taste, add a little more stock and cook until that is absorbed. Remove from heat and stir in the Parmesan cheese, then add the cubed butter and season with salt and pepper. Serve at once in soup plates. *Serves 6.*

Spaghetti with Green Peppercorn and Mushroom Cream Sauce

The better the spaghetti the more superb this dish. If you make your own pasta (fettucine, for instance) it lifts the dish to the realms of magnificence. To make crème fraiche, take a clean jar with a tight-fitting lid, pour in 225 ml/8 fl oz (1 cup) double (heavy) cream, add 15 ml/1 tbsp yoghurt or sour cream (or, preferably, buttermilk, if it is available), screw on the lid and shake hard for 1 minute. Leave with the top on in a warm place for at least 8 hours (this is extremely important); when ready to use it should be very thick. This is superb when fresh strawberries are in season. Wash the strawberries just before serving (leaving the stalks on) and pat dry. Serve with a bowl of unrefined sugar and a bowl of crème fraiche. Roll the strawberry in the crème fraiche then in the sugar, then eat ... magnifico! Back to the spaghetti – sorry about the diversion.

75 g/3 oz UNSALTED BUTTER

30 ml/2 tbsp GREEN PEPPERCORNS, DRAINED AND CHOPPED (MAKES THEM STRONGER)

100 g/4 oz (2 cups) MUSHROOMS, SLICED

225 g/8 oz (1 cup) CRÈME FRAICHE

SALT AND FRESHLY GROUND BLACK PEPPER, TO TASTE (IF REQUIRED)

250 g/9 oz SPAGHETTI, COOKED UNTIL JUST TENDER (AL DENTE)

FRESHLY GRATED PARMESAN CHEESE, TO SERVE

In a heavy-based frying pan, melt the butter over moderate heat and sauté the peppercorns for a few seconds, stirring all the time. Add the mushrooms and cook for about 5 minutes, stirring constantly. Stir in the crème fraiche, stir and cook until hot, but don't let it boil. Add seasoning if you wish. Pour the sauce over the well drained spaghetti and serve. Serve separately a bowl of freshly grated Parmesan cheese. *Serves 2.*

French Bread

This bread really isn't very difficult to make – we have made it many times successfully, and so can you. We have found over the years that the quality of the flour varies from time to time, and also weather has a great effect on how the flour will react. However, the results are usually pretty good. The boiling water helps achieve a crisp crust. Half way through the cooking, some people spray the loaves with iced water . . . go on, we dare you!

15 ml/1 tbsp DRIED YEAST

10 ml/2 tsp SALT

15 ml/1 tbsp SUGAR

450 ml/¾ pint (2 cups) LUKEWARM WATER

ABOUT 600 g/1¼ lb (4 cups) PLAIN FLOUR, SIFTED

A LITTLE CORNMEAL

A LITTLE MELTED BUTTER

In large bowl, dissolve the yeast, salt and sugar in 450 ml/¾ pint (2 cups) lukewarm water. Stir until all ingredients are well dissolved. Gradually stir in the sifted flour. You may need a little more than the 600 g/1¼ lb (4 cups); this is hard to judge accurately, but add flour until the dough will absorb no more. Knead the dough on a large floured surface 3 to 4 minutes, until slightly elastic. Lightly grease a clean bowl, place the kneaded dough in it, cover with a damp tea towel (we rinse it out in hot water), place in a warm spot and let rise for 1 hour.

In the meantime, butter a baking tray and sprinkle with cornmeal; shake off the excess. Divide the risen dough in half and lightly and quickly shape the 2 halves into long, narrow loaves on the baking tray. With a very sharp knife lightly slash diagonal lines across the top of the loaves. Leave to rise for a further 45 minutes, uncovered.

Preheat the oven to 230C/450F/Gas 8. Place one oven rack in the lowest part of the oven and place on it a large shallow pan of boiling water . . . very, very important! Place the other rack in the middle of the oven. Brush the risen loaves with a little melted butter, place on the middle rack and bake for 5 minutes. Lower temperature to 190C/375F/Gas 5 and bake the loaves for another 35 minutes. Remove from oven and place on a rack to cool. *Makes 2 loaves.*

Pagnotta (Italian Bread)

For those who are intimidated by yeast cookery, here is the answer to your prayers – and virtually fail-safe loaf of bread. It is one bread recipe that we have never had a failure with. The taste and keeping qualities, plus of course, the immense satisfaction of making a daily staple which is delicious, make it worth trying this recipe even if you haven't had success before. The texture of this loaf is probably denser than that of most breads made with yeast.

15 ml/1 tbsp DRIED YEAST

100 ml/4 fl oz (½ cup) WARM WATER

2.5 ml/½ tsp SUGAR

562.5 g/22½ oz (4½ cups) PLAIN FLOUR

5 ml /1 tsp SALT

15 ml/1 tbsp OLIVE OIL

EXTRA 225 ml/8 fl oz (1 cup) WARM WATER

Mix the yeast and 100 ml/4 fl oz (½ cup) warm water in a bowl, sprinkle over the sugar, cover and leave to stand in a warm place for 15 to 20 minutes, until it is nice and foamy.

Into a large bowl, sift together the flour and the salt; make a well in the centre and pour in the yeast mixture, olive oil and extra 225 ml/8 fl oz (1 cup) water. With your hands mix it all together until the dough starts to leave the sides of the bowl. Lightly oil the inside of a large polythene bag with some extra olive oil, place the ball of dough in it and tie, leaving slack in the bag to allow the dough to rise. Leave in a warm place for 30 minutes, or more until the dough has doubled in size (be patient about this). In winter the best place to leave it to rise is the airing cupboard, and in sunny (but not windy) weather, leave it outside on a bench or table.

When the dough has doubled in bulk, turn it out onto a lightly floured or smooth surface and knead for 5 minutes, until smooth and elastic. Use as little extra flour as possible to stop it sticking to the surface. Knead with the 'heel' of the hand, pushing it away from you, and folding the stretched dough over and back towards you as you continue to knead it.

Lightly grease a baking tray with some oil or butter, shape the dough into a round (not too flat), and place on the tray. With a sharp knife cut a circle in the top of the dough about 1 cm/½ inch deep and about 4 cm/1¾ inches in from the edge. Dust the top quite thickly with flour.

Place the loaf in the centre of a *cold* oven – unusual, but true! Set the oven to 195C/385F/Gas 5½ once you have put the bread in and bake for 45 to 50 minutes, until lightly golden. The circle you cut into the top should have puffed up a little and cracked. Remove the bread from the oven and leave to cool on a rack. This is a heavy bread, but with a nice firm texture. We find it superb with pastas that have a lot of sauce, cheeses and salamis. It keeps well for several days, and is delicious toasted. *Makes 1 loaf.*

DESSERTS AND CAKES

───────── ⌇⌇⌇ ─────────

Here are a few suggestions for those who have a sweet tooth. Neither of us eats dessert or cake very often, preferring to finish a meal with cheese or something savoury. However, on odd occasions we do have a craving for something sweet, and if you are of the same mind, then this section is for you and your guests.

As this was not intended to be a baking section we have included only the types of cake that are generally served as the ending to a super slap-up meal, and not ones that are consumed with a cuppa in the afternoons or with morning coffee. The 'H & H' Tia Maria Chocolate Mousse Cake (p. 160), for example, may sound a little extravagant, but let us assure you it is worth making, as the taste is terrific and it is so rich that it goes a long way (that is, unless you have tasted a sliver and then can't bear to part with any for your guests). One principle we have always subscribed to when making a dessert or special cake, even a sponge filled with fruit and cream, is make 'em rich. To us it is false economy to make a 1-egg sponge that can turn out rather dry, when with extra eggs and butter you can turn it into a very moist cake that has people singing your praises as a cook.

The simple Frozen Cream with Cherries and Almonds (p. 167) is for those who like frozen ice cream desserts but without the hassle of having to keep re-beating the ingredients when partially frozen. We have not included ice creams, as very few people have an ice cream making machine. If you do have one stuck in a cupboard somewhere we recommend that you use it often, as chocolate or strawberry ice cream made with the aid of one of these machines knock spots off the commercial product.

Leap in and enjoy the following recipes, you can always start that diet tomorrow . . .

'H & H' Tia Maria Chocolate Mousse Cake

We created this cake because we wanted something delicious that could be kept and sliced to go with coffee. It will keep in the fridge for several days, covered with cling film. A little trouble to make, but well and truly worth it.

1 CHOCOLATE CAKE (SPONGE TYPE, BAKED IN A SPRINGFORM PAN)

Syrup

100 ml/4 fl oz (½ cup) WATER

30 ml/2 tbsp SUGAR

100 ml/4 fl oz (½ cup) TIA MARIA

Mousse

200 g/7 oz COOKING CHOCOLATE

15 ml/1 tbsp POWDERED GELATINE

100 ml/4 fl oz (½ cup) BOILING WATER

50 ml/2 fl oz (¼ cup) TIA MARIA

3 EGGS, SIZE 1, SEPARATED

300 ml/½ pint (1¼ cups) WHIPPING CREAM

ICING SUGAR FOR DECORATION

Make the cake (a packet one is perfectly acceptable for this recipe). Bake it in a springform tin; leave to cool completely, then split horizontally into 4. If it breaks up a little don't worry. Next boil the water and sugar for the syrup for 5 minutes, remove from the heat and add the Tia Maria; let cool.

Now melt the chocolate in a large glass or china bowl, either in the microwave or over a pan of boiling water. Dissolve the gelatine in the hot water and stir in the 50 ml/2 fl oz (¼ cup) Tia Maria. Pour this liquid into the melted chocolate and mix well. Add the 3 egg yolks and mix again. Beat the 3 egg whites until stiff, then fold thoroughly into the chocolate mixture. Whip the cream until thick and fold this into the chocolate mixture also. Place in the fridge and leave about 30 minutes or so, until starting to set.

Place the bottom layer of the cake back into the springform tin, place it on a large plate and brush liberally with liqueur-flavoured syrup. Ladle over the moistened cake a third of the setting mousse mixture. Place another slice of cake on top, brush with more syrup and ladle on another third of the mousse mixture. Repeat with the third layer of cake, syrup, mousse and finally the last piece of cake and remaining syrup. Refrigerate overnight and until ready to serve. Run a knife round the edge of the cake to loosen, release the clip on the springform pan and remove the sides of the tin. Carefully invert the cake onto a clean serving plate and sift some icing sugar over to decorate. Serve well chilled. *Serves 12.*

Poached Peaches

You may substitute nectarines for the peaches, but whichever you use make sure the fruit is not overripe or it will lose its shape when poached.

4 to 6 SLIGHTLY UNDERRIPE PEACHES

LEMON JUICE

225 ml/ 8 fl oz (1 cup) SWEET WHITE WINE OR CREAM SHERRY

3 THIN ORANGE SLICES

1 STICK CINNAMON

3 WHOLE CLOVES

50 g/2 oz (¼ cup) SUGAR OR HONEY

Immerse the peaches in boiling water for about 20 seconds, then plunge into cold water. Peel off skins, cut in half and remove stones, turn the halves in the lemon juice to coat to prevent discoloration.

Pour the wine or sherry into a large frying pan, add the orange slices, cinnamon stick, cloves and sugar or honey and simmer for several minutes, until the sugar or honey has dissolved. Place the peaches, cut side down in the liquid, cover gently and cook for 6 to 8 minutes, until the fruit has heated through, turning them once only, about half way through the cooking. Remove pan from heat, place the peach halves in a glass or ceramic bowl and strain the remaining liquid over them. Cool, cover with cling film and place in the fridge to chill until ready to serve.

Here are 2 suggested ways to serve them:

Cheese and Raspberry Peaches

175 g/6 oz FULL-FAT SOFT CHEESE, SOFTENED

60 g /2⅓ oz (⅓ cup) SUGAR

7.5 ml/1½ tsp FINELY GRATED LEMON RIND

1.25 ml/¼ tsp ALMOND ESSENCE

450 g/1 lb RASPBERRIES

Allow the cheese to soften at room temperature, or place in a microwave and soften on Medium for about 30 seconds. Beat the cheese with the sugar, lemon rind and almond essence. If made ahead, chill in a small bowl covered with cling film. Place 2 drained peach halves in each serving dish, cut side up, and spoon about a tablespoon of the cheese mixture into each. Spoon some of the poaching liquid over each serving and scatter over the raspberries. (You can use frozen raspberries if fresh are not available.) *Serves 4 to 6.*

Redcurrant and Almond Peaches

175 g/6 oz (½ cup) REDCURRANT JELLY

75 g/3 oz (¾ cup) FLAKED ALMONDS

SCOOPS OF VANILLA ICE CREAM

Heat the redcurrant jelly in a small, stainless steel saucepan together with 15 ml/1 tbsp water, stirring until melted, then remove from heat.

Place the almonds on a baking tray and place in the oven at 180C/350F/Gas 4 for about 10 minutes, until golden, taking them out and stirring them around occasionally.

Place 2 peach halves, cut side up, on a serving dish; spoon some of the poaching liquid over them. Place a scoop of vanilla ice cream in each half, drizzle some of the liquid redcurrant jelly over the ice cream and sprinkle over the toasted almonds. *Serves 4 to 6.*

Whisky Bread Pudding with Whisky Sauce

Here is a bread pudding that is strictly for the grown-ups. Don't consider making it without the liquor – even if you are not a whisky fan, we are sure you will like the flavour of this delightful dessert. You can use currants or sultanas instead of the raisins, but raisins are definitely our first choice.

ABOUT 1¼ LOAVES DAY-OLD FRENCH BREAD

1.5 litres/2½ pints (6 cups) MILK

250 g/9 oz (1½ cups) SEEDLESS RAISINS

150 ml/5 fl oz (⅔ cup) WHISKY OR BOURBON

5 EGGS, SIZE 1

115 g/4½ oz (⅔ cup) SUGAR

100 g/4 oz BUTTER, MELTED AND COOLED

10 ml/2 tsp VANILLA ESSENCE

2.5 ml/1 tsp SALT

BUTTER

We cannot be specific about the amount of bread because it depends on the size of the loaves used. Cut the bread into 2.5 cm/1 inch cubes, crusts included. Place the cubes of bread in a large glass bowl, pour over the milk, and let stand for 2 hours at room temperature, stirring occasionally.

In another smaller basin, mix the raisins and the whisky and leave to macerate for the same time.

Break the eggs into a jug or basin, add the sugar, melted butter, vanilla essence and salt, then whisk together to combine well. Pour this over the soaked bread, add the macerated raisins and liquor, and mix well with a wooden spoon. Generously butter a large soufflé dish and tip in the mixture. Cover with cling film and chill in the fridge overnight. Next day when ready to cook, remove from fridge and leave to come back to room temperature before commencing to bake. Preheat the oven to 170C/325F/Gas 3 and bake the pudding in the middle of the oven for about 1½ hours, or until the top is puffed and golden brown. When cooked, spoon into warm serving dishes and accompany with Whisky Sauce (below). *Serves 8 to 10.*

Whisky Sauce

As this is egg based, it is best cooked in a double boiler over moderate heat so that it doesn't curdle. If you haven't got a double boiler, place a china bowl over the top of a saucepan of a capacity that will allow at least 3 cm/1⅓ inches of water without the water touching the base of the bowl.

125 g/4 oz UNSALTED BUTTER, SOFTENED

90 g/3½ oz (½ cup) SUGAR

2 EGGS, SIZE 1

225 ml/8 fl oz (1 cup) WHISKY OR BOURBON

In a bowl, cream together the softened butter and sugar until light and fluffy. Beat in the eggs, 1 at a time. Alternatively, place the softened butter, cut up into small pieces, together with the sugar, into a food processor fitted with the steel blade. Blend until creamy, stopping the machine occasionally and pushing down the mixture from the sides of the bowl with a spatula. When the mixture is soft, add the eggs, 1 at a time, through the feed tube, with the motor running, making sure that the first egg has been incorporated with the butter before you add the second egg. Place this mixture in the top of a double boiler and add the whisky. Whisk over moderate heat until the sauce thicken slightly and the sugar has dissolved. We cannot tell you how long this takes, as there are so many variables – the amount of water in the base of the saucepan, the actual heat you are using and the temperature of the ingredients when you start. We will say, however, it is better to cook this slowly so that there is less risk of it curdling, than to cook it quickly and end up with whisky-flavoured scrambled eggs. When the sauce has thickened to the consistency of a pouring custard, transfer it to a warm jug and serve immediately over the pudding portions.

Small Cream Puffs with Praline Filling and Rich Chocolate Sauce

Most people consider choux pastry too difficult, but the food processor makes it very simple. It is the eggs that make the mixture puff up. Once they notice the pastry going a nice golden brown in the oven many people are tempted to take it out. Do not do this, as you have to cook the puffs or rings to a darker colour so that most of the mixture has cooked through.

Choux Pastry

30 g/1¼ oz UNSALTED BUTTER

5 ml/1 tsp CASTER SUGAR

175 g/6 fl oz (¾ cup) WATER

PINCH OF SALT

180 g/6¼ oz (1¼ cups) PLAIN FLOUR

3 EGGS, SIZE 1, PLUS POSSIBLY AN EXTRA EGG

Place the butter, sugar, water and salt in a heavy-based saucepan and bring to the boil over moderate heat. While this is happening, sift the flour onto a piece of kitchen paper. When the water comes to the boil, tip the flour in all at once and stir like crazy with a wooden spoon. The mixture will form a ball. Lower the heat and keep stirring until a light film appears on the bottom of the saucepan, but don't let it burn. Now tip this paste into a food processor fitted with the steel blade and break in 1 egg, switch on and start processing. When the first egg has been incorporated, add the second and then the third. The mixture should be firm enough to stand on its own. You may need to add a little more egg – the more you add, the puffier the end result, but don't add so much that the mixture becomes sloppy. Break the extra egg into a cup and beat with a fork, then if needed add it little by little until the desired consistency is obtained. Preheat the oven to 220C/425 F/Gas 7 while you form the balls. Now transfer the pastry to the piping bag fitted with a plain 1 cm/½ inch nozzle, and pipe onto a baking tray to form small, walnut-sized mounds, spaced well apart for expansion and air circulation. Alternatively, using 2 teaspoons, spoon the mixture onto the tray. Cook in the middle of the preheated oven for about 20 minutes, until well puffed and browned. Turn off the heat and leave for a further 10 minutes, then leave the oven door ajar and leave in for a further 15 minutes to make sure that they are well dried out. (Time depends on the size you make them; this timing is for ones that puff up to golf ball size. If you have made them large, a longer time is required – they must end up crisp.) Transfer to a rack to cool completely, fill with the Praline Filling, stack onto a serving dish to form a pyramid shape and pour over some of the Chocolate Sauce, serving the rest separately.

Hard to say how many this serves, as some people have an enormous appetite for things rich and chocolatey!

Praline Filling

Praline Powder

75 g/3 oz BLANCHED ALMONDS

75 ml/5 tbsp CASTER SUGAR

45 ml/3 tbsp WATER

Pastry Cream

3 EGG YOLKS

45 ml/3 tbsp CASTER SUGAR

15 ml/1 tbsp PLAIN FLOUR

15 ml/1 tbsp CORNFLOUR

300 ml/½ pint (1¼ cups) MILK

1.25 ml/¼ tsp VANILLA ESSENCE

Place the blanched almonds on a baking tray and bake in the oven for about 10 minutes at 180C/350F/Gas 4, until golden brown.

Meanwhile, in a heavy-based stainless steel saucepan, bring the sugar and water to a gradual boil, swirl or stir until the sugar melts and continue boiling until the mixture is light golden brown and gives off a rich caramel aroma. The water will make the mixture froth up at first, so be careful. Adding the water gives you a better degree of control than trying to melt sugar on its own, as many books advocate. When it is a golden colour, tip the toasted nuts in straight away, take off the heat and turn onto a lightly oiled baking tray to cool and harden. The oil you use should be a nut oil, or at least a tasteless one, certainly not olive or similar; don't use too much when oiling the tray, just enough to smear over the surface to prevent the praline sticking.

When the praline is cold, break it into small pieces with a hammer or similar implement and drop bits through the feed tube into a food processor fitted with the steel blade, with the motor running. It's better to do this a little at a time rather than all at once. You want it to end up almost a powder, but if you go mad and it turns into a paste, don't worry, as the flavour will be the same. If you haven't a food processor, you can use a blender, or failing that, crush it in a pestle and mortar. Keep to one side.

Now make the Pastry Cream. Beat the egg yolks and the sugar in a basin with a whisk or electric hand beater until thick and creamy. Whisk in the flour, cornflour and 15 ml/1 tbsp of the milk. Heat the remaining milk over moderate heat until it boils, then whisk it into the egg mixture. Transfer back to the saucepan and continue simmering, whisking all the time, for 2 to 3 minutes, until thick. Remove from heat, add the vanilla esence and pour into a clean basin. Leave to cool, then whisk in the praline powder and chill until needed. *Note:* you have to wait until the custard is cold before whisking in the praline, so that it is distributed through the custard rather than melted in; also press a round of lightly buttered paper or a piece of cling film onto the surface of the custard to help prevent a skin forming.

Rich Chocolate Sauce

100 g/4 oz PLAIN OR COOKING CHOCOLATE

20 ml/4 tsp CASTER SUGAR

10 ml/2 tsp COCOA POWDER

300 ml/½ pint (1¼ cups) WATER

10 ml/2 tsp CORNFLOUR

30 ml/2 tbsp CHOCOLATE- OR COFFEE-FLAVOURED LIQUEUR (OPTIONAL)

Break the chocolate into a heavy-based saucepan together with the sugar, cocoa and water. Bring to the boil, whisking, and simmer about 10 minutes, or until it becomes syrupy. Mix the cornflour with about 15 ml/1 tbsp water and add to the sauce while still whisking. Simmer for a further 2 minutes. Add the liqueur and pour over the filled puffs.

Honey-Almond Cream

This is fantastic and so easy to prepare.

50 g/2 oz (½ cup) FLAKED ALMONDS, TOASTED UNTIL GOLDEN BROWN

2 EGG WHITES

75 g/3 oz (¼ cup) CLEAR HONEY

225 ml/8 fl oz (1 cup) WHIPPING CREAM

1.25 ml/¼ tsp ALMOND ESSENCE

1.25 ml/¼ tsp VANILLA ESSENCE

90 ml/6 tbsp ALMOND-FLAVOUR LIQUEUR

Finely chop a third of the toasted almonds (reserve the rest for decoration). In a bowl, whisk the egg whites until they hold soft peaks (wiping the bowl with a cut lemon aids the whisking). If using an electric beater you are OK ... if doing it by hand you are in trouble, unless of course you have 3 arms! While whisking the egg whites add the honey in a thin stream (see what we mean). (If you heat the measuring jug with boiling water before you measure out the honey, it will pour out more easily. Ditto if using a spoon of honey at any time, heat the spoon ... much easier to handle.) Beat until stiff and glossy. In another clean bowl, whip the cream (unsweetened) until stiff. Fold in the whipped cream, vanilla, almond essence and the chopped nuts. Mix only until blended – you don't want to kill the egg whites. Spoon into 6 elegant freezerproof glasses, cover each with cling film and freeze for 3 hours. When ready to serve, pour 15 ml/1 tbsp of almond liqueur on top of each serving and dust with the slivered almonds. Wow! *Serves 6.*

Frozen Cream with Cherries and Almonds

This is one of those simple, easy-to-make desserts that win acclaim when served. It is not quite an ice cream, as the texture is not as smooth. The best cherries to use are sour ones, such as morello. If they are stoned, well and good, if not, it really isn't worth going to the trouble of stoning them as the stones are quite easy to dispose of when the dessert is being eaten. Warn your guests, though, or there is always the chance that some poor soul might break a tooth, or worse still their plate . . .

400 g/14 oz CAN CHERRIES

2 EGG WHITES, SIZE 1

PINCH OF CREAM OF TARTAR

30 ml/2 tbsp CASTER SUGAR

75 g/3 oz (½ cup) BLANCHED ALMONDS, TOASTED AND FINELY SLIVERED

30 ml/2 tbsp CHERRY-FLAVOURED LIQUEUR, SUCH AS KIRSCH, OR MARSALA OR MADEIRA

300 ml/½ pint (1¼ cups) WHIPPING CREAM, WHIPPED UNTIL SOFT PEAKS FORM

5 ml/1 tsp ARROWROOT

30 ml/2 tbsp LIQUEUR AS ABOVE

Drain the cherries and reserve the liquid. Whisk the egg whites in a fairly large bowl, together with the cream of tartar, until stiff. Add the caster sugar and continue to beat until smooth and glossy. Fold in the drained cherries, toasted slivered almonds and the liqueur of your choice. Finally, gently fold in the whipped cream with a large metal spoon and turn into a lightly oiled 900 g/2 lb loaf tin. Do not in any circumstances use a heavily flavoured oil such as olive; use a nut oil, such as almond or walnut, or a tasteless vegetable oil. Use only enough on a brush to give a very thin coating to the tin to make turning the finished dessert out easier. Cover with a double thickness of foil and freeze until firm, preferably overnight.

Mix the reserved juice with the arrowroot in a small saucepan and bring to the boil over moderate heat, until it boils and thickens, whisking or stirring all the time to prevent any lumps. Take off the heat, add the 30 ml/2 tbsp liqueur, then leave to cool.

To serve, dip the tin into hot water for a few seconds, run a thin knife round the sides of the frozen dessert to loosen, and tip onto a well chilled plate. Slice into portions, place on the centre of a serving plate and pour or spoon some of the cool sauce around the slices, not over the top. Serve straight away. *Serves 6 to 8.*

Baked Pear Pudding

This is a delicious concoction and it is easy to make. Once you have prepared the pears, it can be cooking while you are having your first two courses. The Liqueur Cream enhances the flavour.

30 ml/2 tbsp LEMON JUICE

10 FIRM PEARS, PEELED, CORED AND QUARTERED

BUTTER

325 ml/11 fl oz (1⅓ cups) MILK

150 ml/5 fl oz (⅔ cup) SINGLE (LIGHT) CREAM

200 g/ 7 oz (1 cup) SUGAR

80 g/3¼ oz (⅔ cup) PLAIN FLOUR

4 EGGS, SIZE 1

7.5 ml/1½ tsp VANILLA ESSENCE

30 ml/2 tbsp CASTER SUGAR

10 ml/2 tsp GROUND CINNAMON

50 g/2 oz UNSALTED BUTTER

LIQUEUR CREAM (OPPOSITE)

Place the lemon juice in a large glass or china bowl and add the pear quarters. Toss them with your hands to coat with the lemon juice so as to stop them discolouring. Heavily butter a large flan dish or ovenproof serving dish and lay the pears in it in a decorative manner. The dish has to have sufficient area to hold the pears close together in 1 layer.

In a food processor fitted with the steel blade, place the milk, cream, sugar, flour, eggs and vanilla, then blend until just incorporated, scraping down the mixture if needed with spatula part way through.

Alternatively, place all the ingredients in a deep bowl and whisk together as you would for making a batter. Pour the batter over the pears. Mix together the caster sugar and the cinnamon and sprinkle over the surface. Dot with small pieces of the unsalted butter. Bake in the centre of a preheated oven at 220C/425F/Gas 7 for 15 minutes; lower the heat to 180C/350F/Gas 4 and bake for a further 30 to 40 minutes, until the batter has set and browned. Remove from the oven and let stand to cool slightly as this is best served warm, not hot. Serve with large amounts of Liqueur Cream. *Serves 8.*

Liqueur Cream

This can be made ahead of time and stored, covered, in the fridge till ready to use. If you haven't any pear-flavoured liqueur, use an orange-flavoured one, or calvados, which is apple-flavoured.

450 ml/¾ pint (2 cups) WHIPPING CREAM

60 ml/4 tbsp ICING SUGAR

2.5 ml/½ tsp VANILLA ESSENCE

30 ml/2 tbsp EAU DE VIE DE POIRES WILLIAM (PEAR LIQUEUR)

In a large, cold bowl, beat the cream until soft peaks form, then add the sugar, vanilla and liqueur and continue to beat until thick.

(Take care not to overbeat and turn it into pear butter . . .)

Rum and Lime Cheesecake

You can substitute rum essence for the rum, and make up the difference with water. The end result isn't quite the same, however. (Once met someone who was on a diet and was drinking rum essence in diet cola . . . it tasted abysmal.) The biscuit crumbs can be of your choice – plain, sweet, digestive, almond or even chocolate. You can make extra crumbs and completely line the tin if you wish, rather than have them layered over the base only; or you can spread the amount given over the base and part way up the sides of the tin. If you do this, use a straight-sided jar or milk bottle to press the crumbs against the sides of the tin to form a thin crust.

175 g/6 oz (1¼ cups) BISCUIT CRUMBS

50 g/2 oz (¼ cup) CASTER SUGAR

85 g/3⅓ oz BUTTER, MELTED

15 ml/1 tbsp POWDERED GELATINE

175 ml/6 fl oz (¾ cup) DARK RUM

50 ml/2 fl oz (¼ cup) LIME JUICE

4 EGGS, SIZE 1, SEPARATED

500 g/18 oz FULL-FAT SOFT CHEESE, SOFTENED

PINCH EACH OF CREAM OF TARTAR AND SALT

100 g/4 oz (½ cup) CASTER SUGAR

225 ml/8 fl oz (1 cup) WHIPPING CREAM

LIME SLICES FOR DECORATION

Mix the biscuit crumbs, sugar and melted butter together until well combined and reserve a few tablespoons of the mixture to decorate the cheesecake later. Press the rest onto the base of a buttered 23 cm/9 inch springform pan. Chill the base while you make the filling.

In the top of a double saucepan, sprinkle the gelatine over the rum and lime juice and leave to soften for 10 minutes. Bring the water in the base of the double saucepan to the boil, lower the heat to simmering and stir the gelatine mixture until it is hot and the gelatine has dissolved. With a wire whisk, beat in the egg yolks, 1 at a time, and cook the mixture until it starts to thicken slightly. (As with anything of this nature, be careful that the water doesn't touch the bottom of the top pan, and don't try and rush it or you will scramble the eggs.) Patience is called for in this step, and it is important not to rush it; you want a smooth custard, not a lumpy one. The time depends on how cold the ingredients were to start with, but it should be thick enough in 6 to 10 minutes. Remove the top pan from the double saucepan and let the mixture cool down, stirring it occasionally.

In a large bowl, beat the softened full-fat soft cheese until it is light and fluffy. (We usually microwave it on Medium for a little while to soften it.) Beat it with a wooden spoon, as a whisk gets clogged up too much. Add the egg mixture and beat until combined (now you can use a whisk). Place in the fridge for about 30 minutes, until it thickens slightly.

Whisk the egg whites in a large bowl together with the cream of tartar and salt until soft peaks form, then whisk in the sugar until they hold stiff peaks. In another bowl, whip the cream until it holds fairly stiff peaks, but do not overwhip or it goes buttery. When the cheese mixture has thickened, fold in the egg whites and the cream and pour into the cake tin. Chill for at least 6 hours or overnight. Run a thin knife round the edge of the tin to loosen it and take off the sides; leave the base still under the cake. Decorate the top by sprinkling on the reserved crumb mixture and some thin slices of fresh limes. *Serves 8 to 10.*

Rose Cream with Frozen Fruits

This is a very simple dessert that can be made up to 1 day in advance. It is not advisable to leave it any longer than 2 days at the most as gelatine has a tendency to go a little rubbery if left too long. Although we advocate rose water, you can flavour it with other essences, such as vanilla, almond or coffee, or even chocolate for that matter. Rose water gives you the taste of summer. We suggest frozen tinned fruit to go with this, but fresh fruits, possibly even poached and then chilled, are ideal.

400 g/14 oz CAN FRUIT IN SYRUP, SUCH AS RASPBERRIES, STRAWBERRIES OR BLACKBERRIES

225 ml/8 fl oz (1 cup) WATER

45 ml/3 tbsp CASTER SUGAR

10 ml/2 tsp POWDERED GELATINE

5 ml/1 tsp ROSE WATER OR LESS, DEPENDING ON STRENGTH

1 EGG WHITE, SIZE 1

300 ml/½ pint (1¼ cups) WHIPPING CREAM, WHIPPED UNTIL JUST STIFF

Put the can of fruit of your choice into the freezer 24 hours ahead of serving this dessert. When you open it, depending on the thickness of the syrup, you may find that the fruit is frozen solid; if so, keep it in the fridge for a little while to thaw slightly. If it hasn't frozen at all, possibly because there was a lot of sugar in the syrup, then no matter, as long as it is well chilled.

In a small, stainless steel or enamel saucepan, bring the water and sugar to the boil. Boil for 5 minutes, remove from heat and stir in the gelatine with a fork until dissolved. Strain into a bowl, cool, then add the rose water. Place in the fridge until it starts to turn syrupy.

Whisk the egg white until stiff in a medium-sized bowl, add the syrupy jelly, mix well and fold in the whipped cream. Rinse a 750 ml-1 litre/1¼-1¾ pint (3-4 cup) mould with cold water, and spoon the rose cream into it. Chill until set. Turn out onto a lipped serving dish and surround with the fruit.

Note: if the mould is metal, just place over a low gas flame very quickly to warm the bottom and make the releasing of the cream easy. Otherwise, dip quickly into a bowl of warm water. *Serves 4 to 6.*

Chocolate Almond Terrine

We have always been fans of rich chocolate desserts, and this one is no exception. Don't be tempted to serve it after a rich meal, as the whole thing can become a little overpowering. Try and make this a day or 2 ahead of time. Our use of ground almonds might seem alarming, but as with olive oil, we buy our ground almonds in bulk rather than in packets, and the cost is reduced quite considerably.

Keep them stored in an airtight plastic container somewhere cool and dark. Should the almond flavour dissipate over a period of time, you can always add a little almond essence to the recipe, but don't overdo it or the taste becomes overpowering and can be synthetic rather than subtle.

250 g/9 oz COOKING CHOCOLATE

50 ml/2 fl oz (¼ cup) DARK RUM OR BRANDY

250 g/9 oz UNSALTED BUTTER

75 ml/5 tbsp CASTER SUGAR

3 EGGS, SIZE 1, SEPARATED

175 g/6 oz (1½ cups) GROUND ALMONDS

ABOUT 100g/4 oz SWEET BISCUITS

ALMOND OR WALNUT OIL

GENEROUS 15 ml/ 1 tbsp FINELY GROUND COFFEE AND 100 ml/4 fl oz (½ cup) WATER, OR
10 ml/2 tsp INSTANT COFFEE AND 50 ml/2 fl oz (¼ cup) BOILING WATER

300 ml/½ pint (1¼ cups) WHIPPING CREAM

Break up the chocolate into small pieces and melt in a bowl over simmering water, or place in the microwave and melt for a few minutes on Medium. Add the rum or brandy to the chocolate and keep it warm while you prepare the rest of the ingredients.

Soften the unsalted butter and place in a food processor fitted with the steel blade. Process until creamy and add the caster sugar. Process further until well combined, stopping the machine and scraping down the sides of the bowl occasionally. With the motor running, add the egg yolks, 1 at a time, through the feed tube. When these have been incorporated, add the almonds and mix until just combined. Add this to the melted chocolate and combine well.

Whisk the egg whites until really stiff and fold gently but thoroughly into the almond and chocolate mixture. Break the biscuits up into small pieces and add these also. Lightly brush a 900 g/2 lb loaf tin or terrine with the oil of your choice (never using a strong flavoured one), and tip in the chocolate mixture. Cover with a sheet of foil and put into the freezer for 2 hours. Remove and place in the fridge; leave until required, but no less than 6 hours.

When ready to serve, make up the coffee cream. If using ground coffee, pour over the boiling water and leave for 5 minutes, then strain through a fine sieve and chill. If using instant coffee, dissolve it in the boiling water and leave to cool. Lightly whip the cream until it holds very soft peaks, then add the chilled coffee. Do not be tempted to sweeten it – it should have a slightly bitter taste.

Note: do not whip the cream until thick; the idea is to have it whipped just enough so that when you add the coffee it will still be soft and will subside when placed over the chocolate terrine rather than sit there on top.

Just before serving, dip a knife in hot water to warm, dry it and run it around the edge of the chocolate terrine to loosen; dip the bottom of the tin in hot water for a few seconds. Invert onto a chilled serving dish and shake to turn it out. Cut the terrine into slices and serve with some of the thickened coffee cream. It must be served very cold. *Serves 8 to 12.*

Walnut Coffee Cake with Strawberries

This cake is rather on the dry side, but the lashings of cream and the sliced fruit used to sandwich the layers together make for a stunning and very tasty end result. You can try the old trick of slicing it horizontally with a piece of cotton held tight between both hands, but we prefer to carefully saw through it with a serrated bread knife. To make this operation easier, make the cake a day or 2 in advance of filling and serving it. You can use frozen strawberries when fresh are not available. Thaw them gradually in the fridge with a sprinkling of sugar. Drain before use.

3 EGGS, SIZE 1

100 g/4 oz CASTER SUGAR

80 g/3¼ oz PLAIN FLOUR

70 g/2¾ oz WALNUTS, CHOPPED

15 ml/1 tbsp INSTANT COFFEE POWDER

600 ml/1 pint (2½ cups) WHIPPING CREAM

450 g/1 lb STRAWBERRIES, SLICED

Butter and flour a deep 20 cm/8 inch cake tin and preheat the oven to 175C/340F/Gas 3½. Whisk together the eggs and the sugar in a bowl placed over hot water until the mixture is mousse-like and ribbons form when you trail the mixture across the top to test it. Remove from the heat and whisk for a further minute. (Alternatively, whisk with an electric hand beater until thick; omit the hot water.)

Sift the flour onto a piece of kitchen paper. Place the walnuts and coffee powder in a food processor fitted with the steel blade and chop using the pulse switch, on-off, until walnuts are just chopped. Fold the flour and the processed walnuts into the thick eggs; mix thoroughly and turn into the prepared tin. Bake in the middle of the oven for 40 to 50 minutes. Leave to cool for 5 minutes, then turn out on a rack and leave to go cold.

Split the cake into 3 horizontal layers. Whip the cream until fairly stiff. Slice most of the strawberries, keeping 8 for decoration. Place enough cream into a piping bag fitted with a rose nozzle to allow you to pipe 8 rosettes on the finished cake. Place one third of the cream over the first layer of cake and cover with half of the sliced strawberries. Repeat with the second layer and smooth the remaining third of the cream over the top layer. Pipe on the 8 rosettes of cream and place a whole strawberry on each. Chill before serving. *Serves 8.*

Blueberry Eggnog Pie

This is delicious; we use canned blueberries, drained of their syrup, when fresh are not available.
To prepare fresh blueberries, remove the stalks and any leaves, rinse well and dry thoroughly. Try
strawberries, bilberries or raspberries as well.

Pâté Brisée Case

190 g/6½ oz (1¼ cups) PLAIN FLOUR

90 ml/6 tbsp CHILLED UNSALTED BUTTER, CUBED

25 g/1 oz CHILLED LARD, DICED

1.25 ml/¼ tsp SALT

45 ml/3 tbsp ICED WATER

Filling

30 ml/2 tbsp POWDERED GELATINE

65 ml/2½ fl oz (⅓ cup) WARM WATER

3 EGGS, SIZE 1, SEPARATED

115 g/4½ oz (⅔ cup) SUGAR

PINCH OF SALT

225 ml/8 fl oz (1 cup) MILK

50 ml/2 fl oz (¼ cup) DARK RUM

50 ml/2 fl oz (¼ cup) BRANDY

225 ml/8 fl oz (1 cup) WHIPPING CREAM, CHILLED

30 ml/2 tbsp SUGAR

PINCH OF SALT

PINCH OF CREAM OF TARTAR

225 g/8 oz BLUEBERRIES, FRESH OR CANNED

GRATED PLAIN CHOCOLATE FOR DECORATION

In a large bowl, blend the flour, butter, lard and salt. Mix this until the mixture is crumbly. Add the iced water and toss the dough until the water has been well mixed in. Form into a ball, dust with flour, wrap in greaseproof paper and chill for 1 hour.

Roll the dough into a round to fit into a 25 cm/10 inch pie plate. Prick the bottom with a fork (this is to stop it rising) and chill for 30 minutes. Line the shell with foil, fill with rice to weight it and bake in the lower part of the oven, preheated to 200C/400F/Gas 6, for 10 minutes. Remove the paper and rice and bake a further 10 minutes, until the shell is lightly golden. Cool on a rack.

In a small bowl sprinkle the gelatine on the surface of the warm water and leave about 10 minutes, to soften. In a large bowl, whisk the egg yolks, then whisk in the sugar, little by little, until the egg yolks form ribbons when the beater is lifted. Add a pinch of salt when whisking in the sugar. In a heavy-based saucepan, scald the milk, over moderate heat, stir in the egg yolk mixture and the gelatine and cook, stirring, for 1 minute, until the sauce has thickened and the gelatine dissolved. Transfer this custard to a bowl, stir in the rum and brandy thoroughly. Butter a piece of greaseproof paper, gently press it onto the surface of the custard and chill. Stir several times while cooling, and don't let it set.

In another clean bowl (sorry about all the washing up, but the end result is worth it) whip the chilled cream with the remaining 30 ml/2 tbsp sugar until stiff.

In yet another clean bowl, whisk the egg whites with salt until frothy, then add the cream of tartar and whisk until the egg whites hold soft peaks.

Uncover the custard and carefully fold in the cream and the egg whites.

Spread the blueberries over the base of the shell, then pour over the custard topping. Refrigerate about 3 hours, until the topping has set. Grate the chocolate over the top. Or, whip more cream and pipe rosettes on top, then add grated chocolate. *Serves 8 to 10.*

Fresh Strawberries with Cabbage

What on earth are they talking about, you ask. It's true though – nobody seems to know why, but strawberries have an affinity with cabbage. The cabbage seems to bring out the flavour of strawberries unlike anything else . . . of course you don't eat them with the cabbage – we are not that stupid. Another way to serve fresh strawberries is chilled, then lightly dusted with white pepper. (Bet that one got you! Try it.)
Aways buy nice red firm berries; if they are packed in punnets, turn them upside down and have a look through the air holes to make sure there are no mouldy ones on the bottom. Remove the freshly purchased strawberries from their packet, rip off some large, outer leaves from a cabbage and wrap the strawberries in these, then refrigerate overnight. Now you can prepare the strawberries.
To prepare fresh strawberries, just before serving rinse under cold or ice water with the stalks still on – never, never wash or soak them once you have removed the stalks, or the water will get inside and spoil the taste. Once they are washed, you can remove the stalks and hulls, or let your guests do it.
Take a fairly large cabbage, cut the top off (about a quarter way down) with a sharp knife. Carefully hollow out the bottom to form a bowl, wash the strawberries (with their stalks on), dry them and place them in the cabbage bowl. Replace the top of the cabbage as a lid. You may have to hollow out a bit of the lid so that it sits snugly on top. Cover in foil and chill in fridge. To take on a picnic, wrap it all in a wet tea-towel. It also looks very nice at the table, placed on an attractive plate and perhaps decorated with a few flowers. Don't, of course, throw the cabbage bits away – use them for a slaw.

Ricotta Cheese Pie

Now there are cheesecakes and there are cheesecakes, and in our view this one is the best of all. Cottage cheese makes a fairly good substitute for the ricotta; whichever cheese you use it is essential that it be fresh and moist, not crumbly and slightly dried up (as can be the case if the cheese has been repackaged and in stock too long). The Marsala gives the pastry that certain flavour; should you turn to sherry, use a heavy, sweet sherry. This cheesecake is lovely served with chilled, white, seedless grapes and a glass of well chilled Champagne. On a perfect summer day our favourite meal is homemade fettucine with cream, butter and Parmesan, a crisp fresh mixed green salad with lemon dressing and the Ricotta Cheese Pie and fruit to follow.

Pastry

275 g/10 oz (2 cups) PLAIN FLOUR

175 g/6 oz BUTTER, AT ROOM TEMPERATURE AND DICED

4 EGG YOLKS

GENEROUS 30 ml/2 tbsp CASTER SUGAR

37.5 ml/2½ tbsp MARSALA OR CREAM SHERRY

5 ml/1 tsp FINELY GRATED LEMON RIND

2.5 ml/½ tsp SALT

Filling

1.4 kg/3 lb RICOTTA CHEESE

100 g/4 oz (½ cup) CASTER SUGAR

15 ml/1 tbsp PLAIN FLOUR

2.5 ml/½ tsp SALT

5 ml/1 tsp VANILLA ESSENCE

4 EGG YOLKS

5 ml/1 tsp FINELY GRATED ORANGE RIND

30 ml/2 tbsp SULTANAS, SOAKED AND DRAINED

30 ml/2 tbsp MIXED CANDIED PEEL

30 ml/2 tbsp PINE NUTS OR FLAKED ALMONDS

1 EGG WHITE, MIXED WITH A LITTLE WATER

Although you can make the pastry in a food processor, we prefer to make it by hand in the following way. Do not sift the flour, just tip it into a large bowl, make a well in the centre and add the butter. Tip in the egg yolks, caster sugar, Marsala, lemon rind and salt. With a blunt knife start to mix the ingredients together by cutting into the flour. When this has incorporated most of the flour, use your hands to mix in the rest of the flour to make a ball. Do not overknead. You may have to use a little extra flour so that the dough is not too sticky, but don't make it dry. Place the ball of dough in a polythene bag and pop it in the fridge for up to an hour. Break off a quarter of the dough and keep wrapped while you roll out the remainder. Lightly flour your rolling surface and roll the pastry out to about 30 cm/12 inches. Lightly butter the bottom and sides of a loose-bottom or springform cake tin measuring about 23 cm/9 inches. Carefully place the rolled pastry in the tin, trying not to stretch it too much. Press the pastry well against the sides of the tin and trim off any excess by rolling the rolling pin over the top. Chill in the fridge while you make the filling.

Force the cheese through a sieve, or blend in a food processor until smooth. Place in a large bowl and beat in the sugar, flour, salt, vanilla essence and egg yolks. Thoroughly stir in the orange rind, sultanas and candied peel and spoon into the chilled pastry shell.

Roll the remaining quarter of pastry into a wide strip about 25 cm/10 inches long, and cut into several narrower strips to place over the top of the filling to form a latticed top. Sprinkle the top of the pie with the pine nuts or flaked almonds and form the lattice with the pastry strips, moistening the edges of the pastry shell with water to make them stick. Trim any excess and brush the strips with the egg white and water mixture. Bake in the middle of a preheated oven at 180C/350F/Gas 4 for 1 to 1¼ hours, or until a skewer inserted into the centre comes out clean and the pastry strips are golden brown. Remove from the oven and leave to settle for 15 minutes. Remove the sides of the pan if a springform one; or place the whole tin on a can of food and carefully slide down the side if it is a loose-bottomed tin that you used. When you have removed the sides, leave the cake to cool completely on its base on a wire rack. Chill. Bring back to room temperature before serving. *Serves 8 to 10.*

CONDIMENTS
AND STOCKS

———— ✍ ————

Here we have touched on a few simple things that we have found of tremendous help to us over the years in adding real flavour to many of our recipes. Simple stocks, for instance, are a boon. They add flavour and goodness to soups and are invaluable to have on hand when you want to make a special sauce that can turn something simple like poached chicken into a masterpiece. These stocks, once cooled, strained and the fat removed, keep quite well in the fridge. You have to remember that the containers you store them in must be scrupulously clean and sterile. It is best after several days, if you have stocks left, to re-boil them for about 5 to 10 minutes in an enamel or stainless steel saucepan to stop them going off. Remember these simple rules: cool completely and freeze for longer storage, or keep in the fridge and re-boil every few days – and when in doubt, throw it out.

A good homemade mayonnaise is a must, as you can control the acidity yourself. So many of the commercial products are too vinegary for our taste and we prefer to make our own in fairly small quantities as we need it. With the food processor this is very simple.

Herb butters are a boon and add flavour to cooked vegetables or simple steaks and chops, and herbed jellies and herb vinegars ring the changes when you want to give meat or fish a flavour boost or make a salad dressing with different taste.

If you live where the climate changes dramatically from summer to winter, there is a definite ending to the herb season. When they are at their peak in full summer, it's not a bad idea to make some herb jellies, butters, vinegars and so on, that can be stored for winter use. It takes a bit of effort, but the time you put in will be saved later, when you come to use one of your herb creations. We have nothing against dried herbs, but if you have an abundance of fresh ones in the season, making these sorts of preserves gives another dimension to your cooking as you have prepared them while the herbs retain their natural oils which impart quite a different flavour.

Herb Vinegars

Vinegars are easy to make and handy to use in cooking and salad dressings. You can use any herbs or combinations you want. It is interesting to experiment and not costly. Suggested herbs are: tarragon, rosemary, thyme, lemon balm, mint (apple mint is particularly nice), marjoram and so on. You can also use garlic; naturally you are going to achieve a very strong flavour – still, saves you having to squeeze garlic when making a salad dressing.
Choose an attractive bottle or screw-top jar; make sure it is very clean. Pick enough of the desired herb to loosely fill the container you are using, wash well and pat dry. Place in the container and completely cover with white wine vinegar, cover with cling film and tightly cap. If using a bottle with a cork stopper, wrap the cork in a little cling film to ensure a tight fit. Store at room temperature for 3 weeks, then carefully strain through fine muslin and bottle again. Keeps very well for several months.

Herb Butters

When winter is approaching and herbs are at their peak, the surplus can be made into butters to use during winter. Butters are easy to make and freeze, and make super additions for sauces, steaks and stews. The fresh herbs have a more vibrant flavour than dried and the lemon juice heightens the flavour.

125 g/4 oz BUTTER, AT ROOM TEMPERATURE

15 g/½ oz (½ cup) FRESH HERB LEAVES

5 ml/1 tsp LEMON JUICE

Blend all the ingredients in a blender or food processor or in a bowl by hand. If using a mechanical device, stop and push the butter down over the blades several times, to get even distribution. When creamy, place in a bowl, cover and use in a few days, or roll into logs about the size of a sausage (and we don't mean a salami!) roll up in foil and freeze . . . cut off pieces as required.

If you feel like taking a little more trouble, make the rolls, cover with greaseproof paper and chill until fairly firm. Cut the butter into thick rounds. Re-form the log, but with a piece of non-stick freezer paper in between the slices. Roll in foil and freeze. This way, when you want a few rounds you don't have to spoil the whole log. Takes a bit of time, but saves you time in the end. All sorts of herbs can be used, for example basil (a must), chives, watercress, mint, parsley, sage, rosemary and so on. Nearly forgot – dill for fish. *Makes about 125g/4 oz.*

Herb Jellies

Jellies, aspics and the like have so many uses. Nothing accompanies pink, fresh, juicy roast lamb better than redcurrant or mint jelly. Try quince jelly with roast pork, mint jelly with beautifully grilled (still pink) lamb chops, thick orange jelly (bitter) with roast duck, claret or port jelly with pink roasted beef . . . the mind boggles with pleasure and anticipation. (An aside: you will notice the word pink appearing regularly. Nothing is worse than overcooked meat. It was dead when you purchased it – why kill it any more?) Most herbs can be put down in a jelly and used as a condiment with cooked foods. Here is a good basic recipe for jelly, using mint. The apple gives body and the skin is important, as it provides natural pectin that helps in the setting. After you have tried this recipe, if you wish to make larger quantities, just double or treble the quantities. Using this basis have a go at making other herb jellies.

1 kg/2¼ lb GREEN COOKING APPLES

15 g/½ oz (½ cup) FRESH MINT SPRIGS

1 litre/1¾ pints (4 cups) WATER

450 g/1 lb SUGAR

30 ml/2 tbsp LEMON JUICE

30 ml/2 tbsp WHITE WINE VINEGAR

EXTRA 60 ml/4 tbsp CHOPPED FRESH MINT

Wash the apples and dice them, peel and cores as well. Place in a heavy-based enamel or stainless steel pan with the whole mint sprigs and the water. Bring to the boil, cover and simmer, about 30 minutes, until well cooked and soft. Line a colander with muslin, place over a receptacle that will allow the colander to be suspended, pour in the apple pulp and leave to drain overnight. Do not be tempted to squeeze the pulp to quicken the draining process or the jelly base will be cloudy.

Next day, measure the juice, add 400 g/14 oz (2 cups) sugar to every 600 ml/1 pint (2½ cups) juice. In a heavy-based pan, bring to the boil and boil gently about 30 minutes, until a setting point is reached. Try a little on a saucer, let cool and assess the setting quality. Carefully skim off the surface scum, stir in the lemon juice, vinegar and the extra chopped mint. Pour into jars and seal when cool. Will keep for several months if chilled.

Claret Jelly

This is a delightful accompaniment to roast beef or lamb or game. You can even serve it as a dessert, with some lightly sweetened whipped cream.

1 BOTTLE GOOD CLARET OR BURGUNDY

165 g/5½ oz (¾ cup) SUGAR

GENEROUS 45 ml/3 tbsp REDCURRANT JELLY

JUICE AND RIND OF 1 LEMON

1 CINNAMON STICK

45 ml/3 tbsp WATER

45 ml/3 tbsp BRANDY

30 ml/2 tbsp POWDERED GELATINE

In a heavy-based enamel or stainless steel saucepan, heat the wine, sugar, redcurrant jelly, lemon juice and rind and cinnamon stick over low heat until the sugar has dissolved. Mix the water and brandy. Place the gelatine in a small bowl and sprinkle (not pour) the brandy-water mixture over it; leave to stand for 5 minutes.

Heat the wine mixture until fairly hot, not boiling; stir in the gelatine and continue stirring until it has dissolved. Remove from heat and let cool.

Meanwhile, rinse a 900 ml/1½ pint (3¾ cup) jelly mould with cold water. When the wine jelly has cooled, strain into the jelly mould and place in the fridge to chill until set.

To serve, heat the base of the mould with a warmed cloth, or dip very quickly into very hot water, invert onto a plate and rechill until ready to serve. *Serves 6.*

Beef Stock

As with chicken stock, it is convenient to have frozen beef stock on hand for those special sauces. The more you reduce it the stronger it becomes – almost like an essence. You can reduce it right down; strain and pour into ice-cube trays, freeze, then pop out into a polythene bag and keep for later use.

BONES

FATTY, SCRAPPY BITS OF MEAT

GOOD DRIPPING

2 ONIONS, CHOPPED

WATER

2 CARROTS, CHOPPED

FEW SPRIGS FRESH PARSLEY

2 BAY LEAVES

6 WHOLE BLACK PEPPERCORNS

2 STALKS CELERY, CHOPPED

100 ml/4 fl oz (½ cup) MEDIUM-DRY SHERRY

Roast the bones, meat, dripping and onions at 220C/425F/Gas 7 as though they were a roast. When good and brown and the juices have run, tip into a large, heavy-based pan and add about 1 litre/1¾ pints (4½ cups) fresh water, the carrots, parsley, bay leaves, peppercorns, celery and sherry. Bring to the boil, *don't cover*, and let simmer for about an hour. Skim any froth. When ready (should have reduced by about half), strain into a container or containers. Leave to get cold, de-fat and you have a good stock. *Makes about 600 ml/1 pint (2 ½ cups).*

Fish Stock

If you have eaten prawns, don't throw away the peels . . . they can go into the stock too. Fish stock will not keep longer than 2 days in the refrigerator; if keeping it longer, re-boil for 5 minutes. This stock freezes well.

1.5 kg/3 lb 5 oz FISH TRIMMINGS (BONES, HEAD, SKIN, ETC.)

1 STALK CELERY, SLICED

1 CARROT, SLICED

2 ONIONS, SLICED INTO RINGS

2 TOMATOES, CHOPPED

8 WHOLE BLACK PEPPERCORNS

2 BAY LEAVES

3 SPRIGS FRESH PARSLEY

225 ml/8 fl oz (1 cup) DRY WHITE WINE

WATER, TO COVER

Wash the fish pieces thoroughly. Place in a large pan, add all the other ingredients, cover with water, bring to a boil, lower heat and skim the surface (you may have to do this several times during cooking). Cover and simmer for 30 minutes. Strain and chill.

Chicken Stock

1 LARGE BOILING CHICKEN, ABOUT 2 kg/4½ lb

1 VEAL KNUCKLE, CRACKED

2 CARROTS, CHOPPED

2 STALKS CELERY, TRIMMED AND SLICED

2 ONIONS, QUARTERED

8 WHOLE BLACK PEPPERCORNS

5 ml/1 tsp SALT

3 BAY LEAVES

2 or 3 SPRIGS FRESH PARSLEY

WATER, TO COVER

Place all the ingredients in a large pan, cover with water, bring to the boil, lower the heat, cover and simmer for 2 hours. When the chicken is tender (about an hour), remove from the pan and take off the flesh (use for a chicken pie). Return all the bones to the stock and go on simmering. Strain and chill.

Green Sauce (Salsa Verde)

This classic sauce is served with mixed boiled meats, but is also very good with cold meats or poached fish. When we saw it served in Sabatini's Restaurant in Florence, we were a bit taken back by the quantity of meats presented with it. There was an enormous trolley that supported a huge pan, from which were taken half a calf's head, a large boiling fowl, an Italian pork sausage and a great piece of beef. This was placed on a huge platter and the waiter proceeded to carve pieces for the solitary diner. On a separate plate were potatoes, onions and cabbage. The man added the 'salsa verde' to his plate and washed the whole thing down with a litre of Chianti that was held in a special cradle so all he had to do was to tilt the bottle and the wine flowed into his glass in copious quantities.

22.5 g/¾ oz (¾ cup) FINELY CHOPPED FRESH PARSLEY

22.5 ml/1½ tbsp CAPERS, WELL DRAINED

22.5 ml/1½ tbsp FINELY CHOPPED SOUR PICKLED CUCUMBER

1 CLOVE GARLIC, CRUSHED

1 SLICE BREAD, CRUSTS REMOVED, THEN CRUMBLED

SOME FRESHLY GROUND BLACK PEPPER

1.25 ml/¼ tsp SUGAR

50 ml/2 fl oz (¼ cup) OLIVE OIL

ABOUT 50 ml/2 fl oz (¼ cup) WINE VINEGAR

Place the parsley, capers, pickled cucumber, garlic and the crumbled bread into a bowl or a large mortar and mix together well with a wooden spoon. Add some black pepper and the sugar and gradually whisk in the oil. Stir in the wine vinegar – the quantity depends on the sourness of the capers and the cucumber, so you may need to add slightly more or less; the end result must be quite tart. Keep beating, check seasoning and leave covered at room temperature for several hours for the tastes to develop.

There should be enough of the sauce to serve 6 portions of food, whatever you decide to serve it with.

Béarnaise Sauce

Making Béarnaise Sauce usually means spending ages standing over a double saucepan. This recipe is quicker, but you must take care! The critical thing is having the butter at the right temperature to amalgamate with the egg yolks, but not turn them into scrambled eggs. Catch the butter just as the bubbles subside and make sure the egg yolks are at room temperature, not straight from the fridge. Should the sauce curdle, take a fresh bowl and place over a pan of simmering water, place in it 15 ml/1 tbsp warm water and an egg yolk and gently beat in the curdled mixture.

45 ml/3 tbsp WATER

45 ml/3 tbsp WHITE VINEGAR

5 ml/1 tsp DRIED TARRAGON, OR 10 ml/2 tsp FINELY CHOPPED FRESH

15 ml/1 tbsp FINELY CHOPPED FRESH PARSLEY

2.5 ml/½ tsp FINELY GROUND BLACK PEPPER

250 g/9 oz BUTTER, DICED

4 EGG YOLKS, SIZE 1

In a heavy-based saucepan, bring to a boil the water, vinegar, tarragon, parsley and pepper. Lower the heat and cook, uncovered, until all the liquid has nearly evaporated. Add the butter and melt.

In a clean bowl, whisk the egg yolks until light and fluffy. Bring the butter to a boil and let it froth; remove from the heat at once, let the froth almost subside, then pour onto the egg yolks; whisk all the time until the ingredients are blended and emulsified. Serve immediately. *Serves 6.*

Béchamel Sauce

The recipe is the basis and there are many alternative ways of using it. You can thin it with a little medium-dry sherry (sweetens the sauce), or chicken stock (for flavour). Or, try whisking in some sour cream (when reheating, don't let it boil or it will curdle) . . . makes a really silky sauce. Chopped capers can be added, or finely chopped parsley (for fish).

15 ml/1 tbsp BUTTER

30 ml/2 tbsp PLAIN FLOUR

225 ml/8 fl oz (1 cup) MILK

1 BAY LEAF

PINCH OF GRATED NUTMEG

2.5 ml/½ tsp SALT

1.25 ml/¼ tsp GROUND WHITE PEPPER

In a heavy-based saucepan, melt the butter over moderate heat, then stir in the flour. Remove from the heat and slowly whisk in the milk (the whisk gets rid of any lumps). Add the bay leaf, nutmeg, salt and pepper, return to the heat and stir cook for about 5 minutes, until the sauce is thick. If too thick, add a little more milk and whisk; do this till you reach the consistency you want. *Makes about 225 ml/8 fl oz (1 cup).*

Mayonnaise

This is a basic mayonnaise. About 2.5 ml/½ tsp paprika, or more if you wish, will spike it up and give it a delicate pink tinge.

1 EGG, PLUS 1 YOLK

5 ml/1 tsp SALT

5 ml/1 tsp SUGAR

5 ml/1 tsp DRY MUSTARD

45 ml/3 tbsp WHITE VINEGAR OR LEMON JUICE

350 ml/12 fl oz (1½ cups) VEGETABLE OIL

Place all the ingredients, except the oil, in a blender or food processor fitted with the steel blade. Blend on slow speed (if blender) for a few seconds. With the motor still on slow speed, slowly add the oil. Blend until thick and smooth.

Tartare Sauce. Add to the prepared mayonnaise some chopped gherkins, capers and ground black pepper. Use with fish or seafood. *Makes about 450 ml/¾ pint (2 cups).*

Dijon Mustard

This is a nice smooth soft-tasting mustard. Store it in the refrigerator, well covered. When making anything that contains vinegar that you wish to keep, such as this mustard for example, do not use a jar or container with a metal lid. Even when the top of the jar is covered with cling film or greaseproof paper, the vapour of the vinegar always manages to get through and turn the lid rusty, which of course affects the taste of the contents. This recipe is only a guideline. Play around with it, add and subtract ingredients to suit your own palate.

100 g/4 oz (1 cup) DRY MUSTARD

100 ml/4 fl oz (½ cup) COLD WATER

350 ml/12 fl oz (1⅓ cups) DRY WHITE WINE

350 ml/12 fl oz (1⅓ cups) WHITE WINE VINEGAR

1 SMALL ONION, FINELY CHOPPED

3 LARGE CLOVES GARLIC, FINELY CHOPPED

2 BAY LEAVES

8 WHOLE ALLSPICE

10 ml/2 tsp SALT

10 ml/2 tsp SUGAR

5 ml/1 tsp DRIED TARRAGON

Mix together the mustard and water and let stand for at least 15 minutes – the longer it stands the softer the taste of the mustard becomes.

In a large, heavy-based, non-metal saucepan, boil the rest of the ingredients, uncovered, about 20 minutes, until reduced by half. When you consider your mustard powder is ready, strain the hot liquid into it and press out all the juices. Whisk well with a balloon whisk. In the top of a double boiler over simmering water, cook the mustard, stirring occasionally, until the consistency of thick cream. Cool, pour into a container and cover with a close-fitting lid. Refrigerate for a week before using. *Makes about 750 ml/1 ¼ pints (3 cups).*

INDEX